AN ESSAY ON THE PRINCIPLE OF POPULATION

Thomas Robert Malthus was born in Guilford in 1766. He was educated first privately and then at Jesus College, Cambridge. There he graduated in 1788 as ninth Wrangler, taking Holy Orders in the same year. In 1793 he was elected to a fellowship of his college, which he held until his marriage in 1804. The first version of *An Essay on the Principle of Population* (the *First Essay*) appeared anonymously in 1798 achieving immediate notoriety. Mainly in order to collect further material, he made extensive tours abroad in 1799 and 1802, and the results appeared in 1803 as what was nominally a second edition but really a further book. Later Malthus summarized his thesis in a short essay, *A Summary View of the Principle of Population*, published in 1830.

In 1805 Malthus was appointed to the faculty of the East India Company's newly-founded college at Haileybury, where he occupied until his death in 1834 the first professorship of political economy established in the British Isles. He was survived by his widow, his only son and one of his two daughters.

His honours included a Fellowship of the Royal Society, and membership of both the French Institute and Berlin Royal Academy. Among his other publications were *An Enquiry into the Nature and Progress of Rent* and *Principles of Political Economy considered with a View to their Practical Application*.

Antony Flew was born in 1923 and went to St John's College, Oxford, where he took a first in 'Greats' and won the John Locke Scholarship in Mental Philosophy. During the war he learnt Japanese. He lectured in philosophy in Oxford and Aberdeen Universities, before becoming Professor of Philosophy at the University of Keele in 1954. He has also taught in the United States, Australia, and Malawi. He was Professor of Philosophy at the University of Reading from 1973 to 1982, and from 1983 to 1985. He is now part-time Distinguished Research Fellow at Bowling Green State University, Ohio. He is married and has two daughters.

His publications include: *A New Approach to Psychical Research* (1953), *Hume's Philosophy of Belief* (1961), *God and Philosophy* (1966), *Evolutionary Ethics* (1967), *An Introduction to Western Philosophy* (1971), *Crime or Disease?* (1973), *Thinking About Thinking* (1975), *The Presumption of Atheism* (1976), *Sociology, Equality and Education* (1976), *A Rational Animal* (1978), *Philosophy: an introduction* (1979), *The Politics of Procrustes* (1981), *Darwinian Evolution* (1984) and *The Logic of Mortality* (1987).

THOMAS ROBERT MALTHUS

AN ESSAY ON THE
PRINCIPLE OF POPULATION

AND

A SUMMARY VIEW OF
THE PRINCIPLE OF
POPULATION

EDITED WITH AN INTRODUCTION
BY ANTONY FLEW

PENGUIN BOOKS

PENGUIN BOOKS

Published by the Penguin Group
Penguin Books Ltd, 27 Wrights Lane, London W8 5TZ, England
Penguin Books USA Inc., 375 Hudson Street, New York, New York 10014, USA
Penguin Books Australia Ltd, Ringwood, Victoria, Australia
Penguin Books Canada Ltd, 10 Alcorn Avenue, Toronto, Ontario, Canada M4V 3B2
Penguin Books (NZ) Ltd, 182–190 Wairau Road, Auckland 10, New Zealand

Penguin Books Ltd, Registered Offices: Harmondsworth, Middlesex, England

First published in 1798 and 1830
Published in Pelican Books 1970
Reissued in the Penguin English Library 1982
Reprinted in Penguin Classics 1985
9 10 8

Printed in England by Clays Ltd, St Ives plc
Set in Linotype Granjon

CONTENTS

INTRODUCTION

THOMAS ROBERT MALTHUS (1766–1834) is a member of that heterogeneous élite from whose names we have derived words. In this he stands with such various figures as Charles Macintosh (mackintosh), Captain Boycott (boycott), and Duns Scotus (dunce). However, as is so often the case, what Malthus himself actually advocated differs in important ways from what has become associated with his name.

Thus in Aldous Huxley's novel *Brave New World* the expression 'malthusian drill' is applied to the taking of contraceptive precautions, although those few references to such devices which Malthus brings himself to make are all in terms of horrified disapproval. Again – and more seriously, since here there can be no question of artistic licence – we find acknowledged experts on population and resources attributing to Malthus, and then indignantly rejecting, policies which Malthus himself categorically and equally indignantly repudiated. Thus in 1948 at Cheltenham, at an International Congress on Population and World Resources in Relation to the Family, Lord Boyd Orr (then Sir John Boyd Orr) marked an anniversary occasion by saying:

Exactly a hundred and fifty years ago a reverend gentleman called Malthus wrote a pamphlet pointing out that the population of the world was growing, that the physical capacities were limited, and that a stage would soon be reached where there was not sufficient food to feed the people of the world. It was therefore wrong, he suggested, to bring in measures of social amelioration, for preventing the death of infants and for keeping people healthy, because if that were done more people would survive and the problem would become worse.[1]

Even as an account of the earliest views of Malthus this statement is a tendentious distortion. The fact that such

1. *Conference Report*, pp. 10–11.

misunderstandings and mispresentations are so common is one very good reason for reproducing this 'pamphlet' as a Penguin Classic. 'The classics', as the cynic said, 'are like the aristocracy; we learn their titles and thereafter claim acquaintance with them.'

THE LIFE AND WORKS OF MALTHUS

Before starting to investigate what Malthus really said, it helps to have some biographical and bibliographical framework. Thomas Robert Malthus was the second and last son in a family of eight. His father Daniel Malthus seems to have been a rather unusual man, the friend of both David Hume and Jean-Jacques Rousseau. These two indeed visited him together when the future author of the *Essay on Population* was a bare three weeks old. It was under the influence of Rousseau's *Émile* that the father arranged for both his sons to be educated privately. In 1784, at the age of eighteen, Thomas Malthus entered Jesus College, Cambridge. There he had an excellent undergraduate career. He read widely in both English and French literature. He won prizes for declamations in Latin, Greek, and English – and this notwithstanding his cleft palate, something which ran in the family. (His great-great grandfather's parishioners at Northolt in Middlesex had given this as one of many reasons for petitioning Cromwell to eject their Vicar from his living!) His Italian seems to have been acquired later. We know that he took special notice of Edward Gibbon's *History of the Decline and Fall of the Roman Empire*, the last three volumes of which first appeared in 1788. He also played cricket, skated, and enjoyed a lively social life. Yet clearly none of these extra-curricular activities were allowed to get in the way of his main work. For in 1788 he succeeded in graduating as ninth Wrangler, the only one from Jesus College in his year.

This achievement is significant, since to be a Wrangler is the Cambridge equivalent of obtaining first class honours in mathematics. Malthus was thus, as the educationalists say nowadays, fully numerate. Nor did he confine himself to pure, as opposed to applied, mathematics. As he said, he was from the start 'remarked in college for talking of what actually exists in nature or may be put to real practical use' rather than for abstract speculations. Certainly while he was reading mathematics he also learnt his way around Newtonian physics. He was literate too, and had some acquaintance with history. It would be good if the same could truly be said of all our contemporaries aspiring to the diploma title 'social scientist'.

In the year of his graduation Malthus also took Holy Orders. Then in 1793, at the age of twenty-seven, he was admitted to a fellowship of his college. He resided there intermittently until 1804, when he married, and had in consequence to resign the fellowship. In 1796 he accepted a curacy at Albury, where his father lived. Two years later he published, anonymously, *An Essay on the Principle of Population as it affects the future Improvement of Society, with Remarks on the Speculations of Mr Godwin, M. Condorcet, and other Writers*. This is the pamphlet previously mentioned, and it is this which constitutes the greater part of the present volume. For reasons which will emerge soon enough, I shall refer to this as the *First Essay*.

*

This *First Essay* was, as its full title suggests, an occasional polemic provoked by the optimistic speculations of certain currently fashionable utopian writers. 'M. Condorcet' was Marie-Jean-Antoine-Nicolas Caritat, Marquis de Condorcet (1743–94). His famous book was the *Esquisse d'un Tableau Historique des Progrès de l'Ésprit Humain*, first published in Paris in 1794 and then in an English translation in London in 1795. This remarkable work was written while the author was in hiding under sentence of death. He had been active and influential in the first phases of the French Revolution. But later he fell foul of the Jacobin extremists who came to dominate the Convention. For instance, he was one who voted against the execution of the King, urging that the Republic ought to abolish the death penalty. Condorcet protested too against the arrest of the Girondins, telling the Convention that Robespierre had neither ideas in his head nor feelings in his heart. The key idea of the *Esquisse* is of a natural order of progress, extending through ten successive stages. The ninth of these began with Descartes and ended with the establishment of the first French Republic; while the tenth is to move on from there towards a world of abundance in which racial and national animosities will disappear, along with all inequalities of sex, wealth and opportunity.

'Mr Godwin' was William Godwin (1756–1836), the father-in-law of the poet Shelley. Godwin's *Enquiry concerning Political Justice* was published in 1793, with second and third editions in 1796 and 1798. Godwin, like Condorcet, was inspired by the French Revolution, albeit from a safer distance. He too foresaw a society of social and economic equality: 'There will be no war, no crimes, no administration of justice, as it is called, and no government. Besides this, there will be neither disease, anguish, melancholy, nor resentment. Every man will seek, with ineffable ardour, the good of all.'

Daniel Malthus was enchanted by these visions. In 1797 his enthusiasms were further fanned by the publication of Godwin's *Enquirer*. One essay in particular, that on 'Avarice and Profusion', the father pressed upon the son. In it Godwin urged the advantages of a state of social and economic equality, maintaining that this state is 'most consonant to the nature of man, and most conductive to the diffusion of felicity'. But the son, in his own words, had not 'acquired that command over his understanding which would enable him to believe what he wished without evidence'. Instead he deployed an objection which was, he contended, 'decisive against the possible existence of a society, all the members of which should live in ease, happiness, and comparative leisure; and feel no anxiety about providing the means of subsistence for themselves and their families'.[2]

This objection is based upon a comparison; between, on the one hand, our powers of multiplying the numbers of our own species by reproduction, and, on the other hand, the possibilities of increasing the resources available for the support of these numbers. The paragraph of which the previous quotation is the conclusion begins: 'This natural inequality of the two powers, of population, and of production in the earth, and that great law of our nature which must constantly keep their effects

2. *First Essay*, p. 72. Page references are to this edition.

equal, form the great difficulty that appears to me insurmountable in the way to the perfectibility of society.'[3]

But where Lord Boyd Orr thought of Malthus as warning us against a disaster still to come – 'a stage would soon be reached where there was not sufficient food to feed the people of the world' – Malthus himself saw his principle of population quite differently: 'this constantly subsisting cause of periodical misery has existed ever since we have had any histories of mankind, does exist at present, and will for ever continue to exist, unless some decided change takes place in the physical constitution of our nature.'[4]

Again, it would be false to say that Malthus advocated the policies which, according to Lord Boyd Orr, he suggested. Certainly Malthus did throughout his life contend, with this principle of population mainly in mind, that the actual effects of the Poor Laws were, despite all good intentions, positively harmful. Certainly he did always, for the same reason, reject all utopian programmes for the construction of a perfect and egalitarian society. But never at any stage did Malthus himself see his discoveries as providing a warrant for abandoning piecemeal and realistic efforts for improvement. Perhaps in consistency he ought to have drawn such a moral. In fact he did not.

The last two chapters of the *First Essay* are an attempt to put his principle of population into the context of God's providence. Thus the whole work ends with a statement which was surely as sincere as it now seems sanctimonious:

Evil exists in the world not to create despair, but activity. We are not patiently to submit to it, but to exert ourselves to avoid it. It is not only the interest, but the duty of every individual, to use his utmost efforts to remove evil from himself, and from as large a circle as he can influence; and the more he exercises himself in the duty, the more wisely he directs his efforts, and the more successful these efforts are; the more he will probably improve and exalt his own mind, and the more completely does he appear to fulfil the will of his Creator.[5]

It is perhaps no wonder that after a sermon such as this William Cobbett and other radical opponents snarled at 'Parson Malthus'!

3. ibid., p. 72.   4. ibid., p. 124.   5. ibid., p. 217.

The *First Essay*, like Hume's *Treatise*, was published anonymously. But Malthus could not complain, as Hume did, that his first 'literary attempt ... fell dead-born from the press.' On the contrary, it was this occasional polemic rather than any of his more laboriously considered later works which immediately made Malthus famous or – if you like – notorious. Since that first publication no one concerned for the general human welfare has been able, whatever his convictions, to ignore those problems of the pressures of population which are now labelled 'malthusian'.

Among his first distinguished converts Malthus was proud to number both William Paley and the younger Pitt. Paley was perhaps in this matter the less clear-headed of the two. But there certainly is a big shift towards a malthusian concern between the *Moral and Political Philosophy* of 1785 and the *Natural Theology* of 1802. Pitt had in 1796, in a debate on a Bill introduced by Samuel Whitbread, promised to amend the Poor Laws in such a way as to encourage large families. But in 1800 he decided not to proceed with this legislation, and explained to the House of Commons that his decision had been taken in deference to 'those whose opinions he was bound to respect'. Jeremy Bentham and Robert Malthus were the two whom he had in mind.

*

Despite, or because of, the stir caused by the *First Essay* Malthus was not satisfied with the book. He at once started work on what was to be in name though not in fact a second edition. The *First Essay*, as he said in the Preface to this second edition, 'was written on the impulse of the occasion, and from the few materials which were then within my reach in a country situation.' Now he settled down to a thorough examination of all the available literature. In 1799 with three college friends he made a study tour of all the countries then open to British tourists: Norway, Sweden, Finland, and Russia. In 1802 he took advantage of the truce which was called the Peace of Amiens to make a similar study tour of France and Switzerland. The results appeared late in 1803 as *An Essay on the Principle of*

Population; or, a View of its Past and Present Effects on Human Happiness; with an Inquiry into our Prospects respecting the Future Removal or Mitigation of the Evils which it occasions.

This, as its author said in his Preface, 'may be considered as a new work.' We shall, therefore, refer to it in this second edition, and in the author's four subsequent editions of 1806, 1807, 1817 and 1826, as the *Second Essay*. Whereas the first edition, the *First Essay*, was an octavo volume of 396 pages and 55,000 words; the *Second Essay* first appeared as a quarto of 610 pages and 200,000 words. Whereas the *First Essay* is, as we have repeatedly insisted, an occasional polemic designed to debunk utopian visions inspired by the French Revolution, the *Second Essay* is a painstaking sociological treatise deploying a mass of detailed evidence. J. M. Keynes described the *First Essay* as 'bold and rhetorical in style with much bravura of language and sentiment'. By contrast, in the *Second Essay* 'political philosophy gives way to political economy, general principles are overlaid by the inductive verifications of a pioneer in sociological history, and the brilliance and high spirits of a young man writing in the last years of the Directory disappear.' A third great Cambridge economist, Alfred Marshall, rated the *Second Essay* 'one of the most crushing answers that patient and hard-working science has ever given to the reckless assertions of its adversaries'.[6]

For our present purposes the most important difference is the introduction into the *Second Essay* of the notion of 'moral restraint'. This amendment to his theoretical scheme, which will be explained in the next section, was possibly first suggested to Malthus by his correspondence with Godwin, initiated by Godwin within weeks of the publication of the *First Essay*. Certainly it was this innovation which enabled Malthus to claim in his later Preface:·

Throughout the whole of the present work I have so far differed in principle from the former as to suppose the action of another

---

6. J. M. Keynes, *Essays in Biography*, Macmillans, 1933, p. 117, and A. Marshall, *The Economics of Industry*, 2nd ed., Macmillans, 1896, p. 30.

check to population which does not come under the head of either vice or misery; and in the latter part I have endeavoured to soften some of the harshest conclusions of the *First Essay*. In doing this I hope I have not violated the principles of just reasoning; nor expressed any opinion respecting the probable improvement of society, in which I am not borne out by the experience of the past.

Thanks to the reputation consolidated by the publication of this *Second Essay* in 1803, Malthus was in 1805 appointed to the faculty of the new East India College at Haileybury. This college was founded at the suggestion, made in August 1800, of the then Governor-General of India, the Marquis of Wellesley, elder brother of the future victor of Waterloo and Duke of Wellington. The idea was to give a two year course of general education and language study to the servants of the East India Company before they proceeded overseas. The chair which Malthus occupied until his death in 1834 was the first professorship of political economy in Britain. (Adam Smith at Glasgow in the previous century had been a professor of moral philosophy.) Malthus said that the sometimes turbulent students at Haileybury not only understood his lectures 'but did not even find them dull.' The appointment, though not lucrative, must have been timely for Malthus since it was in the previous year that he had married Harriet Eckersall.

Besides fulfilling his teaching and other duties at the East India College, Malthus, like a good academic, continued to research and publish. These publications included: *Observations on the Effects of the Corn Laws, and of a Rise or Fall in the Price of Corn on the Agriculture and General Wealth of the Country*, in 1814; *Grounds of an Opinion on the Policy of Restricting the Importation of Foreign Corn* and *An Inquiry into the Nature and Progress of Rent, and the Principles by which it is Regulated*, in 1815; *Principles of Political Economy Considered with a View to their Practical Application*, in 1820; *The Measure of Value stated and illustrated, with an Application of it to the Alterations in the Value of the English Currency since 1790*, in 1823; and the article on 'Population' for the 1824 *Supplement* to the *Encyclopaedia Britannica*. Most of this last was in 1830 issued separately with a few amendments as *A Summary View of the Principle of Population*. This is the second work reprinted here. We shall from now on refer to it simply as *A Summary View*, giving page references to the present volume.

The two other minor sources for the views of Malthus on population also belong to the Haileybury period. They are what were nominally the third and fifth editions of the *First Essay*, but really the second and fourth of the *Second Essay*, which appeared in 1806 and 1817 respectively. Both had important new appendices. We shall refer to these by their dates as the *1806 Appendix* and the *1817 Appendix*. Page references will be given to what is the last and nominally the sixth edition of Malthus' lifetime, that of 1826. In these appendices Malthus 'wished to correct some of the misrepresentations which have gone abroad respecting two or three of the most important points of the *Essay*.'[7]

It was while he was at Haileybury that Malthus got to know another of the great classical economists, David Ricardo. In June 1811 Malthus wrote to Ricardo in hopes that in private discussion they 'might supersede the necessity of a long controversy in print respecting the points in which we differ.' The wish of Malthus was reciprocated, and the two became close friends. The letters of Ricardo to Malthus were discovered by his biographer James Bonar, and published by him in 1887. But it was only in 1930 that the other part of the correspondence, the letters of Malthus to Ricardo, fell into the hands of Mr Piero Sraffa, who had been commissioned by the Royal Economic Society to prepare a complete and definitive edition of the *Works and Correspondence of David Ricardo*. The exchanges between Malthus and Ricardo, which extended over the twelve years from 1811 until the death of the latter in 1823, do not treat population, since about this the two were in substantial agreement. Indeed Ricardo, in his *Principles of Political Economy and Taxation*, paid tribute: 'Of Mr Malthus' *Essay on Population*, I am happy in the opportunity here afforded me of expressing my admiration. The assaults of the opponents of this great work have only served to prove its strength; and I am

7. *Second Essay*, Vol. II, p. 443.

persuaded that its just reputation will spread with the cultivation of that science of which it is so eminent an adornment.'[8]

Because these exchanges do not deal with population they are not of direct concern to us now. But as an indication of the stature of Malthus in economics generally it is worth quoting the judgement of Keynes:

One cannot rise from a perusal of this correspondence without a feeling that the almost total obliteration of Malthus' line of approach and the complete domination of Ricardo's for a period of a hundred years has been a disaster to the progress of economics. ... If only Malthus, instead of Ricardo, had been the parent stem from which nineteenth-century economics proceeded, what a much wiser and richer place the world would be today.[9]

Malthus felt the death of Ricardo deeply, and his own comment of their transactions magnifies mankind: 'I never loved anybody out of my own family so much. Our interchange of opinion was so unreserved, and the object after which we were enquiring was so entirely the truth, and nothing else, that I cannot but think that sooner or later we must have agreed.'[10]

The family life of Malthus seems, as this comment would suggest, to have been extremely happy. His wife was apparently a woman of quality, and certainly a very successful hostess. They had three children, of whom the younger daughter, Lucy, to their great grief died in 1825 at the age of seventeen. The other two survived them both: one as the Reverend Henry Malthus; and the other, Emily, as Mrs Pringle, the wife of Captain John Pringle, a veteran of Waterloo.[11] Thomas Robert Malthus died, suddenly, in 1834 while on a visit to his wife's former home at Claverton. He is buried in Bath Abbey, in the North aisle of the nave.

8. David Ricardo, *Principles of Political Economy and Taxation*, ch. 32.

9. J. M. Keynes, *Essays in Biography*, pp. 140, 144.

10. Reported by W. Empson in the *Edinburgh Review*, January 1837, p. 499.

11. Kenneth Boulding is mistaken in saying: 'Malthus ... confined himself to three children, only one of which survived to maturity' (Malthus, *Population*, University of Michigan, 1959, p. xii).

The inscription on the wall above is probably by his lifelong friend Bishop Otter, whom Malthus first met when they were both undergraduates at Jesus College, Cambridge. This lapidary oration makes no mention of any of the public honours awarded to its subject, such as his Fellowship of the Royal Society, or his memberships of the French Institute and of the Berlin Royal Academy. Let us for a moment savour its fine period character before proceeding to examine the timeless structure of his ideas:

Sacred to the memory of the Rev. Thomas Robert Malthus, long known to the lettered world by his admirable writings on the social branches of political economy, particularly by his *Essay on Population*. One of the best men and truest philosophers of any age or country, raised by native dignity of mind above the misrepresentation of the ignorant and the neglect of the great, he lived a serene and happy life devoted to the pursuit and communication of truth, supported by a calm but firm conviction of the usefulness of his labours, content with the approbation of the wise and good. His writings will be a lasting monument to the extent and correctness of his understanding. The spotless integrity of his principles, the equity and candour of his nature, his sweetness of temper, urbanity of manners, and tenderness of heart, his benevolence and his piety, are the still dearer recollections of his family and friends.

THE CONCEPTUAL STRUCTURE EXPLICATED

From the *First Essay* to the final *A Summary View* all Malthus' thinking about population was framed by what was fundamentally the same simple yet very powerful theoretical scheme. This scheme has to be mastered by anyone who wants to come to terms with what Malthus really said, and it is this which constitutes his main permanent contribution.

The basis of the whole structure is in every successive treatment essentially the same. But the presentation in *A Summary View* is perhaps the most effective. 'In taking a view of animated nature, we cannot fail to be struck with a prodigious power of increase in plants and animals.' [12] 'Elevated as man is above all other animals by his intellectual faculties, it is not to

12. *A Summary View*, p. 223.

be supposed that the physical laws to which he is subjected should be essentially different from those which are observed to prevail in other parts of animated nature.'[13] '... all animals, according to the known laws by which they are produced, must have a capacity of increasing in a geometrical progression.'[14]

These general contentions are, when properly understood, obviously true. Malthus supports his thesis with regard to the case of our own species, and makes it more precise, by appealing to what some human populations have in fact achieved. For, as Aristotle once remarked, a thing must be possible if it in fact happens; so there must be such a power of multiplication if ever this power actually is exercised. In the light of present knowledge of the population explosions occurring now, the estimate of the strength of this power which Malthus made appears to be cautious, as indeed he intended: 'It may be safely asserted therefore, that population, when unchecked, increases in a geometrical progression of such a nature as to double itself every twenty-five years.'[15]

The key expressions to underline here are 'a capacity' and 'when unchecked'. Malthus never claimed, what is not true, that this power of multiplication is ever – much less that it is always – fully exercised and realized. On the contrary, he was from the very beginning of the *First Essay* careful to insist that 'in no state that we have yet known, has the power of population been left to exert itself with perfect freedom.'[16] If it were 'left to exert itself unchecked, the increase of the human species would evidently be much greater than any increase that has been hitherto known.'[17] After referring to 'the United States of America, where ... the population has been found to double itself in twenty-five years', Malthus concludes that 'This ratio of increase, though short of the utmost power of population, yet as a result of actual experience, we will take as our rule; and say, "That population, when unchecked, goes on doubling itself every twenty-five years, ... increases in a geometrical ratio." '[18]

*

13. ibid., p. 225.   15. ibid., p. 238.   17. ibid., pp. 73-4.
14. ibid., p. 226.   16. ibid., p. 73.   18. ibid., p. 74.

The next stage in Malthus' theory construction is to urge that:

... the means of subsistence, under circumstances most favourable to human industry, could not possibly be made to increase faster than in an arithmetical ratio[19] ... by the laws of nature in respect to the powers of a limited territory, the additions which can be made in equal periods to the food which it produces must, after a short time, either be constantly decreasing, which is what would really take place; or, at the very most, must remain stationary, so as to increase the means of subsistence only in arithmetical progression.[20]

The status of this second principle of the theory is very different from that of the first. For that human, like animal, populations – with certain freak exceptions to be noticed later – possess a power to multiply is a matter of fact. (Surely some more domestic version of this principle must have been among those awkward 'facts of life' into which embarrassed parents, in a less blatant age, used to have conscientiously to initiate their young?) Even the precision of the geometrical progression, doubling every twenty-five years, is a sober extrapolation from something which Malthus knew had actually happened in favourable though never absolutely ideal conditions. But the supposition of a limiting rate to the possibilities of increasing the output of food is for Malthus at best a plausible conjecture, while his formulation of this limiting rate as a particular arithmetical progression was a piece of entirely unwarranted exactness, which later developments in agricultural technology have shown to have been just wrong.

However, in fairness to Malthus, it must be emphasized that he himself offered the arithmetical ratio not as any sort of discovery but as a reasonable maximum supposition. Thus in *A Summary View* he wrote:

... it must be allowable, if it throws light on the subject, to make a supposition respecting the increase of food in a limited territory, which, without pretending to accuracy, is clearly more favourable to the power of the soil to produce the means of subsistence for an increasing population, than an experience which we have of its qualities will warrant.[21]

19. *Second Essay*, Vol. I, p. 10. 20. *A Summary View*, p. 242.
21. ibid., pp. 239-40.

In the *First Essay* as in the final *Summary* the stress is on such expressions as 'can be supposed' and 'if I allow'. Thus, immediately after the statement of his first principle, he writes:

> Let us now take any spot of earth, this Island for instance, and see in what rate the subsistence it affords can be supposed to increase. We will begin with it under its present state of cultivation. If I allow that by the best possible policy, by breaking up more land, and by great encouragements to agriculture, the produce of this Island may be doubled in the first twenty-five years, I think it will be allowing as much as any person can well demand. In the next twenty-five years, it is impossible to suppose that the produce could be quadrupled. It would be contrary to all our knowledge of the qualities of land. The very utmost we can conceive is that the increase in the second twenty-five years might equal the present produce. Let us then take this for our rule, though certainly far beyond the truth; and allow that by great exertion, the whole produce of the Island might be increased every twenty-five years, by a quantity of subsistence equal to what it at present produces. The most enthusiastic speculator cannot suppose a greater increase than this. ... Yet this ratio of increase is evidently arithmetical. It may fairly be said, therefore, that the means of subsistence increase in an arithmetical ratio.[22]

*

All is now ready for the third stage in the construction of the theory: 'Let us now bring the effects of these two ratios together.'[23] It is easy to see the disproportion between the geometrical (1, 2, 4, 8, 16, 32 etc.) and the arithmetical (1, 2, 3, 4, 5, 6 etc.). In every subsequent statement of his position it is with the help of the observation of this disproportion that Malthus tries to draw the conclusion that in fact there must always be some check or checks operating against this inordinate power of reproduction. Thus in the first chapter of the *First Essay* he says:

> By that law of our nature which makes food necessary to the life of man, the effects of these two unequal powers must be kept equal. This implies a strong and constantly operating check on population

22. *First Essay*, p. 74.　　　　23. ibid., p. 74.

from the difficulty of subsistence. This difficulty must fall somewhere; and must necessarily be severely felt by a large portion of mankind.[24]

So again in the *Second Essay* Malthus insists that

the power of population being in every period so much superior, the increase of the human species can only be kept down to the level of the means of subsistence by the constant operation of the strong law of necessity, acting as a check upon the greater power.[25]

By the time he came to write *A Summary View*, however, Malthus seems to have developed some slight scruple as to exactly how much and what this comparison does prove:

it follows necessarily that the average rate of the actual increase of population over the greatest part of the globe, obeying the same laws as the increase of food, must be totally of a different character from the rate at which it would increase *if unchecked*. The great question, then, which remains to be considered, is the manner in which this constant and necessary check upon population practically operates.[26]

Certainly, whatever Malthus himself may or may not have seen, there are differences: between, on the one hand, inferring that sooner or later, like it or not, there will have to be checks; and, on the other hand, concluding that it follows necessarily that checks are in fact operating constantly and everywhere. The distinctions required here can be important, both theoretically and practically. To these we shall return.

*

But the immediate next business is to appreciate that the fourth stage in the development of the theory is to raise 'the great question' which has been generated by the first three. Because the thrust of the *First Essay* is practical, it is only in the *Second Essay* that this theoretical question comes into its own. Thus early in the *Second Essay* Malthus quotes 'The question that is asked in Captain Cook's *First Voyage*, with respect to the thinly scattered savages of New Holland, "By what means are the inhabitants of this country reduced to such a number as it can subsist?"' Malthus remarks that it 'may be asked with

24. ibid., p. 71. 25. *Second Essay*, Vol. I, p. 11.
26. *A Summary View*, p. 242: italics in original.

equal propriety respecting the most populous islands in the
South Sea, or the best peopled countries in Europe and Asia'.[27]
It becomes his master speculative question:

> The question, applied generally, appears to me to be highly curious,
> and to lead to the elucidation of some of the most obscure, yet im-
> portant, points in the history of human society. I cannot so clearly and
> concisely describe the precise aim of the first part of the present work as
> by saying that it is an endeavour to answer this question so applied.[28]

In a later passage Malthus brings out most clearly how this master
speculative question is generated by his own fundamental principle of population, and how the attempt to answer it gives rise
to the notion of checks:

> The natural tendency to increase is everywhere so great that it will
> generally be easy to account for the height at which the population is
> found in any country. The more difficult, as well as the more inter-
> esting, part of the inquiry is to trace the immediate causes which stop
> its further progress. . . . What then becomes of this mighty power . . .
> what are the kinds of restraint, and the forms of premature death,
> which keep the population down to the means of subsistence.[29]

Although this master speculative question becomes prominent
only in the *Second Essay*, in which the interests of Malthus are
at least as much theoretical as practical, there is of course a cor-
responding practical question. The speculative question is: what
checks in fact are operating? The practical question is: what is
to be done about the principle of population, and, in particular,
which checks ought we to choose in preference to which? This
latter question is not formulated until the beginning of the
fourth book of the *Second Essay*, where Malthus insists that,
taking the operation of some great check as 'an inevitable law of
nature; . . . the only inquiry that remains is, how it may take
place with the least possible prejudice to the virtue and happiness of human society.'[30]

*

The fifth stage in the theory construction consists in distinguish-

27. *Second Essay*, Vol. III, p. 240.   28. ibid., Vol. I, p. 67.
29. ibid., Vol. I, p. 218.   30. ibid., Vol. II, p. 255.

ing and classifying kinds of check. Always, from the *First Essay* to the final *A Summary View*, Malthus employs two quite different systems of classification. The first of these is neutral and detached. The second is committed and engaged. About this second system the second thoughts of Malthus were, as has been said already, importantly different from the first. But even the first system was, and needed to be, improved in the *Second Essay*.

(i) Thus in the *First Essay* the two neutral categories of preventive check and positive check are presented always as mutually exclusive: 'a foresight of the difficulties attending the rearing of a family acts as a preventive check; and the actual distresses of some of the lower classes, by which they are disabled from giving the proper food and attention to their children, act as a positive check. ...'[31] But then later in the same work it emerges that though always mutually exclusive the two notions are not, after all, together exhaustive: 'To these two great checks to population in all long occupied countries, which I have called the preventive and the positive checks, may be added vicious customs with respect to women, great cities, unwholesome manufactures, luxury, pestilence, and war.'[32]

This is very clumsy. Not only does it try to squeeze in a third category where there is, surely, room for only two; it also insinuates irrelevantly evaluative notions into a system of classification which is otherwise uncommitted. This awkwardness is corrected in the *Second Essay*, and thereafter 'positive checks' and 'preventive checks' become labels for categories which are taken to be both mutually exclusive and together exhaustive. The former

are extremely various, and include every cause ... which in any degree contributes to shorten the natural duration of human life. Under this head, therefore, may be enumerated all unwholesome occupations, severe labour and exposure to the seasons, extreme poverty, bad nursing of children, great towns, excesses of all kinds, the whole train of common diseases and epidemics, wars, plague, and famine.[33]

31. *First Essay*, p. 89.   32. ibid., p. 103.
33. *Second Essay*, Vol. I, p. 15.

The latter are clearly intended to be complementary and opposite; although, thanks to the strength of the author's commitments and the delicacy of his expressions, the outlines remain a little blurred. These preventive checks now comprehend all checks to the birthrate. They range from 'the restraint from marriage which is not followed by irregular gratifications'; through 'promiscuous intercourse, unnatural passions', and 'violations of the marriage bed'; and so on, up to and including 'improper arts to conceal the consequences of irregular connections'.[34] This last is presumably a reference to abortion. Elsewhere Malthus even brings himself to mention contraception under the description 'something else as unnatural', as 'promiscuous concubinage'.[35]

(ii) In addition to the first and fundamentally neutral division of checks into positive and preventive, Malthus also employs a second system. This is uninhibitedly prescriptive and committed. Its terms too are taken to be mutually exclusive and together exhaustive. But its divisions cut across the lines drawn by the first system. Thus in the *First Essay*, as the sentence immediately following the passage quoted at the end of the last paragraph but one, Malthus writes: 'All these checks may be fairly resolved into misery and vice', and, a little later, 'In short it is difficult to conceive any check to population, which does not come under the description of some species of misery or vice.'[36]

This once granted, the practical conclusions are inescapable. We must virtuously eschew vice, and realistically resign ourselves to what are inescapable miseries of the human condition. Hence Malthus in the *First Essay* recommends an active stoicism:

The perpetual tendency in the race of man to increase beyond the means of subsistence is one of the general laws of animated nature, which we can have no reason to expect will change. Yet, discouraging as the contemplation of this difficulty must be to those whose exertions are laudably directed to the improvement of the human species, it is evident that no possible good can arise from any endeavours to slur it over, or keep it in the background. On the contrary, the most baleful

34. ibid., Vol. I, p. 16.   35. ibid., Vol. II, p. 8.
36. *First Essay*, pp. 103 and 106.

mischiefs may be expected from the unmanly conduct of not daring to face truth, because it is unpleasing. Independent of this great obstacle sufficient yet remains to be done for mankind, to animate us to take the most unremitted exertion.[37]

The only way to escape this strenuous, manly, but discouraging conclusion must be to challenge the premise that 'All ... checks may be fairly resolved into misery and vice.' Malthus did precisely this between the *First Essay* and the *Second Essay*. I have quoted the key sentence on this already from the Preface to the latter. But the change introduced is so crucial that this sentence will bear repetition:

Throughout the whole of the present work I have so far differed in principle from the former as to suppose the action of another check to population which does not come under the head of either vice or misery; and in the latter part I have endeavoured to soften some of the harshest conclusions of the *First Essay*.

The new third category thus admitted is 'moral restraint'. This is defined, strictly and narrowly, as 'the restraint from marriage which is not followed by irregular gratifications'.[38] With this transforming modification the old claim to exhaustiveness is then repeated: 'The checks which repress the superior power of population, and keep its effects on a level with the means of subsistence, are all resolvable into moral restraint, vice and misery.'[39]

Before moving to the sixth and final stage of his theory construction it is worth remarking that just as Malthus seems not to envisage the possibility that a married couple might resort to abortion in order to remove the consequences of their regular connexions, so he never explicitly entertains the thought that there could be restraint not just from and before marriage, but after and within it. Much later, in 1848, we find John Stuart Mill writing, in a book addressed to a public familiar with the ideas of Malthus:

That it is possible to delay marriage, and to live in abstinence while unmarried, most people are willing to allow; but when persons

37. ibid., p. 199.   38. *Second Essay*, Vol. I, p. 15.
39. ibid., Vol. I, p. 24n.

are once married, the idea, in this country, never seems to enter any-one's mind that having or not having a family, or the number of which it shall consist, is amenable to their own control.[40]

It appears that the ideas both of prudential (as opposed to ascetic) sexual restraint within marriage and of contraception within marriage first began to win currency in England in the 1820s. Certainly a kind of condom had been employed by English – and Scottish – rakes in the previous century. But this device was then by those who knew of it associated exclusively with extra-marital or pre-marital activities; and it was to be used – in what later was to become a cant phrase – 'for the prevention of disease only'. Readers of James Boswell's *Journals* will recall those frequent references to his using, or not using, his 'armour'.

Although James Mill, the father of J. S. Mill, had ventured a strong hint in his *Elements of Political Economy* in 1821, the credit for beginning to break these discreditable associations, and for being the first in England, explicitly and in print, to advo-cate contraception as a check on population, belongs to Francis Place. For in his *Illustrations and Proofs of the Principle of Population*, completed early in 1822, he wrote:

> If, above all, it were once clearly understood, that it was not dis-reputable for married persons to avail themselves of such precaution-ary means as would, without being injurious to health, or destructive of female delicacy, prevent conception, a sufficient check might at once be given to the increase of population beyond the means of sub-sistence; vice and misery, to a prodigious extent, might be removed from society; and the object of Mr Malthus, Mr Godwin, and every philanthropic person, be promoted by the increase of comfort, of intelligence and of moral conduct, in the mass of the population.

*

The sixth and last stage in the development of the theory of Malthus consists in the recognition of the relatedness of the various variables. This point will perhaps be understood best by considering two very simple diagrams (Fig. 1 and Fig. 2). Assuming that in each case the different sorts of check specified constitute an exhaustive list of mutually exclusive alternatives,

40. John Stuart Mill, *Principles of Political Economy*, II, xiii, 1.

then for a stable population the sums of the various checks must be sufficient to neutralize the power of increase. If in either case the force of one of the sorts of check is reduced then either the population must rise or there must be an exactly compensating increase in the force of the other sort (Fig.1) or, possibly, sorts (Fig. 2) of check. So if, further, we know that there must be some inhibition on the enormous power of increase, it must follow that to the extent that it is not one of the possible sorts of check it will be either the other, or one of the others, as the case may be.

FIG. I. THE NEUTRAL SYSTEM

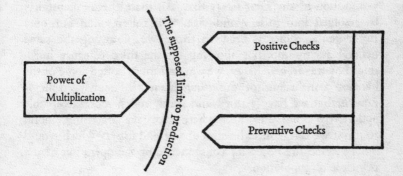

FIG. 2. THE ENGAGED SYSTEM

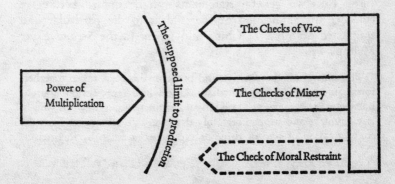

Thus, taking the first figure first, and granting the assumptions already stated, if the preventive checks are insufficient then the necessary work will be done instead by the positive – above all by the unholy trinity of War, Pestilence and Famine. And furthermore, although both figures for the sake of simplicity represent only the relations between different categories of check, with appropriate alterations the same conclusions will follow about the relations between the individual members of these categories. Considered simply as a check on population, war is an alternative to abortion, and pestilence to famine.

The second of our two figures is slightly complicated by the important shift described previously. Granting the general assumption that checks are inevitable, and adding the particular assumption of the *First Essay* that 'All these checks may fairly be resolved into misery and vice,' [41] it follows that our only fundamental choice is between these two. Granting the same general assumption, but allowing for the third category introduced by the *Second Essay*, we can and must 'soften some of the harshest conclusions of the *First Essay*'.[42] For what follows now is that we have a third and surely much more acceptable option. By promoting, and where necessary practising, moral restraint we can reduce the sum of vice and misery which would otherwise be the necessary consequence of the operation of the principle of population.

Malthus himself does not make his point about the relatedness of the various variables in quite this generalized way. Instead he prefers to bring it out by elucidating the relations in particular cases. But two general statements can be quoted before we consider his application of these ideas to the particular and contrasted examples of China and Japan. In the *Second Essay* Malthus writes:

The sum of all the positive and preventive checks, taken together, forms undoubtedly the immediate cause which represses population; but we never can expect to obtain and estimate accurately this sum in any country; and we can certainly draw no safe conclusion from the contemplation of two or three of these checks taken by themselves,

41. *First Essay*, p. 103. 42. *Second Essay*, Vol. I, p. viii.

because it so frequently happens that the excess of one check is balanced by the defect of some other.[43]

Again in *A Summary View* we read:

... consider ... the nature of those checks which have been classed under the general heads of preventive and positive. It will be found that they are all resolvable into moral restraint, vice, and misery. And if, from the laws of nature, some check to the increase of population be absolutely inevitable, and human institutions have any influence on the extent to which each of these checks operates, a heavy responsibility will be incurred, if all that influence, whether direct or indirect, be not exerted to diminish the amount of vice or misery.[44]

The abstract logical relationships become cruelly concrete in the discussion 'Of the Checks to Population in China and Japan': chapter 12 of Book I of the *Second Essay*. Malthus begins by marvelling at the enormous numbers of the Chinese, and picks on three causes of this immense population:

First, the excellence of the natural soil, and its advantageous position in the warmest parts of the temperate zone ...; secondly, the very great encouragement that from the beginning of the monarchy has been given to agriculture, which has directed the labours of the people to the production of the greatest possible quantity of human subsistence ... lastly, the extraordinary encouragements that have been given to marriage, which has caused the immense produce of the country to be divided into very small shares, and have consequently rendered China more populous, in proportion to its means of subsistence, than perhaps any other country in the world.

Given policies so opposed to moral restraint, in the very restricted and technical sense here given to that expression, we must expect a correspondingly high level of either vice or misery or both.

Sure enough, that is just what we find. Malthus cites, among other authorities, 'the Jesuit Premare, writing to a friend of the same society'. Premare says:

I will tell you a fact, which may appear to be a paradox, but is nevertheless strictly true. It is, that the richest and most flourishing

43. ibid., Vol. I, p. 256.   44. *A Summary View*, p. 249–50.

empire in the world is notwithstanding, in one sense, the poorest and the most miserable of all. The country, however extensive and fertile it may be, is not sufficient to support its inhabitants. Four times as much territory would be necessary to place them at their ease. ... A third part of this infinite population would hardly find sufficient rice to support itself properly. It is well known that extreme misery impels people to the most dreadful excesses. A spectator in China who examines things closely will not be surprised that mothers destroy or expose many of their children; that parents sell their daughters for a trifle; ... and that there should be such a number of robbers. The surprise is that nothing still more dreadful should happen, and that in times of famine, which are here but too frequent, millions of people should perish with hunger without having recourse to those dreadful extremities of which we read examples in the histories of Europe.

After citing various other sinologues to the same effect, and making or quoting the sort of calculations which could be made without census data and other modern statistical material, Malthus points his lesson of the need for moral restraint:

The population which has arisen naturally from the fertility of the soil, and the encouragements to agriculture, may be considered as genuine and desirable; but all that has been added by the encouragements to marriage has not only been an addition of so much pure misery in itself, but has completely interrupted the happiness which the rest might have enjoyed.

It is after drawing his moral that Malthus begins to compare China with Japan. Thus he cites 'the Jesuit Parennim, writing to a member of the Royal Academy of Sciences', who says 'Another thing which you can scarcely believe is, that dearths should be so frequent in China'; and in the conclusion of his letter he remarks that, if famine did not, from time to time, thin the immense number of inhabitants which China contains, it would be impossible for her to live in peace. The work which is not done by one check has to be undertaken by others.

Having as best he might reviewed the various checks operating in China, Malthus turns briefly to Japan. His treatment is brief because 'The state of Japan resembles in so many respects that of China, that a particular consideration of it would lead into too many repetitions.' Its interest for us lies in the insistence that, whenever the values of the other variables are held constant, the force of any one check must be inversely proportional to that of the sum of the others. For 'With regard to the positive checks to population from disease and famine, the two countries seem to be nearly on a level.' But

The Japanese are distinguished from the Chinese in being much more warlike, seditious, dissolute, and ambitious: and it would appear, from Kaempfer's account, that the check to population from infanticide, in China, is balanced by the greater dissoluteness of manners with regard to the sex, and the greater frequency of wars and intestine commotions, which prevail in Japan.

THE CONCEPTUAL STRUCTURE EXAMINED

Having allowed Malthus to speak for himself through quotations, I shall now examine his theoretical structure systematically. His fundamental principle is the proposition that human populations, like those of other living creatures, have the power to multiply by reproduction, on a conservative estimate, once every twenty-five years. There are five things to be said about this.

First, Malthus was not maintaining that human populations always do and always will increase at this rate. It is unfortunately necessary to labour this rather obvious point since many of his critics, including some who must surely have read him, have failed to grasp it fully. Thus Dr Kenneth Smith, in an elaborate polemic, remarks: 'Although his illustrations and proofs have a first appearance of careful inductive work, the basis of all his ideas is the postulate of the geometrical ratio, which he does not find in practice.'[45] But no one knew better than Malthus that the geometrical ratio was not always 'found in practice'. His purpose was to draw attention to the disparity between the rate one might expect and the rate usually observed; to deduce that therefore checks must already be operating; and to raise questions about their nature and interaction.

The Malthusian conceptual scheme here bears some resem-

45. Kenneth Smith, *The Malthusian Controversy*, Routledge & Kegan Paul, 1951, p. 331.

blance to classical mechanics. For the First Law of Motion states: 'Every body continues in its state of rest or of uniform motion in a right line unless it is compelled to change that state by forces impressed upon it.' Since in actual fact most, if not all, bodies are in motion and since this motion never continues for long in a right line, the questions arise: Why do bodies not continue in a state of rest or of uniform motion in a right line, what forces operate to prevent this, and how? As the First Law of Motion generates the notion of a force, so the principle of population gives rise to the malthusian concept of a check.[46]

Yet Dr Smith writes:

Man cannot live without food. Hence the two ratios would both be arithmetical. What then becomes of the geometrical series? It is reduced to the rate of food production in each period. ... The invalidity of Malthus' ratios could never have escaped detection if he had stated the real series of increase and hence deduced all that it implied.[47]

One might as well argue the invalidity of the First Law of Motion on the ground that real bodies do not for long continue in a state of rest or of uniform motion.

Second, it follows that the absence, spread, or presence of contraceptive practices have no effect on Malthus' fundamental argument. Thus Smith remarks that Francis Place's 'advocacy of birth control was the beginning of a movement which can completely nullify the geometrical or any other ratio'.[48] Later Smith

46. Of course, this analogy should not be pressed too far. But that there is some resemblance is certainly no coincidence. We know that Malthus was soundly grounded in Newtonian physics at Cambridge. In the *First Essay* he goes out of his way to express admiration for 'the grand and consistent theory (p. 126) and 'the immortal mind' (p. 205) of Newton; and he argues strongly that 'the causes of population and depopulation have probably been as constant as any of the laws of nature with which we are acquainted' (p. 114). In seeing classical mechanics as the model for the human studies Malthus put himself in a long and distinguished tradition extending back at least as far as the Hume of the *Treatise* (published 1739–40) and on well into the nineteenth century, and after. On this aspiration to be 'the Newton of the moral [i.e. human] sciences' see, for instance, E. Halévy, *The Growth of Philosophic Radicalism*, Faber & Faber, 1928, especially Chapter I.

47. op. cit., p. 234.   48. ibid., p. 325.

says 'Malthus opposed birth control, yet it has become so widespread that where it is practised the notion of a geometrical ratio can have no validity at all.' [49] But, on the contrary, it is precisely, and only in order to put a check on, this formidable power to be fruitful and multiply that contraception is and has to be employed. There would be no scope for a birth-control movement if there were not a Malthusian power for it to control.

Third, Malthus always and explicitly makes the reasonable but by no means unquestionable assumption that sexual desire and the capacities to fertilize and to conceive are constants. Thus in the *First Essay* he denies that there has been 'a decay of the passion between the sexes. We have sufficient reason to think that this natural propensity exists still in undiminished vigour.' [50] In the *1817 Appendix* he still insists 'that neither theory nor experience will justify us in believing either that the passion between the sexes, or the natural prolificness of women, diminishes in the progress of society.' [51] Over a century later the *Report* of the British Royal Commission on Population recorded its verdict in the same sense: 'It is just possible that there has been some decline in reproductive capacity, though there is no positive evidence to this effect; and indeed so far as we know reproductive capacity may have risen.' [52] Maybe some day such positive evidence will appear. But already we can be certain that the time scale of any such natural adjustment as may in fact be occurring is that of biological evolution rather than of practical politics; and, therefore, that it is not safe just to leave it complacently to 'the wisdom of nature' to dispose of this vast power of multiplication.

Fourth, both in defending his basic proposition that there is such a power and in estimating the sort of rate at which the multiplication would progress if there were no checks, Malthus takes for granted a population normally balanced. For consider one extreme case: a freak population consisting entirely of men or entirely of women would possess no power to reproduce at

49. ibid., p. 329.   50. *First Essay*, p. 89.
51. *1817 Appendix* to *Second Essay*, Vol. II, p. 483.
52. H.M.S.O., 1949, p. 34.

all – much less to multiply by reproduction. Or you might have a population more or less equally divided between the sexes but with such a very small proportion of women of child-bearing age, and such a very high proportion of the old at death's door, that total numbers could not start to increase until after a period when they would be lower than they had been at the beginning. On the other hand you can, and nowadays very frequently do, have populations in which – thanks to recent high actual rates of growth – the young of both sexes predominate, and which in consequence possess exceptional potential for still further rapid growth. But these are all refinements which Malthus left to his successors. The first writer to bring out the importance of age and sex distribution generally, and of the proportions of women of child-bearing age in particular, seems in fact to have been one of the early critics of Malthus, David Booth.[53]

Fifth, and finally here, it is perhaps just worth mentioning, as another assumption, that Malthus always takes the norm of strict monogamy for granted. This is an institution which must itself in some aspects be regarded as a check. It must be so regarded, for instance, in so far as it ever requires a fertile woman to stay faithful to a sterile man. This particular possible predicament will not, of course, arise in reality among those who observe the custom epitomized in that memorable exclamation of the gossiping Welsh matron: 'Married, you say? Why, I did not even realize she was pregnant!'

*

In the previous section I emphasized that Malthus himself presented the arithmetical limit only as a reasonable maximum supposition, and I then suggested that later developments have shown this estimate to have been far too low as a supposed universal maximum. But it is only fair to remember that Malthus made it in the light of the then available evidence, and with what seemed all reasonable generosity towards the opposition. Thus his biographer James Bonar was able to write, giving supporting authority:

53. See his 'Mathematical Dissertation' in W. Godwin, *Of Population*, London, 1820.

If the Napoleonic times were the times of a forced population in England, they were also the times of a forced agricultural production. Yet we ourselves, long after this stimulus, and after much high farming unknown to our fathers, have reached only an average produce of twenty-eight bushels per acre of arable land as compared with twenty-three in 1770, while the population has risen from about six millions to twenty-five.[54]

The counter-argument will be familiar to everyone nowadays, made so especially perhaps by the prestige advertisements of growth-minded corporations.[55] For piquant comparison I will here quote a formulation by Friedrich Engels, who is not usually thought of as an industrialist, which he was for most of his life. It comes from his *Outlines of a Critique of Political Economy*, published in 1844 when Malthus was already ten years in his grave. Engels asks:

has it been proved that the productivity of the land increases in an arithmetical progression? The extent of land is limited – that is perfectly true. But the labour power to be employed on this area increases along with the population; and even if we assume that the increase in yield due to this increase does not always rise in proportion to the labour, there still remains a third element – which the economists, however, never consider as important – namely, science, the progress of which is just as unceasing and at least as rapid as that of populations. What progress does the agriculture of this century owe to chemistry alone – and indeed to two men alone, Sir Humphrey Davy and Justus Liebig? But science increases at least as fast as population. The latter increases in proportion to the size of the previous generation. Science advances in proportion to the knowledge bequeathed to it by the previous generation, and thus under the most ordinary conditions it also grows in geometrical progression – and what is impossible for science?[56]

*

54. James Bonar, *Malthus and His Work*, 2nd ed., Allen & Unwin, 1924, p. 69.

55. See, for instance, the passage from L. H. and A. T. Day, *Too Many Americans*, quoted in *Population in Perspective*, edited by B. Young, O.U.P. 1968.

56. This is found most conveniently in the form of an Appendix to K. Marx, *The Economic and Philosophic Manuscripts of 1884*, edited by

The third stage in the development of Malthus' theory is to compare the arithmetical power of production with the geometrical power of reproduction, from which – with the help of 'that law of our nature which makes food necessary for the life of man' – Malthus proceeds to infer that the latter must always somehow be held back by the insufficiency of the former.

This argument as it stands is not valid on three counts. First, and most obviously, because the two progressions are in step for the first two phases and only begin to diverge in the third. (Compare 1, 2, 4, 8 etc. with 1, 2, 3, 4 etc.). Thus, whenever you suppose them to begin to operate, so long as they begin together, there is bound to be an initial period in which the productive is not checking the reproductive power.

The second reason is less slick and more compelling. It is that in supposing the arithmetical limit Malthus is surely offering it as an average: 'considering the present average state of the earth, the means of subsistence, under circumstances the most favourable to human industry ...', and so on.[57] Yet from the subsistence of such a general average limit you cannot validly deduce that the same limit will be effective all the time in every particular case. On the contrary, if there is to be any point in talking of an average, there must be room for cases falling both above and below that average. It is for instance absurd, albeit all too common and all too humanly understandable, for people to accept some average figure as the norm for pay rises, or for other desirable increases; and then to insist that, while their group must of course get more, it is only fair and proper that everyone else should have at least the average.

The third reason is the most significant for the student of population. We may very well allow that, from the premises given, you can validly infer that the power of reproduction

---

D. J. Struik and translated by M. Milligan, International Publishers, New York, 1964. The present passage, except in so far as I have made some small translation changes not affecting the sense, occurs at p. 222.

57. *Second Essay*, Vol. I, p. 10.

always, in the long run, would be checked by the insufficiency of the power of production, provided that it is not checked first by anything else. But this is not at all the same as saying that from these premises alone you can validly infer that this ultimate check is already operating now; or that if – exceptionally – it is not operating, then sooner or later it certainly will be. Quite apart from the two other lapses just noticed, Malthus is also at fault in overlooking that other checks might forestall the pressure of any such ultimate necessity. It is, therefore, trebly mistaken to think that the disproportion between the two ratios 'implies a strong *and constantly operating* check from the difficulty of subsistence' (my italics).

The observation of the third of these three fallacies can be exploited in two important and useful ways. First, it can draw attention to the failure of Malthus ever to recognize the possibility that people may inhibit their reproductive powers for reasons totally unconnected with any foresight of difficulties in providing subsistence for children. Thus in *A Summary View*, speaking of a possible increase of population 'in the well-peopled countries of Europe', Malthus maintains that 'there is no reason whatever to suppose that anything besides the difficulty of procuring in adequate plenty the necessaries of life should either indispose this greater number of persons to marry early, or disable them from rearing in health the largest families.'[58] The sovereign remedy of moral restraint is defined accordingly in terms of 'prudential considerations', which Malthus usually construes as referring exclusively to this difficulty: 'abstinence from marriage, either for a time or permanently, from prudential considerations, with a strictly moral conduct towards the sex in the interval. And this is the only mode of keeping population on a level with the means of subsistence which is perfectly consistent with virtue and happiness.'[59]

Once the point has been made, and especially for us for whom it is so much easier than it was for Malthus to think of the question of sex as different from the question of offspring, it surely cannot be denied that there are here frequently realized

---

58. *A Summary View*, pp. 242–5.
59. ibid., p. 250: compare *Second Essay*, Book I, Chapter II, passim.

possibilities of a prudential restraint which is not concerned primarily, or even at all, with financial difficulties. Many of us who have families would admit that we could afford more children than we intend to have; and many more would say the same if they were as frank. Most of us can point to others at similar income levels who are married but by choice have no children; and this class would, I suspect, be much larger were the social pressures towards procreation less than they are.

The second point which can usefully be brought out, in the context of the identification of the third of the fallacies involved in Malthus' argument here, is the need to distinguish two concepts of tendency. In the *1817 Appendix* Malthus defended his appeal to the idea of an enormous power, which is in fact always to a greater or lesser extent checked by counter-acting forces, by appealing to the practice 'of the natural philosopher ... observing the different velocities and ranges of projectiles passing through resisting media of different densities'. He complains that he cannot see why 'the moral and political philosopher should proceed upon principles so totally opposite'.[60] So far, so good.

Unfortunately Malthus is apt to misinterpret his own contention that the power of populations to multiply is inordinately greater than their power to increase their food supplies. Specifically, he is inclined to construe it as if it were the same as saying, or at any rate involved to saying that population at all times does and inevitably must press hard upon the means of subsistence. This must have made it harder for him to detect any fallacy in the argument dissected on pp. 36–7, while his acceptance of that argument necessarily reinforced the inclination.

The crucial difference was brought out well in 1832 by Archbishop Whately when he distinguished between two senses of the word 'tendency': that in which a tendency to produce something is a cause which, operating unimpeded, would produce it; and that in which to speak of a tendency to produce something is to say that that result may reasonably be expected in fact to occur.[61] Very much the same point had been made a year earlier

60. *1817 Appendix* to *Second Essay*, Vol. II, p. 485.
61. *Lectures on Political Economy*, Lecture IX.

by Nassau Senior in his *Two Lectures on Population*. It was accepted tacitly and rather grudgingly by Malthus in the ensuing correspondence, printed as an Appendix to the *Two Lectures on Population*, although he apparently never grasped that it might be relevant to his argument of the comparison of the ratios.

This comparison was described by John Stuart Mill in his *Principles of Political Economy* as 'a passing remark of Mr Malthus, hazarded chiefly by way of illustration, that the increase of food may perhaps be assumed to take place in an arithmetical ratio, while the population increases in a geometrical'. He proceeds to claim that 'every candid reader knows that Mr Malthus laid no stress on this unlucky attempt to give numerical precision to things which do not admit of it, and every person capable of reasoning must see that it is wholly superfluous to his argument.' [62]

Mill is, I am afraid, being far too generous. For this comparison, as the candid reader of the present volume will soon start to discover for himself, is given prominence by Malthus from the beginning of the *First Essay* right up to *A Summary View*. It is, indeed, to the appearance of 'mathematical certainty' which this provided that the immediate import of Malthusian ideas must largely be attributed. Nor is the comparison by any means superfluous to the argument, if this is to say that the conclusions which Malthus tries to derive in this way are themselves inessential and peripheral.

But though in one way Mill is being far too generous, in another way he is not being quite generous enough. It was not for nothing that Malthus had been ninth Wrangler in the University of Cambridge: 'We begin with mechanics and Maclaurin, Newton, and Keill's *Physics*.' [63] The supposition of the arithmetical ratio may indeed have been 'an unlucky attempt to give numerical precision to things which do not admit of it'. But there was nothing either unlucky or inappropriate about expressing our human animal power of multiplication as a geometrical progression, nor yet about the concern of Malthus to

62. John Stuart Mill, *Principles of Political Economy*, II, xi, 6.
63. Letter to his father, dated 14 November 1784.

extend the sway of numerical precision within his chosen vital field of population studies and population policies.

*

The fourth stage in the development of the theory consists in raising two general questions: first, how and in what forms 'this constant and necessary check on population practically operates'; [64] and, second, how we ought to adjust to the supposedly universal and unalterable fact that this check always does operate and always will.

I have argued that the conclusions which Malthus attempts to derive from a comparison of the two ratios do not follow from his premises as stated. Fortunately we do not need this particular comparison in order to generate an adequate speculative question. Thus there is no need to try to patch the argument up by adding as further premises any dubious generalizations either about populations invariably multiplying up to the limits of available subsistence, or about everyone wanting to have as many children as they can afford. Nor do we need to make controversial suppositions about a specifiable limit to the possibilities of food production.

Suppose instead that we simply compare the power to multiply, at a rate of the order estimated by Malthus, with the undisputed fact that actual populations often rise, sometimes remain stationary, and occasionally fall, but scarcely ever multiply at anything like such a rate. Then we can validly infer that usually some check or checks are in fact operating against this mighty power. If we now go on to notice that even in the exceptional populations in the exceptional periods some women die without having exhausted their procreative possibilities, then we can conclude not merely that checks are usually operating, but that they always do operate. The question to which this conclusion gives rise is not exactly that of Malthus. For whereas he, following Captain Cook, asked: 'By what means the inhabitants of this country are reduced to such a number as it can subsist?' we, guided by a different argument, will ask instead: 'By what means the inhabitants of this country are reduced to such a

64. *A Summary View*, p. 242.

number as it in fact does subsist?' This alternative master question is for speculative purposes equally fruitful, while it has, as we have just seen, the great advantage of being generable without recourse to any questionable assertions or controversial suppositions.

But besides the speculative, academic, interest, there is in Malthus always – and surely creditably – a strong practical concern. The drive behind the *First Essay* was indeed primarily practical; and even when, in 1820, he produced his *Principles of Political Economy* he was at pains to add as part of the full title, *considered with a View to their Practical Application*. So the conclusion which he draws from his comparison of the ratios is seen as raising also the practical question of how we ought to adjust to this supposedly unalterable fact of 'a strong and constantly operating check on population from the difficulty of subsistence'. In this second case the substitute argument suggested for the first will not do. For it does not yield what is here required, the idea of fundamental and universal necessity.

The conclusion that there always is 'a strong and constantly operating check on population from the difficulty of subsistence' is one which it would probably be wrong to try to salvage. For there have been and are, or at any rate could be, populations which, thanks to the unexploited richness of their territory and to the technical possibilities available to them, could multiply at the full biologically possible rate for a few generations without feeling any shortage of the means of mere subsistence; and this even allowing that that rate is in fact considerably larger than Malthus estimated. So if we are to find some universal practical necessity for checks we shall have to resort to one or both of two other ideas: that of some unsurmountable limit in the long run, as opposed to a 'constantly operating check'; or that of a general standard of living, in contrast to mere subsistence.

Although his theoretical scheme never made provision for either of these relaxations Malthus from the beginning recognized the second, and at the end had some inclination towards the first also. Thus in the *First Essay*, after first insisting that reason asks man 'whether he may not bring beings into the world for whom he cannot provide the means of subsistence', Malthus at once notices – notwithstanding that his argument is officially concerned only with food supplies – that 'In the present state of society, other considerations occur. Will he not lower his rank in life? Will he not subject himself to greater difficulties than he at present feels?' [65]

Once we firmly raise our aims above mere subsistence and towards the achievement and maintenance of prosperous standards of living, then it becomes fairly easy to demonstrate the need for checks on fertility. For suppose the population is rising at three per cent a year, then the whole economy will have to expand at three per cent a year if the average income per head is not to decline; and so only the amount by which the economic growth exceeds the population rise can be available to increase the average standard of living. Since rates of population expansion of three per cent per year or even more are today common among the less developed countries it should not be surprising that, from a national point of view, a birth control programme is often the most profitable of all possible investments.[66] Nor are such advantages available for the less developed only. Consider, for instance, how much more quickly we in Britain could hope to replace those existing schools which are out of date if only we could divert to this purpose some of the funds which are at present required to pay for the provision of new school places for additional children.[67] The whole obvious yet constantly and

65. *First Essay*, p. 76.

66. See 'The Effect of Fewer Births on Average Income', S. Enke and R. Zind, in the *Journal of Biosocial Science*, Vol. I, No. 1, Jan. 1969, pp. 41–55. They conclude: that a modest birth control programme costing thirty U.S. cents per year per head of population could, over only fifteen years, raise the average income in a less developed country by almost twice the percentage by which it could be raised without such a programme; that such an investment could yield an undiscounted return on cost of thirteen-fold in five years, and eightyfold in thirty years; that the value of the permanent prevention of a birth in such a country is twice the average income per head therein.

67. For a development of this point see 'Population Control: Who Needs Persuading?', Madeleine Simms, in *Question 4*, Pemberton, 1971. Mrs Simms argues that in Britain a drive to ensure that children were only born to parents who want them when they want them could, for a cost which in terms of the national budget would be derisory, secure two enormous

often wilfully neglected point is summed up for me by a poster which I saw recently in Singapore. Under a picture of a couple enjoying two lively children and a car the legend in bold print ran: 'Small families own more', followed by details of the government-backed family planning services available for all those who got, and wanted to act upon, that sales message.

If we are looking for 'some unsurmountable limit in the long run', as opposed to a 'constantly operating check', we may take a hint from something which Malthus himself said, in another connection: 'Though I may not be able, in the present instance, to mark the limit at which further improvement will stop, I can very easily mention a point at which it will not arrive.' [68] In 1956 Professor W. A. Lewis calculated that if the present world population were to double itself every twenty-five years it 'would reach 173,500 thousand million by the year A.D. 2330, at which time there would be standing room only, since this is the number of square yards on the land surface of the earth.' [69]

*

Stage five in the construction of the Malthusian theory consists in classifying possible checks on the multiplicative power of populations.

Even after the improvements introduced in the *Second Essay* the distinction between positive and preventive checks still needs more tidying. First, the dividing line has to be drawn more clearly, and put definitely either at conception or at birth. Since Malthus was presumably thinking of induced abortions when he wrote of 'improper arts to conceal the consequences of

---

goods. First, it would relieve all those directly concerned. It ought to be intolerable that there still are unpremeditated pregnancies and unwanted children. Second, it would by at least stabilizing our population relieve all those growing pressures on amenity, space, and social services which are constantly being increased by our present population growth of up to a quarter of a million a year.

68. *First Essay*, p. 127–8.

69. W. A. Lewis in *The Duke of Edinburgh's Study Conference; Background Papers*, O.U.P., 1957, Vol. II, p. 94.

irregular connections', it looks as if, when pressed to an indelicate precision, he would have drawn it at birth. This spares us the paradox of having to count unborn foetuses as units of population; though at the price of being required to rate even spontaneous miscarriages as preventive, while every other sort of pestilence counts as positive.

Second, we need to amend even the *Second Essay* definition of 'positive checks'. Where that made them 'include every cause ... which in any degree contributes to shorten the natural duration of human life' [70] we must read instead just 'every cause of death'. The reference to 'the natural duration of human life' serves no useful purpose; it raises unnecessary issues of definition; it must complicate arguments and calculations made in terms of the theory; and in any case even deaths in the ripest of old age still belong on the debit side of the population ledger. The phrase 'which in any degree contributes' serves only sententiously to remind that deaths may have remoter as well as immediate causes; and it does this at the unacceptably high cost of making any measurement of the effective force of different checks virtually impossible.

When these two changes are made the concepts of positive check and of preventive check become much less fuzzy. The latter are just checks on the birth rate, while the former are simply causes of death. So it becomes fairly easy to make exhaustive classifications of kinds of check in both categories. Again, once positive checks are made to be just causes of death, the measurement of their different effective forces presents no difficulties which are not already actuarial commonplaces. Nor have we in our time – mindful of the investigations of the late Dr Kinsey and his many successors – any business to despair of the possibility of constructing quantitative indices of the force of different preventive checks. Waiving questions of the indelicacy inherent in inquiries of this second sort, we can say that the general aim of quantification in social studies was close to the heart of Malthus: 'It would be a most curious, and to every philosophical mind a most interesting, piece of information, to know the exact share of the full power of increase

70. *Second Essay*, Vol. I, p. 15.

which each existing check prevents; but at present I see no mode of obtaining such information.' [71]

Of the other set of categories in which Malthus classifies checks there is, I think, little good to be said and nothing much to be made. In his presentation and employment of these he lies wide open to damaging criticism. First, he was careless, hasty, and – on his own later admission – mistaken, to rush in the *First Essay*, without listing possible checks systematically, to the conclusion that they could all 'be resolved into misery and vice' – the conclusion which in turn immediately determines the gloomy morals of the whole work. Even after in the *Second Essay* he has brought himself to recognize moral restraint as a third member of his second set of categories, Malthus still provides no systematic review from this standpoint of possible checks. He just insists again that the list, as now extended, really is exhaustive and complete; he sees this finding as happily enabling him 'to soften some of the harshest conclusions of the *First Essay*'. Such carelessness and haste in matters of such importance cannot easily be excused; not, that is, of course, by any of us who can truly claim to be qualified to cast the first stone!

Second, Malthus does not attempt to offer any rationale for this tripartite classification; something which could either reinforce, or be a substitute for, a systematic review from this standpoint of all possible checks. Some rationale is surely required: the tripartite system looks awkward and unbalanced. In it the two very general and comprehensive categories of vice and misery are harnessed alongside what is for Malthus the narrow and specific notion of moral restraint. This system also looks arbitrary and factitious, in so far as there is no very obvious reason for taking the famous three to be both mutually exclusive and together exhaustive. On the contrary, for even if we agree to defer as in some way anachronistic our own enlightened conviction that contraception as such is neither miserable nor vicious, we cannot be equally indulgent to the failure of Malthus to consider the option of some sexual restraint within marriage; and this is something which, granted the consent of both parties,

71. *1806 Appendix* to *Second Essay*, Vol. II, p. 453 n.

no catholic Christian could think to be wrong. (Indeed, the small size of his own family may to some suggest, though it certainly cannot prove, that Professor and Mrs Malthus themselves practised this discipline.) And if the reply comes that this would be not vice but misery, then much the same could fairly be said of the prolonged and often permanent celibacy demanded by moral restraint, in the narrow Malthusian definition.

If we wanted to salvage anything from this second system of classification, we could try dividing checks first into those beyond human control and those within human control, and then subdividing the latter into the licit and the illicit. But this, though undoubtedly an improvement, would represent a radical departure from the Malthusian originals.

*

The final stage in the erection of the Malthusian conceptual scheme is to point out that the values of the various checks must be connected. Malthus himself, as I urged earlier (p. 28), made curiously little of this implication in his general arguments, but much more in his particular applications.

Given the tidying of the notions of positive check and preventive check suggested above, and always for simplicity assuming an isolated population with neither emigration nor immigration, this classification is obviously both exclusive and exhaustive. If such a population is to remain stable the total of births must balance the total of deaths. If it rises, then this can only be because there are more births than deaths. And if it falls, then this must be because deaths have exceeded births.

It is in terms of this simple but compulsive Malthusian scheme that we can best understand the explosive increases of population which are today affecting most of the less developed countries. For these are not in fact to any significant extent the result of increases in either fertility or sexual activity. For present purposes at any rate these can be taken, as Malthus took them, to be constant. What is happening is that the positive checks are being weakened without any compensating strengthening of the preventive. The crux is that it is enormously easier to introduce modern methods of death-control than it is to introduce any methods of birth-control.

I have already suggested that Malthus' other system for classifying checks may be beyond redemption. But, before leaving the subject of functional relationships between different sorts of Malthusian check, there are one or two consequences of the bipartite division in the *First Essay* which need to be brought out. Thus, at the beginning of this Introduction I quoted Lord Boyd Orr's charge against Malthus: 'It was therefore wrong, he suggested, to bring in measures of social amelioration, for preventing the death of infants and for keeping people healthy, because if that were done more people would survive and the problem would become worse.' Later I attacked Lord Boyd Orr's statement as a misrepresentation of Malthus: 'Perhaps for consistency he ought to have drawn such a moral. In fact he did not.' The question remains whether it would not after all be right to draw it.

Consider what an earlier editor of this *First Essay*, Kenneth Boulding, has happily christened the Dismal Theorem.[72] Since population tends to press to the limit of available subsistence; since the power of production is beyond all comparison weaker than the power of reproduction; and since the equilibrium between population and resources can be maintained only by the constant operation of various checks, all of which are kinds of either vice or misery; then populations will always grow until there is enough misery, or enough vice, or – more likely – a sufficient mixture of both, to achieve equilibrium. It would seem, still following Boulding, that a corollary to the Dismal Theorem is the Utterly Dismal Theorem. Since equilibrium between resources and population can be maintained only by misery and/or vice, and since population tends to rise to the limit of available subsistence, any improvements leading to an increase in the production of food must increase the equilibrium population, and hence, presumably, increase the sum of human misery and vice.

Now, strictly, the Utterly Dismal Theorem is not valid. For

72. See the foreword to the work mentioned in note 11, above.

this conclusion will follow necessarily only if we may also assume that the total sum of misery and/or vice required must be directly proportionate to the size of the population. Although this would in the context of the early Malthus appear to be a plausible assumption, it is never explicitly stated as such nor, I think, are we ever provided with premises from which it could validly be inferred. However, notwithstanding that the *First Essay* neither advocates nor strictly warrants such a conclusion, we must allow that the book does suggest what Lord Boyd Orr wrongly said that its author suggested. (The point is, it is as unfair as it is common to accuse an opponent of advocating what was in fact far from his intentions, on the irrelevant grounds that you think – perhaps wrongly – that what you say he advocates is the logical or causal consequence of what he recommends. The difficulty is to remember how often our opponents are less wicked – but more ignorant, or more stupid – than we are inclined to think.)

But even if the Utterly Dismal Theorem does not, strictly, follow as a corollary of the Dismal Theorem, the latter really does carry one wry and – for Malthus – embarrassing implication. For in so far as the sum of (the relevant sorts of) vice and misery provides a necessary check and in so far as such vice and misery are alternatives, it follows that to indulge in (any relevant form of) vice must be to reduce misery. This unnoticed moral of the *First Essay* is very similar to the notorious paradox of Bernard de Mandeville's *Fable of the Bees*: 'private vices, public benefits' !

MALTHUS AND DARWIN: MALTHUS AND MARX

The influence of Malthus, by both action and reaction, has been immense. .His biographer begins: 'He was the "best-abused man of the age". ... Malthus from the first was not ignored. For thirty years it rained refutations.'[73] One partial bibliography of the controversy, confined to items published up to

73. James Bonar, *Malthus and His Work*, 2nd ed., Allen & Unwin, 1924. pp. 1–2.

1880 and within the British Isles, is over thirty pages long.[74] And a recent historian of the thought of the period writes of how 'Malthus had raised a spectre which haunted half the century.' [75] But I will confine myself here to noticing only two influences: first, that by action on Charles Darwin and Alfred Russell Wallace, the independent inventors of the theory of the evolution of species by natural selection; and, second, that by reaction on Karl Marx and Friedrich Engels, the joint creators of what they and their disciples would have us call scientific socialism.

I drew attention to a certain limited resemblance between the Malthusian conceptual scheme and that of Newtonian mechanics, and I indicated that this resemblance is not accidental. The resemblance between that scheme and the theory of Darwin and Wallace is far greater, and this is even less accidental. I will not here describe and discuss this analogy. I have done this fully elsewhere.[76] But the influence of Malthus on both of the two men who separately invented this theory of biological evolution constitutes a most remarkable text-book case-study in the history of scientific thought. It is ideal material, both because for once history did, almost exactly, repeat itself, and because the evidence for the influence on each independent discoverer is about as clear and decisive as could be desired.

Take Darwin first, since he was the first to invent the theory. The crucial passage comes in the *Autobiography*. This passage reads:

In October 1838, that is, fifteen months after I had begun my systematic inquiry, I happened to read for amusement Malthus on *Population*, and being well prepared to appreciate the struggle for existence which everywhere goes on, from long-continued observation of the habits of animals and plants, it at once struck me that under

74. 'A List of Books, Pamphlets and Articles on the Population Question, published in Britain in the period 1793–1880', J. A. Banks and D. V. Glass, in *Introduction to Malthus*, ed. D. V. Glass, pub. C. A. Watts, 1953.

75. Professor Basil Willey, 'Origins and Development of the Idea of Progress' in a collection of talks by various authors first broadcast by the B.B.C., *Ideas and Beliefs of the Victorians*, Sylvan Press, 1949, p. 43.

76. 'The Structure of Darwinism', in *New Biology 28*, Penguin Books, 1959, especially pp. 33–5.

these circumstances favourable variations would tend to be preserved, and unfavourable ones to be destroyed. The result of this would be the formation of a new species. Here, then, I had at last got a theory by which to work; but I was so anxious to avoid prejudice that I determined not for some time to write even the briefest sketch of it.[77]

It is a statement well worth pondering in all its aspects. Now compare it with another. As Darwin reflected on the evidence he had gathered during the voyage of the *Beagle* he faced the

inexplicable problem how the necessary degree of modification could have been effected, and it would have thus remained forever, had I not studied domestic productions, and thus acquired a just idea of the power of selection. As soon as I had fully realized this idea, I saw, on reading Malthus on Population, that natural selection was the inevitable result of the rapid increase of all organic beings; for I was prepared to appreciate the struggle for existence by having long studied the habits of animals.[78]

Both these passages were written up to three decades after the events which they record. But these memories of Darwin's later years can now be confirmed and supplemented by his private notes written at the time.[79] The evidence in the case of Wallace is similarly clear and first-hand but, in default of similar contemporary confirmation, perhaps not quite equally decisive. He too tells us in his autobiography, *My Life* (1905), how, at about the same time as Darwin had had his great inspiration,

perhaps the most important book I read was Malthus' *Principle of Population*. ... It was the first work I had yet read treating of any of the problems of philosophical biology, and its main principles remained with me as a permanent possession, and twenty years later gave me the long-sought clue to the effective agent in the evolution of organic species.[80]

77. C. Darwin, *Autobiography*, ed. N. Barlow, Collins, 1958, p. 120.

78. C. Darwin, *The Variations of Animals and Plants under Domestication*, J. Murray, 1868. Vol. I, p. 10.

79. See C. Darwin and A. R. Wallace, *Evolution by Natural Selection*, C.U.P. 1958, pp. 46–7 and 116–17. This and other relevant material is to be found in R. M. Young, 'Malthus and the Evolutionists', *Past and Present*, No. 43, 1969, pp. 109–45.

80. *My Life*, Chapman and Hall, 1905, Vol. I, p. 232.

His own inspiration came about twelve years later, during an attack of malaria. He gave several accounts, of which the fullest and best is also in *My Life*:

One day something brought to my recollection Malthus' *Principle of Population*, which I had read about twelve years before. I thought of his clear exposition of 'the positive checks' to increase ... which keep down the population. ... It then occurred to me that these causes or their equivalents are continually acting in the case of animals also; and, as animals usually breed much more rapidly than does mankind, the destructions every year from these causes must be enormous in order to keep down the numbers of each species, since they evidently do not increase regularly from year to year, as otherwise the world would long ago have become densely crowded with those that breed most quickly. ... Why do some die and some live? And the answer was clearly, that on the whole the best fitted live. From the effects of disease the most healthy escaped; from enemies the strongest, the swiftest, or the most cunning; from famine, the best hunters or those with the best digestion; and so on. Then it flashed upon me that this self-acting process would necessarily improve the race, because in every generation the inferior would inevitably be killed off and the superior would remain – that is, the fittest would survive. Then at once I seemed to see the whole effect of this. ... The more I thought over it the more I became convinced that I had at length found the long-sought-for law of nature that solved the problem of the origin of species.[81]

The reaction of Marx and Engels to Malthus was apoplectic. In the same early work from which I have quoted already Engels railed at the 'sham philanthropy' which 'produced the Malthusian population theory – the crudest, most barbarous theory that ever existed, a system of despair which struck down all those beautiful phrases about love of neighbour and world citizenship'.[82] Later he asks, starting with words which sound a little incongruous on the lips of an atheist: 'Am I to go on any longer elaborating this vile, infamous theory, this revolting blasphemy against nature and mankind? Am I to pursue its consequences any further? Here at last we have the immorality

81. ibid., Vol. I, pp. 361–2.
82. F. Engels, 'Outlines of a Critique of Political Economy', 1844, p. 199.

of the economist brought to its highest pitch.' [83] In this violent reaction Marx followed Engels: 'The hatred of the English working class against Malthus – the "mountebank-parson" as Cobbett rudely calls him – is therefore entirely justified. The people were right here in sensing instinctively that they were confronted not with a man of science but with a bought advocate, a pleader on behalf of their enemies, a shameless sycophant of the ruling classes.' [84]

The reason why this is more than an historical curiosity is, of course, that Marx and Engels have turned out to be the founders of a great crusading religion. They were, so to speak, the prophets of the secular Islam of the twentieth century. It is in the light of their vehement reaction to Malthus, therefore, that we have to understand the reluctance of those who bear the Marxist name to admit that there ever is or can be any need to check the increase of population. Thus we find a Soviet spokesman at the international conference on population in Rome in 1954, T. V. Ryabushkin, laying down the party line in these terms:

In the conditions of the capitalistic mode of production a certain part of the population systematically becomes relatively superfluous. ... In a socialist society ... the problem of excessive population no longer arises ... the Malthusian theory is completely wrong, and fruitless to explain historical facts. But maybe it has some sense for population policy in the future? Maybe it makes some sense to reduce the rate of increase in population in any economically backward country in order to increase to some extent the level of well-being of

83. ibid., p. 219.

84. This passage comes from what was originally intended to be a final volume of *Capital*, but in fact appeared in two volumes, edited K. Kautsky, as *Theorien über den Mehrwert* (Theories of Surplus Value). The relevant section of this book and other material is found most conveniently in R. L. Meek, *Marx and Engels on Malthus*, Lawrence and Wishart, 1953. It is to be regretted that Meek speaks throughout in His Moscow's Voice. Thus his long Introductory Essay concludes: 'The struggle against Malthusianism is an integral part of the struggle for peace in the world today' (p. 50) – a conclusion which only begins to have some modest degree of plausibility if the word 'peace' is read as roughly equivalent, in this sort of context, to 'Soviet power' or 'Communism'.

the population in the immediate future? To these questions also we give a sharp negative answer. The Malthusian theory is harmful because it distracts attention from really scientific ways of increasing the well-being of the working people.[85]

Enough has, I hope, been said already to show that the correct answers to both Ryabushkin's questions is not 'No' but 'Yes'. It is scandalous to pretend, as he and his masters do, that policies to limit reproduction are incompatible with policies to increase production. There is no sort of impossibility about pursuing both at once. Of course, whatever proportion of available resources is put into a birth-control programme cannot also be expended on the direct development of agriculture and industry. But that is not to say that you cannot have some of one and some of the other. In fact you may well find that you can only get a strong response to that programme when the economy is developing too, just as you cannot get the maximum possible rises in income per head if you allow economic development to be swallowed up by population growth.

Since this last is a demonstrable truth, we have here one of those situations in which ideology may conflict with practice. Fortunately for the secular theologians of Marxism there is one saving text. It comes in a rather late letter from Engels to Kautsky (1 February 1881):

There is, of course, the abstract possibility that the number of people will become so great that limits will have to be set to their increase. But if at some stage communist society finds itself obliged to regulate the production of human beings, just as it has already come to regulate the production of things, it will be precisely this society, and this society alone, which can carry this out without difficulty. It does not seem to me that it would be at all difficult in such a society to achieve by planning a result which has already been produced spontaneously, without planning, in France and Lower Austria.

The other thing which can ease or altogether remove the

85. *World Population Conference 1954*, United Nations, 1955, Vol. V, Meeting 28, pp. 1032–3 and 1038. One of the paradoxes of this conference was the way in which Roman Catholic and Communist ideologues kept finding themselves in Holy–Unholy Alliance.

practical problems for a Marxist-Leninist party, once it has installed itself in power, is that there is no obstacle in Marxist principle to making contraception and abortion freely available, provided this is not done for Malthusian reasons. (Connoisseurs of casuistry will find it illuminating, as well as maliciously agreeable, to add this to their lists of possible applications of the Principle of Double Effect; thus while, for instance, it is, in Roman Catholic eyes, utterly wrong to assist in euthanasia it is very good to relieve pain – and the side effect of a necessarily large dose of painkiller may just happen to be heart failure; and then again while in some jurisdictions the sale or advertisement of contraceptives is illegal, the traffic in condoms 'For the prevention of disease only' is not; and so on.)

It is perhaps indicative of who the 'sham philanthropists' really were, that neither Marx nor Engels ever showed any interest in or sympathy for the English birth-control movement, though this had been started by the impeccably radical Francis Place. In general both Marx and Engels were concerned with the future of an abstract social class rather than with the present welfare of human beings, even if these happened to be members of that class. (Who even tries to prove that Engels was a model employer?) And both Marx and Engels seem to have been as blind as the hated Malthus himself to the possibility that people might want to inhibit their reproductive powers for reasons which are not wholly, or even at all, economic. The same certainly cannot be said against Lenin and the élite of the Old Bolsheviks. For he and they insisted that the availability of both contraception and – as a longstop – abortion are necessary conditions of human emancipation, and especially of the emancipation of women : which they are.

THE ACHIEVEMENT OF MALTHUS

The aims of the *First Essay* were primarily practical. It was only in the *Second Essay* that the conceptual scheme devised for these purposes became the theoretical framework for a major descriptive and explanatory treatise which at once achieved its present status as the one indispensible landmark in the history of population studies. It was later still, years after the death of Malthus, that his fundamental ideas provided the crucial stimulus to the development of the theory of the origin of species by natural selection. So it is perhaps fitting if now, when we look back through all the dust and hubbub of the still continuing controversy, the main achievement of Malthus appears to be practical.

This main achievement is to have brought questions of national population and individual family size within the sphere of morality and prudence, of policy and decision. Of course, to say this is not to say that individuals and organizations do not still pretend that this is not so. On the contrary, it is precisely because they very often do make these pretences, and do show this form of what Sartrean existentialists would call bad faith, that Malthus remains so relevant. Consider, for instance, how most people in Britain still go on as if the present and expected future increase in the total national population were something entirely beyond human control – like the weather; and as if, consequently, it were something to which everyone and everything just has to adjust or be adjusted as best may be. (Significantly, perhaps, such bad faith was far less common in the thirties when the immediate prospect was of a population decline.) Nor, again, is my picking on this expansion of the realm of policy and decision as the great lesson which Malthus taught intended to imply that Malthus himself fully took his own lesson. On the contrary, the fact is, he did not. For he left it to others to point out that there could be moral restraint, in a wider sense, not merely from but within marriage.

No, the point is not that the lesson is nowadays fully mastered and taken to heart by everyone, but that since Malthus there is no excuse for those many who would ignore it. There is no excuse for those in Britain who take extrapolations of present population trends as unalterable data, and then ask how in an already congested country we are to accommodate another five Birminghams by 1984, or whatever it may be. Their offence is compounded by the certainty that a large part of our annual increase would disappear if only we had a strenuous and effective programme to ensure that no woman has more children than she wants to have, nor has these before she wants. Such a programme should in any case appear independently desirable to anyone genuinely concerned about welfare and emancipation.

Again – and far more important, if only because of the vaster numbers affected – there is now no excuse for those who in prescribing for developing countries attend only to production and never to reproduction. Nassau Senior, in his over-generous summing up of the agreement reached in his controversy with Malthus, put his finger on the crucial point: 'No plan for social improvement can be complete, unless it embraces the means both of increasing production, and of preventing population making a proportionate advance.' [86]

January 1970   A.G.N.F.

86. Nassau Senior, *Two Lectures on Population*, p. 90.

A NOTE ON THE TEXT

THE material below is in general exactly what Malthus himself originally published, with the following exceptions. Quite extensive changes have been made in the lesser punctuation, although Malthus's sentence divisions are always followed. Many spellings have been modernized. In this respect I should like to thank Miss Carol Filby for her useful suggestions, and mention that the engagingly archaic versions of some geographical and personal names, and of a few other words, have been retained against her protests. References which Malthus gave as footnotes have been elevated into the text as parentheses, and, where necessary, corrected and extended. Discursive footnotes – which are in fact all very relevant illustrations and developments of his argument – have also been inserted in the main text, where they belong. These deviations from the strict originals have been made in the interest of smoother reading.

The Editor's Notes, which are grouped separately (pp. 273–86) in order to remove any possible excuse for confusing what was said by Malthus with what is added by Flew, are intended to err, if at all, in the direction of over-fullness. By providing rather more than the minimum of information about persons mentioned by Malthus, and especially by noticing some of their connections with one another, I hoped to help a little to make them all seem more real. Where, as is the case with Godwin and Condorcet, the necessary background information has already been provided in the Introduction, it is not repeated in the Notes.

Facsimile of the title page of the first edition of
An Essay on the Principle of Population

AN

ESSAY

ON THE

PRINCIPLE OF POPULATION,

AS IT AFFECTS

THE FUTURE IMPROVEMENT OF SOCIETY

WITH REMARKS

ON THE SPECULATIONS OF MR. GODWIN,

M. CONDORCET,

AND OTHER WRITERS.

———————

LONDON:

PRINTED FOR J. JOHNSON, IN ST. PAUL'S
CHURCH-YARD.

———

1798.

PREFACE

THE following *Essay* owes its origin to a conversation with a friend, on the subject of Mr Godwin's essay on 'Avarice and Profusion' in his *Enquirer*. The discussion started the general question of the future improvement of society; and the Author at first sat down with an intention of merely stating his thoughts to his friend, upon paper, in a clearer manner than he thought he could do in conversation. But as the subject opened upon him, some ideas occurred, which he did not recollect to have met with before; and as he conceived that every least light, on a topic so generally interesting, might be received with candour, he determined to put his thoughts in a form for publication.

The *Essay* might, undoubtedly, have been rendered much more complete by a collection of a greater number of facts in elucidation of the general argument. But a long and almost total interruption from very particular business, joined to a desire (perhaps imprudent) of not delaying the publication much beyond the time that he originally proposed, prevented the Author from giving to the subject an undivided attention. He presumes, however, that the facts which he has adduced will be found to form no inconsiderable evidence for the truth of his opinion respecting the future improvement of mankind. As the Author contemplates this opinion at present, little more appears to him to be necessary than a plain statement, in addition to the most cursory view of society, to establish it.

It is an obvious truth, which has been taken notice of by many writers, that population must always be kept down to the level of the means of subsistence; but no writer that the Author recollects has inquired particularly into the means by which this level is effected: and it is a view of these means which forms, to his mind, the strongest obstacle in the way to any very great future improvement of society. He hopes it will appear that, in the discussion of this interesting subject, he is actuated solely by a love of truth, and not by any prejudices against any particular set of men, or of opinions. He professes to have read some of the speculations on the future improvement of society in a temper very different from a wish to find them visionary, but he has not acquired that command over his understanding which would enable him to believe what he wishes, without evidence, or to refuse his assent to what might be unpleasing, when accompanied with evidence.

The view which he has given of human life has a melancholy hue, but he feels conscious that he has drawn these dark tints from a conviction that they are really in the picture, and not from a jaundiced eye or an inherent spleen of disposition. The theory of mind which he has sketched in the two last chapters accounts to his own understanding in a satisfactory manner for the existence of most of the evils of life, but whether it will have the same effect upon others must be left to the judgement of his readers.

If he should succeed in drawing the attention of more able men to what he conceives to be the principal difficulty in the way to the improvement of society and should, in consequence, see this difficulty removed, even in theory, he will gladly retract his present opinions and rejoice in a conviction of his error.

7 June 1798

CONTENTS

of society – All the checks to population may be resolved into misery or vice.

CHAPTER I

Question, stated – Little prospect of a determination of it, from the enmity of the opposing parties – The principal argument against the perfectibility of man and of society has never been fairly answered – Nature of the difficulty arising from population – Outline of the principal argument of the *Essay*.

THE great and unlooked for discoveries that have taken place of late years in natural philosophy, the increasing diffusion of general knowledge from the extension of the art of printing, the ardent and unshackled spirit of inquiry that prevails throughout the lettered and even unlettered world, the new and extraordinary lights that have been thrown on political subjects which dazzle and astonish the understanding, and particularly that tremendous phenomenon in the political horizon, the French Revolution, which, like a blazing comet, seems destined either to inspire with fresh life and vigour, or to scorch up and destroy the shrinking inhabitants of the earth, have all concurred to lead many able men into the opinion that we were touching on a period big with the most important changes, changes that would in some measure be decisive of the future fate of mankind.

It has been said that the great question is now at issue, whether man shall henceforth start forwards with accelerated velocity towards illimitable, and hitherto unconceived improvement, or be condemned to a perpetual oscillation between happiness and misery, and after every effort remain still at an immeasurable distance from the wished-for goal.

Yet, anxiously as every friend of mankind must look forwards to the termination of this painful suspense, and eagerly as the inquiring mind would hail every ray of light that might assist its view into futurity, it is much to be lamented that the writers on each side of this momentous question still keep far aloof from each other. Their mutual arguments do not meet with a candid examination. The question is not brought to rest on fewer points, and even in theory scarcely seems to be approaching to a decision.

The advocate for the present order of things is apt to treat the sect of speculative philosophers either as a set of artful and designing knaves who preach up ardent benevolence and draw captivating pictures of a happier state of society only the better to enable them to destroy the present establishments and to forward their own deep-laid schemes of ambition, or as wild and mad-headed enthusiasts whose silly speculations and absurd paradoxes are not worthy the attention of any reasonable man.

The advocate for the perfectibility of man, and of society, retorts on the defender of establishments a more than equal contempt. He brands him as the slave of the most miserable and narrow prejudices; or as the defender of the abuses of civil society only because he profits by them. He paints him either as a character who prostitutes his understanding to his interest, or as one whose powers of mind are not of a size to grasp any thing great and noble, who cannot see above five yards before him, and who must therefore be utterly unable to take in the views of the enlightened benefactor of mankind.

In this unamicable contest the cause of truth cannot but suffer. The really good arguments on each side of the question are not allowed to have their proper weight. Each pursues his own theory, little solicitous to correct or improve it by an attention to what is advanced by his opponents.

The friend of the present order of things condemns all political speculations in the gross. He will not even condescend to examine the grounds from which the perfectibility of society is inferred. Much less will he give himself the trouble in a fair and candid manner to attempt an exposition of their fallacy.

The speculative philosopher equally offends against the cause of truth. With eyes fixed on a happier state of society, the blessings of which he paints in the most captivating colours, he allows himself to indulge in the most bitter invectives against every present establishment, without applying his talents to consider the best and safest means of removing abuses and without seeming to be aware of the tremendous obstacles that threaten, even in theory, to oppose the progress of man towards perfection.

It is an acknowledged truth in philosophy that a just theory will always be confirmed by experiment. Yet so much friction, and so many minute circumstances occur in practice, which it is next to impossible for the most enlarged and penetrating mind to foresee, that on few subjects can any theory be pronounced just, till all the arguments against it have been maturely weighed and clearly and consistently refuted.

I have read some of the speculations on the perfectibility of man and of society with great pleasure. I have been warmed and delighted with the enchanting picture which they hold forth. I ardently wish for such happy improvements. But I see great, and, to my understanding, unconquerable difficulties in the way to them. These difficulties it is my present purpose to state, declaring, at the same time, that so far from exulting in them, as a cause of triumph over the friends of innovation, nothing would give me greater pleasure than to see them completely removed.

The most important argument that I shall adduce is certainly not new. The principles on which it depends have been explained in part by Hume, and more at large by Dr Adam Smith. It has been advanced and applied to the present subject, though not with its proper weight, or in the most forcible point of view, by Mr Wallace, and it may probably have been stated by many writers that I have never met with.[1] I should certainly therefore not think of advancing it again, though I mean to place it in a point of view in some degree different from any that I have hitherto seen, if it had ever been fairly and satisfactorily answered.

The cause of this neglect on the part of the advocates for the perfectibility of mankind is not easily accounted for. I cannot doubt the talents of such men as Godwin and Condorcet. I am unwilling to doubt their candour. To my understanding, and probably to that of most others, the difficulty appears insurmountable. Yet these men of acknowledged ability and penetration scarcely deign to notice it, and hold on their course in such speculations with unabated ardour and undiminished confidence. I have certainly no right to say that they purposely shut their eyes to such arguments. I ought rather to doubt the validity of them, when neglected by such men, however forcibly their truth may strike my own mind. Yet in this respect it must be acknowledged that we are all of us too prone to err. If I saw a glass of wine repeatedly presented to a man, and he took no notice of it, I should be apt to think that he was blind or uncivil. A juster philosophy might teach me rather to think that my eyes deceived me and that the offer was not really what I conceived it to be.

In entering upon the argument I must premise that I put out of the question, at present, all mere conjectures, that is, all suppositions, the probable realization of which cannot be inferred upon any just philosophical grounds. A writer may tell me that he thinks man will ultimately become an ostrich. I cannot properly contradict him. But before he can expect to bring any reasonable person over to his opinion, he ought to shew that the necks of mankind have been gradually elongating, that the lips have grown harder and more prominent, that the legs and feet are daily altering their shape, and that the hair is beginning to change into stubs of feathers. And till the probability of so wonderful a conversion can be shewn, it is surely lost time and lost eloquence to expatiate on the happiness of man in such a state; to describe his powers, both of running and flying, to paint him in a condition where all narrow luxuries would be contemned, where he would be employed only in collecting the necessaries of life, and where, consequently, each man's share of labour would be light, and his portion of leisure ample.

I think I may fairly make two postulata.

First, That food is necessary to the existence of man.

Secondly, That the passion between the sexes is necessary and will remain nearly in its present state.

These two laws, ever since we have had any knowledge of mankind, appear to have been fixed laws of our nature, and, as we have not hitherto seen any alteration in them, we have no right to conclude that they will ever cease to be what they now are, without an immediate act of power in that Being who first arranged the system of the universe, and for the advantage of his creatures, still executes, according to fixed laws, all its various operations.

I do not know that any writer has supposed that on this earth man will ultimately be able to live without food. But Mr Godwin has conjectured that the passion between the sexes may in time be extinguished. As, however, he calls this part of his work a deviation into the land of conjecture, I will not dwell longer upon it at present than to say that the best arguments for the perfectibility of man are drawn from a contemplation of the great progress that he has already made from the savage state and the difficulty of saying where he is to stop. But towards the extinction of the passion between the sexes, no progress whatever has hitherto been made. It appears to exist in as much force at present as it did two thousand or four thousand years ago. There are individual exceptions now as there always have been. But, as these exceptions do not appear to increase in number, it would surely be a very unphilosophical mode of arguing to infer, merely from the existence of an exception, that the exception would, in time, become the rule, and the rule the exception.

Assuming then my postulata as granted, I say, that the power of population is indefinitely greater than the power in the earth to produce subsistence for man.

Population, when unchecked, increases in a geometrical ratio. Subsistence increases only in an arithmetical ratio. A slight acquaintance with numbers will shew the immensity of the first power in comparison of the second.

By that law of our nature which makes food necessary to the life of man, the effects of these two unequal powers must be kept equal.

This implies a strong and constantly operating check on population from the difficulty of subsistence. This difficulty must fall somewhere and must necessarily be severely felt by a large portion of mankind.

Through the animal and vegetable kingdoms, nature has scattered the seeds of life abroad with the most profuse and liberal hand. She has been comparatively sparing in the room and the nourishment necessary to rear them. The germs of existence contained in this spot of earth, with ample food, and ample room to expand in, would fill millions of worlds in the course of a few thousand years. Necessity, that imperious all pervading law of nature, restrains them within the prescribed bounds. The race of plants and the race of animals shrink under this great restrictive law. And the race of man cannot, by any efforts of reason, escape from it. Among plants and animals its effects are waste of seed, sickness, and premature death. Among mankind, misery and vice. The former, misery, is an absolutely necessary consequence of it. Vice is a highly probable consequence, and we therefore see it abundantly prevail, but it ought not, perhaps, to be called an absolutely necessary consequence. The ordeal of virtue is to resist all temptation to evil.

This natural inequality of the two powers of population and of production in the earth, and that great law of our nature which must constantly keep their effects equal, form the great difficulty that to me appears insurmountable in the way to the perfectibility of society. All other arguments are of slight and subordinate consideration in comparison of this. I see no way by which man can escape from the weight of this law which pervades all animated nature. No fancied equality, no agrarian regulations in their utmost extent, could remove the pressure of it even for a single century. And it appears, therefore, to be decisive against the possible existence of a society, all the members of which should live in ease, happiness, and comparative leisure; and feel no anxiety about providing the means of subsistence for themselves and families.

Consequently, if the premises are just, the argument is conclusive against the perfectibility of the mass of mankind.

I have thus sketched the general outline of the argument, but I will examine it more particularly, and I think it will be found that experience, the true source and foundation of all knowledge, invariably confirms its truth.

CHAPTER II

The different ratios in which population and food increase
– The necessary effects of these different ratios of increase –
Oscillation produced by them in the condition of the lower
classes of society – Reasons why this oscillation has not been
so much observed as might be expected – Three propositions
on which the general argument of the *Essay* depends – The
different states in which mankind have been known to
exist proposed to be examined with reference to these three
propositions.

I SAID that population, when unchecked, increased in a geometrical ratio, and subsistence for man in an arithmetical ratio.

Let us examine whether this position be just.

I think it will be allowed, that no state has hitherto existed
(at least that we have any account of) where the manners were
so pure and simple, and the means of subsistence so abundant,
that no check whatever has existed to early marriages, among
the lower classes, from a fear of not providing well for their
families, or among the higher classes, from a fear of lowering
their condition in life. Consequently in no state that we have yet
known has the power of population been left to exert itself with
perfect freedom.

Whether the law of marriage be instituted or not, the dictate
of nature and virtue seems to be an early attachment to one
woman. Supposing a liberty of changing in the case of an un-
fortunate choice, this liberty would not affect population till it
arose to a height greatly vicious; and we are now supposing the
existence of a society where vice is scarcely known.

In a state therefore of great equality and virtue, where pure
and simple manners prevailed, and where the means of subsistence were so abundant that no part of the society could have
any fears about providing amply for a family, the power of
population being left to exert itself unchecked, the increase of

the human species would evidently be much greater than any increase that has been hitherto known.

In the United States of America, where the means of subsistence have been more ample, the manners of the people more pure, and consequently the checks to early marriages fewer, than in any of the modern states of Europe, the population has been found to double itself in twenty-five years.

This ratio of increase, though short of the utmost power of population, yet as the result of actual experience, we will take as our rule, and say, that population, when unchecked, goes on doubling itself every twenty-five years or increases in a geometrical ratio.

Let us now take any spot of earth, this Island for instance, and see in what ratio the subsistence it affords can be supposed to increase. We will begin with it under its present state of cultivation.

If I allow that by the best possible policy, by breaking up more land and by great encouragements to agriculture, the produce of this Island may be doubled in the first twenty-five years, I think it will be allowing as much as any person can well demand.

In the next twenty-five years, it is impossible to suppose that the produce could be quadrupled. It would be contrary to all our knowledge of the qualities of land. The very utmost that we can conceive, is, that the increase in the second twenty-five years might equal the present produce. Let us then take this for our rule, though certainly far beyond the truth, and allow that, by great exertion, the whole produce of the Island might be increased every twenty-five years, by a quantity of subsistence equal to what it at present produces. The most enthusiastic speculator cannot suppose a greater increase than this. In a few centuries it would make every acre of land in the Island like a garden.

Yet this ratio of increase is evidently arithmetical.

It may be fairly said, therefore, that the means of subsistence increase in an arithmetical ratio. Let us now bring the effects of these two ratios together.

The population of the Island is computed to be about seven

millions, and we will suppose the present produce equal to the support of such a number. In the first twenty-five years the population would be fourteen millions, and the food being also doubled, the means of subsistence would be equal to this increase. In the next twenty-five years the population would be twenty-eight millions, and the means of subsistence only equal to the support of twenty-one millions. In the next period, the population would be fifty-six millions, and the means of subsistence just sufficient for half that number. And at the conclusion of the first century the population would be one hundred and twelve millions and the means of subsistence only equal to the support of thirty-five millions, which would leave a population of seventy-seven millions totally unprovided for.

A great emigration necessarily implies unhappiness of some kind or other in the country that is deserted. For few persons will leave their families, connections, friends, and native land, to seek a settlement in untried foreign climes, without some strong subsisting causes of uneasiness where they are, or the hope of some great advantages in the place to which they are going.

But to make the argument more general and less interrupted by the partial views of emigration, let us take the whole earth, instead of one spot, and suppose that the restraints to population were universally removed. If the subsistence for man that the earth affords was to be increased every twenty-five years by a quantity equal to what the whole world at present produces, this would allow the power of production in the earth to be absolutely unlimited, and its ratio of increase much greater than we can conceive that any possible exertions of mankind could make it.

Taking the population of the world at any number, a thousand millions, for instance, the human species would increase in the ratio of – 1, 2, 4, 8, 16, 32, 64, 128, 256, 512, etc. and subsistence as – 1, 2, 3, 4, 5, 6, 7, 8, 9, 10, etc. In two centuries and a quarter, the population would be to the means of subsistence as 512 to 10: in three centuries as 4096 to 13, and in two thousand years the difference would be almost incalculable, though the produce in that time would have increased to an immense extent.

No limits whatever are placed to the productions of the earth; they may increase for ever and be greater than any assignable quantity; yet still the power of population being a power of a superior order, the increase of the human species can only be kept commensurate to the increase of the means of subsistence by the constant operation of the strong law of necessity acting as a check upon the greater power.

The effects of this check remain now to be considered.

Among plants and animals the view of the subject is simple. They are all impelled by a powerful instinct to the increase of their species, and this instinct is interrupted by no reasoning or doubts about providing for their offspring. Wherever therefore there is liberty, the power of increase is exerted, and the super-abundant effects are repressed afterwards by want of room and nourishment, which is common to animals and plants, and among animals by becoming the prey of others.

The effects of this check on man are more complicated. Impelled to the increase of his species by an equally powerful instinct, reason interrupts his career and asks him whether he may not bring beings into the world for whom he cannot provide the means of subsistence. In a state of equality, this would be the simple question. In the present state of society, other considerations occur. Will he not lower his rank in life? Will he not subject himself to greater difficulties than he at present feels? Will he not be obliged to labour harder? and if he has a large family, will his utmost exertions enable him to support them? May he not see his offspring in rags and misery, and clamouring for bread that he cannot give them? And may he not be reduced to the grating necessity of forfeiting his independence, and of being obliged to the sparing hand of charity for support?

These considerations are calculated to prevent, and certainly do prevent, a very great number in all civilized nations from pursuing the dictate of nature in an early attachment to one woman. And this restraint almost necessarily, though not absolutely so, produces vice. Yet in all societies, even those that are most vicious, the tendency to a virtuous attachment is so strong that there is a constant effort towards an increase of population. This constant effort as constantly tends to subject the lower classes of the society to distress and to prevent any great permanent amelioration of their condition.

The way in which these effects are produced seems to be this. We will suppose the means of subsistence in any country just equal to the easy support of its inhabitants. The constant effort towards population, which is found to act even in the most vicious societies, increases the number of people before the means of subsistence are increased. The food therefore which before supported seven millions must now be divided among seven millions and a half or eight millions. The poor consequently must live much worse, and many of them be reduced to severe distress. The number of labourers also being above the proportion of the work in the market, the price of labour must tend toward a decrease, while the price of provisions would at the same time tend to rise. The labourer therefore must work harder to earn the same as he did before. During this season of distress, the discouragements to marriage, and the difficulty of rearing a family are so great that population is at a stand. In the mean time the cheapness of labour, the plenty of labourers, and the necessity of an increased industry amongst them, encourage cultivators to employ more labour upon their land, to turn up fresh soil, and to manure and improve more completely what is already in tillage, till ultimately the means of subsistence become in the same proportion to the population as at the period from which we set out. The situation of the labourer being then again tolerably comfortable, the restraints to population are in some degree loosened, and the same retrograde and progressive movements with respect to happiness are repeated.

This sort of oscillation will not be remarked by superficial observers, and it may be difficult even for the most penetrating mind to calculate its periods. Yet that in all old states some such vibration does exist, though from various transverse causes, in a much less marked, and in a much more irregular manner than I have described it, no reflecting man who considers the subject deeply can well doubt.

Many reasons occur why this oscillation has been less obvious, and less decidedly confirmed by experience, than might naturally be expected.

One principal reason is that the histories of mankind that we possess are histories only of the higher classes. We have but few accounts that can be depended upon of the manners and customs of that part of mankind where these retrograde and progressive movements chiefly take place. A satisfactory history of this kind, on one people, and of one period, would require the constant and minute attention of an observing mind during a long life. Some of the objects of inquiry would be, in what proportion to the number of adults was the number of marriages, to what extent vicious customs prevailed in consequence of the restraints upon matrimony, what was the comparative mortality among the children of the most distressed part of the community and those who lived rather more at their ease, what were the variations in the real price of labour, and what were the observable differences in the state of the lower classes of society with respect to ease and happiness, at different times during a certain period.

Such a history would tend greatly to elucidate the manner in which the constant check upon population acts and would probably prove the existence of the retrograde and progressive movements that have been mentioned, though the times of their vibrations must necessarily be rendered irregular from the operation of many interrupting causes, such as the introduction or failure of certain manufactures, a greater or less prevalent spirit of agricultural enterprise, years of plenty, or years of scarcity, wars and pestilence, poor laws, the invention of processes for shortening labour without the proportional extension of the market for the commodity, and, particularly, the difference between the nominal and real price of labour, a circumstance which has perhaps more than any other contributed to conceal this oscillation from common view.

It very rarely happens that the nominal price of labour universally falls, but we well know that it frequently remains the same, while the nominal price of provisions has been gradually increasing. This is, in effect, a real fall in the price of labour, and during this period the condition of the lower orders of the community must gradually grow worse and worse. But the farmers and capitalists are growing rich from the real cheapness of labour. Their increased capitals enable them to employ a greater number of men. Work therefore may be plentiful, and the price of labour would consequently rise. But the want of freedom in the market of labour, which occurs more or less in all communities, either from parish laws, or the more general cause of the facility of combination among the rich, and its difficulty among the poor, operates to prevent the price of labour from rising at the natural period, and keeps it down some time longer; perhaps till a year of scarcity, when the clamour is too loud and the necessity too apparent to be resisted.

The true cause of the advance in the price of labour is thus concealed, and the rich affect to grant it as an act of compassion and favour to the poor, in consideration of a year of scarcity, and, when plenty returns, indulge themselves in the most unreasonable of all complaints, that the price does not again fall, when a little reflection would shew them that it must have risen long before but from an unjust conspiracy of their own.

But though the rich by unfair combinations contribute frequently to prolong a season of distress among the poor, yet no possible form of society could prevent the almost constant action of misery upon a great part of mankind, if in a state of inequality, and upon all, if all were equal.

The theory on which the truth of this position depends appears to me so extremely clear that I feel at a loss to conjecture what part of it can be denied.

That population cannot increase without the means of subsistence is a proposition so evident that it needs no illustration.

That population does invariably increase where there are the means of subsistence, the history of every people that have ever existed will abundantly prove.

And that the superior power of population cannot be checked without producing misery or vice, the ample portion of these too bitter ingredients in the cup of human life and the continuance of the physical causes that seem to have produced them bear too convincing a testimony.

But, in order more fully to ascertain the validity of these three propositions, let us examine the different states in which mankind have been known to exist. Even a cursory review will, I think, be sufficient to convince us that these propositions are incontrovertible truths.

CHAPTER III

The savage or hunter state shortly reviewed – The shepherd
state, or the tribes of barbarians that overran the Roman
Empire – The superiority of the power of population to the
means of subsistence – the cause of the great tide of Northern
Emigration.

In the rudest state of mankind, in which hunting is the principal occupation, and the only mode of acquiring food, the
means of subsistence being scattered over a large extent of territory, the comparative population must necessarily be thin. It
is said that the passion between the sexes is less ardent among
the North American Indians than among any other race of
men. Yet, notwithstanding this apathy, the effort towards population, even in this people, seems to be always greater than the
means to support it. This appears from the comparatively rapid
population that takes place whenever any of the tribes happen
to settle in some fertile spot and to draw nourishment from
more fruitful sources than that of hunting, and it has been
frequently remarked that when an Indian family has taken up
its abode near any European settlement and adopted a more
easy and civilized mode of life, that one woman has reared five,
or six, or more children, though in the savage state it rarely
happens that above one or two in a family grow up to maturity.
The same observation has been made with regard to the Hot-
tentots near the Cape. These facts prove the superior power of
population to the means of subsistence in nations of hunters,
and that this power always shews itself the moment it is left to
act with freedom.

It remains to inquire whether this power can be checked, and
its effects kept equal to the means of subsistence, without vice
or misery.

The North American Indians, considered as a people, cannot
justly be called free and equal. In all the accounts we have of
them, and, indeed, of most other savage nations, the women are

represented as much more completely in a state of slavery to the men than the poor are to the rich in civilized countries. One half the nation appears to act as Helots to the other half, and the misery that checks population falls chiefly, as it always must do, upon that part whose condition is lowest in the scale of society. The infancy of man in the simplest state requires considerable attention, but this necessary attention the women cannot give, condemned as they are to the inconveniences and hardships of frequent change of place and to the constant and unremitting drudgery of preparing every thing for the reception of their tyrannic lords. These exertions, sometimes during pregnancy or with children at their backs, must occasion frequent miscarriages, and prevent any but the most robust infants from growing to maturity. Add to these hardships of the women the constant war that prevails among savages, and the necessity which they frequently labour under of exposing their aged and helpless parents, and of thus violating the first feelings of nature, and the picture will not appear very free from the blot of misery. In estimating the happiness of a savage nation, we must not fix our eyes only on the warrior in the prime of life: he is one of a hundred: he is the gentleman, the man of fortune, the chances have been in his favour; and many efforts have failed ere this fortunate being was produced, whose guardian genius should preserve him through the numberless dangers with which he would be surrounded from infancy to manhood. The true points of comparison between two nations seem to be the ranks in each which appear nearest to answer to each other. And in this view, I should compare the warriors in the prime of life with the gentlemen, and the women, children, and aged, with the lower classes of the community in civilized states.

May we not then fairly infer from this short review, or rather, from the accounts that may be referred to of nations of hunters, that their population is thin from the scarcity of food, that it would immediately increase if food was in greater plenty, and that, putting vice out of the question among savages, misery is the check that represses the superior power of population and keeps its effects equal to the means of subsistence. Actual observation and experience tell us that this check, with a few local and temporary exceptions, is constantly acting now upon all savage nations, and the theory indicates that it probably acted with nearly equal strength a thousand years ago, and it may not be much greater a thousand years hence.

Of the manners and habits that prevail among nations of shepherds, the next state of mankind, we are even more ignorant than of the savage state. But that these nations could not escape the general lot of misery arising from the want of subsistence, Europe, and all the fairest countries in the world, bear ample testimony. Want was the goad that drove the Scythian shepherds from their native haunts, like so many famished wolves in search of prey. Set in motion by this all powerful cause, clouds of Barbarians seemed to collect from all points of the northern hemisphere. Gathering fresh darkness and terror as they rolled on, the congregated bodies at length obscured the sun of Italy and sunk the whole world in universal night. These tremendous effects, so long and so deeply felt throughout the fairest portions of the earth, may be traced to the simple cause of the superior power of population to the means of subsistence.

It is well known that a country in pasture cannot support so many inhabitants as a country in tillage, but what renders nations of shepherds so formidable is the power which they possess of moving all together and the necessity they frequently feel of exerting this power in search of fresh pasture for their herds. A tribe that was rich in cattle had an immediate plenty of food. Even the parent stock might be devoured in a case of absolute necessity. The women lived in greater ease than among nations of hunters. The men bold in their united strength and confiding in their power of procuring pasture for their cattle by change of place, felt, probably, but few fears about providing for a family. These combined causes soon produced their natural and invariable effect, an extended population. A more frequent and rapid change of place became then necessary. A wider and more extensive territory was successively occupied. A broader desolation extended all around them. Want pinched the less fortunate members of the society, and, at length, the impossibility of supporting such a number together became too evident to be resisted. Young scions were then pushed out from the parent-stock and instructed to explore fresh regions and to gain happier seats for themselves by their swords. 'The world was all before them where to choose.'[2] Restless from present distress, flushed with the hope of fairer prospects, and animated with the spirit of hardy enterprise, these daring adventurers were likely to become formidable adversaries to all who opposed them. The peaceful inhabitants of the countries on which they rushed could not long withstand the energy of men acting under such powerful motives of exertion. And when they fell in with any tribes like their own, the contest was a struggle for existence, and they fought with a desperate courage, inspired by the reflection that death was the punishment of defeat and life the prize of victory.

In these savage contests many tribes must have been utterly exterminated. Some, probably, perished by hardship and famine. Others, whose leading star had given them a happier direction, became great and powerful tribes, and, in their turns, sent off fresh adventurers in search of still more fertile seats. The prodigious waste of human life occasioned by this perpetual struggle for room and food was more than supplied by the mighty power of population, acting, in some degree, unshackled from the constant habit of emigration. The tribes that migrated towards the South, though they won these more fruitful regions by continual battles, rapidly increased in number and power, from the increased means of subsistence. Till at length the whole territory, from the confines of China to the shores of the Baltic, was peopled by a various race of Barbarians, brave, robust, and enterprising, inured to hardship, and delighting in war. Some tribes maintained their independence. Others ranged themselves under the standard of some barbaric chieftain who led them to victory after victory, and what was of more importance, to regions abounding in corn, wine, and oil, the long wished for consummation, and great reward of their labours. An Alaric, an Attila, or a Zingis Khan,[3] and the chiefs around them, might fight for glory, for the fame of extensive conquests, but the true cause that set in motion the great tide of northern emigration, and that continued to propel it till it rolled at different periods against China, Persia, Italy, and even Egypt, was a scarcity of food, a population extended beyond the means of supporting it.

The absolute population at any one period, in proportion to the extent of territory, could never be great, on account of the unproductive nature of some of the regions occupied; but there appears to have been a most rapid succession of human beings, and as fast as some were mowed down by the scythe of war or of famine, others rose in increased numbers to supply their place. Among these bold and improvident Barbarians, population was probably but little checked, as in modern states, from a fear of future difficulties. A prevailing hope of bettering their condition by change of place, a constant expectation of plunder, a power even, if distressed, of selling their children as slaves, added to the natural carelessness of the barbaric character, all conspired to raise a population which remained to be repressed afterwards by famine or war.

Where there is any inequality of conditions, and among nations of shepherds this soon takes place, the distress arising from a scarcity of provisions must fall hardest upon the least fortunate members of the society. This distress also must frequently have been felt by the women, exposed to casual plunder in the absence of their husbands, and subject to continual disappointments in their expected return.

But without knowing enough of the minute and intimate history of these people, to point out precisely on what part the distress for want of food chiefly fell, and to what extent it was generally felt, I think we may fairly say, from all the accounts that we have of nations of shepherds, that population invariably increased among them whenever, by emigration or any other cause, the means of subsistence were increased, and that a further population was checked, and the actual population kept equal to the means of subsistence, by misery and vice.

For, independently of any vicious customs that might have prevailed amongst them with regard to women, which always operate as checks to population, it must be acknowledged, I think, that the commission of war is vice, and the effect of it misery, and none can doubt the misery of want of food.

CHAPTER IV

State of civilized nations – Probability that Europe is much more populous now than in the time of Julius Caesar – Best criterion of population – Probable error of Hume in one of the criterions that he proposes as assisting in an estimate of population – Slow increase of population at present in most of the states of Europe – The two principal checks to population – The first, or preventive check examined with regard to England.

IN examining the next state of mankind with relation to the question before us, the state of mixed pasture and tillage, in which with some variation in the proportions the most civilized nations must always remain, we shall be assisted in our review by what we daily see around us, by actual experience, by facts that come within the scope of every man's observation.

Notwithstanding the exaggerations of some old historians, there can remain no doubt in the mind of any thinking man that the population of the principal countries of Europe, France, England, Germany, Russia, Poland, Sweden, and Denmark is much greater than ever it was in former times. The obvious reason of these exaggerations is the formidable aspect that even a thinly peopled nation must have, when collected together and moving all at once in search of fresh seats. If to this tremendous appearance be added a succession at certain intervals of similar emigrations, we shall not be much surprised that the fears of the timid nations of the South represented the North as a region absolutely swarming with human beings. A nearer and juster view of the subject at present enables us to see that the inference was as absurd as if a man in this country, who was continually meeting on the road droves of cattle from Wales and the North, was immediately to conclude that these countries were the most productive of all the parts of the kingdom.

The reason that the greater part of Europe is more populous now than it was in former times, is that the industry of the inhabitants has made these countries produce a greater quantity of human subsistence. For I conceive that it may be laid down as a position not to be controverted, that, taking a sufficient extent of territory to include within it exportation and importation, and allowing some variation for the prevalence of luxury, or of frugal habits, *that population constantly bears a regular proportion to the food that the earth is made to produce*. In the controversy concerning the populousness of ancient and modern nations, could it be clearly ascertained that the average produce of the countries in question, taken altogether, is greater now than it was in the times of Julius Caesar,[4] the dispute would be at once determined.

When we are assured that China is the most fertile country in the world, that almost all the land is in tillage, and that a great part of it bears two crops every year, and further, that the people live very frugally, we may infer with certainty that the population must be immense, without busying ourselves in inquiries into the manners and habits of the lower classes and the encouragements to early marriages. But these inquiries are of the utmost importance, and a minute history of the customs of the lower Chinese would be of the greatest use in ascertaining in what manner the checks to a further population operate; what are the vices, and what are the distresses that prevent an increase of numbers beyond the ability of the country to support.

Hume, in his essay on the populousness of ancient and modern nations, when he intermingles, as he says, an inquiry concerning causes with that concerning facts, does not seem to see with his usual penetration how very little some of the causes he alludes to could enable him to form any judgement of the actual population of ancient nations. If any inference can be drawn from them, perhaps it should be directly the reverse of what Hume draws, though I certainly ought to speak with great diffidence in dissenting from a man who of all others on such subjects was the least likely to be deceived by first appearances. If I find that at a certain period in ancient history, the encouragements to have a family were great, that early marriages were consequently very prevalent, and that few persons remained single, I should infer with certainty that population was rapidly increasing, but by no means that it was then actually very great, rather; indeed, the contrary, that it was then thin and that there was room and food for a much greater number. On the other hand, if I find that at this period the difficulties attending a family were very great, that, consequently, few early marriages took place, and that a great number of both sexes remained single, I infer with certainty that population was at a stand, and, probably, because the actual population was very great in proportion to the fertility of the land and that there was scarcely room and food for more. The number of footmen, housemaids, and other persons remaining unmarried in modern states, Hume allows to be rather an argument against their population. I should rather draw a contrary inference and consider it an argument of their fullness, though this inference is not certain, because there are many thinly inhabited states that are yet stationary in their population. To speak, therefore, correctly, perhaps it may be said that the number of unmarried persons in proportion to the whole number, existing at different periods, in the same or different states will enable us to judge whether population at these periods was increasing, stationary, or decreasing, but will form no criterion by which we can determine the actual population.

There is, however, a circumstance taken notice of in most of the accounts we have of China that it seems difficult to reconcile with this reasoning. It is said that early marriages very generally prevail through all the ranks of the Chinese. Yet Dr Adam Smith supposes that population in China is stationary. These two circumstances appear to be irreconcilable. It certainly seems very little probable that the population of China is fast increasing. Every acre of land has been so long in cultivation that we can hardly conceive there is any great yearly addition to the average produce. The fact, perhaps, of the universality of early marriages may not be sufficiently ascertained. If it be supposed true, the only way of accounting for the difficulty, with our present knowledge of the subject, appears to be that the redundant population, necessarily occasioned by the prevalence of early marriages, must be repressed by occasional famines, and by the custom of exposing children, which, in times of distress, is probably more frequent than is ever acknowledged to Europeans. Relative to this barbarous practice, it is difficult to avoid remarking, that there cannot be a stronger proof of the distresses that have been felt by mankind for want of food, than the existence of a custom that thus violates the most natural principle of the human heart. It appears to have been very general among ancient nations, and certainly tended rather to increase population.

In examining the principal states of modern Europe, we shall find that though they have increased very considerably in population since they were nations of shepherds, yet that at present their progress is but slow, and instead of doubling their numbers every twenty-five years they require three or four hundred years, or more, for that purpose. Some, indeed, may be absolutely stationary, and others even retrograde. The cause of this slow progress in population cannot be traced to a decay of the passion between the sexes. We have sufficient reason to think that this natural propensity exists still in undiminished vigour. Why then do not its effects appear in a rapid increase of the human species? An intimate view of the state of society in any one country in Europe, which may serve equally for all, will enable us to answer this question, and to say that a foresight of the difficulties attending the rearing of a family acts as a preventive check, and the actual distresses of some of the lower classes, by which they are disabled from giving the proper food and attention to their children, act as a positive check to the natural increase of population.

England, as one of the most flourishing states of Europe, may be fairly taken for an example, and the observations made will apply with but little variation to any other country where the population increases slowly.

The preventive check appears to operate in some degree through all the ranks of society in England. There are some men, even in the highest rank, who are prevented from marrying by the idea of the expenses that they must retrench, and the fancied pleasures that they must deprive themselves of, on the supposition of having a family. These considerations are certainly trivial, but a preventive foresight of this kind has objects of much greater weight for its contemplation as we go lower.

A man of liberal education, but with an income only just sufficient to enable him to associate in the rank of gentlemen, must feel absolutely certain that if he marries and has a family he shall be obliged, if he mixes at all in society, to rank himself with moderate farmers and the lower class of tradesmen. The woman that a man of education would naturally make the object of his choice would be one brought up in the same tastes and sentiments with himself and used to the familiar intercourse of a society totally different from that to which she must be reduced by marriage. Can a man consent to place the object of his affection in a situation so discordant, probably, to her tastes and inclinations? Two or three steps of descent in society, particularly at this round of the ladder, where education ends and ignorance begins, will not be considered by the generality of people as a fancied and chimerical, but a real and essential evil. If society be held desirable, it surely must be free, equal, and reciprocal society, where benefits are conferred as well as received, and not such as the dependent finds with his patron or the poor with the rich.

These considerations undoubtedly prevent a great number in this rank of life from following the bent of their inclinations in an early attachment. Others, guided either by a stronger passion, or a weaker judgement, break through these restraints, and it would be hard indeed, if the gratification of so delightful a passion as virtuous love, did not, sometimes, more than counterbalance all its attendant evils. But I fear it must be owned that the more general consequences of such marriages are rather calculated to justify than to repress the forebodings of the prudent.

The sons of tradesmen and farmers are exhorted not to marry, and generally find it necessary to pursue this advice till they are settled in some business or farm that may enable them to support a family. These events may not, perhaps, occur till they are far advanced in life. The scarcity of farms is a very general complaint in England. And the competition in every kind of business is so great that it is not possible that all should be successful.

The labourer who earns eighteen pence a day and lives with some degree of comfort as a single man, will hesitate a little before he divides that pittance among four or five, which seems to be but just sufficient for one. Harder fare and harder labour he would submit to for the sake of living with the woman that he loves, but he must feel conscious, if he thinks at all, that should he have a large family, and any ill luck whatever, no degree of frugality, no possible exertion of his manual strength could preserve him from the heart-rending sensation of seeing his children starve, or of forfeiting his independence, and being obliged to the parish for their support. The love of independence is a sentiment that surely none would wish to be erased from the breast of man, though the parish law of England, it must be confessed, is a system of all others the most calculated gradually to weaken this sentiment, and in the end may eradicate it completely.

The servants who live in gentlemen's families have restraints that are yet stronger to break through in venturing upon marriage. They possess the necessaries, and even the comforts of life, almost in as great plenty as their masters. Their work is easy and their food luxurious compared with the class of labourers. And their sense of dependence is weakened by the conscious power of changing their masters, if they feel themselves offended. Thus comfortably situated at present, what are their prospects in marrying? Without knowledge or capital, either for business, or farming, and unused and therefore unable, to earn a subsistence by daily labour, their only refuge seems to be a miserable alehouse, which certainly offers no very enchanting prospect of a happy evening to their lives. By much the greater part, therefore, deterred by this uninviting view of their future situation, content themselves with remaining single where they are.

If this sketch of the state of society in England be near the truth, and I do not conceive that it is exaggerated, it will be allowed that the preventive check to population in this country operates, though with varied force, through all the classes of the community. The same observation will hold true with regard to all old states. The effects, indeed, of these restraints upon marriage are but too conspicuous in the consequent vices that are produced in almost every part of the world, vices that are continually involving both sexes in inextricable unhappiness.

CHAPTER V

The second, or positive check to population examined, in
England – The true cause why the immense sum collected
in England for the poor does not better their condition –
The powerful tendency of the poor laws to defeat their own
purpose – Palliative of the distresses of the poor proposed –
The absolute impossibility, from the fixed laws of our nature,
that the pressure of want can ever be completely removed
from the lower classes of society – All the checks to population may be resolved into misery or vice.

THE positive check to population, by which I mean the check
that represses an increase which is already begun, is confined
chiefly, though not perhaps solely, to the lowest orders of society.
This check is not so obvious to common view as the other I have
mentioned, and, to prove distinctly the force and extent of its
operation would require, perhaps, more data than we are in
possession of. But I believe it has been very generally remarked
by those who have attended to bills of mortality that of the number of children who die annually, much too great a proportion
belongs to those who may be supposed unable to give their offspring proper food and attention, exposed as they are occasionally
to severe distress and confined, perhaps, to unwholesome habitations and hard labour. This mortality among the children of
the poor has been constantly taken notice of in all towns. It
certainly does not prevail in an equal degree in the country, but
the subject has not hitherto received sufficient attention to enable
anyone to say that there are not more deaths in proportion
among the children of the poor, even in the country, than
among those of the middling and higher classes. Indeed, it
seems difficult to suppose that a labourer's wife who has six
children, and who is sometimes in absolute want of bread,
should be able always to give them the food and attention necessary to support life. The sons and daughters of peasants will not
be found such rosy cherubs in real life as they are described to

be in romances. It cannot fail to be remarked by those who live much in the country that the sons of labourers are very apt to be stunted in their growth, and are a long while arriving at maturity. Boys that you would guess to be fourteen or fifteen are, upon inquiry, frequently found to be eighteen or nineteen. And the lads who drive plough, which must certainly be a healthy exercise, are very rarely seen with any appearance of calves to their legs: a circumstance which can only be attributed to a want either of proper or of sufficient nourishment.

To remedy the frequent distresses of the common people, the poor laws of England have been instituted; but it is to be feared, that though they may have alleviated a little the intensity of individual misfortune, they have spread the general evil over a much larger surface. It is a subject often started in conversation and mentioned always as a matter of great surprise that, notwithstanding the immense sum that is annually collected for the poor in England, there is still so much distress among them. Some think that the money must be embezzled, others that the churchwardens and overseers consume the greater part of it in dinners. All agree that somehow or other it must be very ill-managed. In short the fact that nearly three millions are collected annually for the poor and yet that their distresses are not removed is the subject of continual astonishment. But a man who sees a little below the surface of things would be very much more astonished if the fact were otherwise than it is observed to be, or even if a collection universally of eighteen shillings in the pound, instead of four, were materially to alter it. I will state a case which I hope will elucidate my meaning.

Suppose that by a subscription of the rich the eighteen pence a day which men earn now was made up five shillings, it might be imagined, perhaps, that they would then be able to live comfortably and have a piece of meat every day for their dinners. But this would be a very false conclusion. The transfer of three shillings and sixpence a day to every labourer would not increase the quantity of meat in the country. There is not at present enough for all to have a decent share. What would then be the consequence? The competition among the buyers in the market of meat would rapidly raise the price from sixpence or sevenpence, to two or three shillings in the pound, and the commodity would not be divided among many more than it is at present. When an article is scarce, and cannot be distributed to all, he that can shew the most valid patent, that is, he that offers most money, becomes the possessor. If we can suppose the competition among the buyers of meat to continue long enough for a greater number of cattle to be reared annually, this could only be done at the expense of the corn, which would be a very disadvantagous exchange, for it is well known that the country could not then support the same population, and when sub-sistence is scarce in proportion to the number of people, it is of little consequence whether the lowest members of the society possess eighteen pence or five shillings. They must at all events be reduced to live upon the hardest fare and in the smallest quantity.

It will be said, perhaps, that the increased number of pur-chasers in every article would give a spur to productive industry and that the whole produce of the island would be increased. This might in some degree be the case. But the spur that these fancied riches would give to population would more than counterbalance it, and the increased produce would be to be divided among a more than proportionably increased number of people. All this time I am supposing that the same quantity of work would be done as before. But this would not really take place. The receipt of five shillings a day, instead of eighteen pence, would make every man fancy himself comparatively rich and able to indulge himself in many hours or days of leisure. This would give a strong and immediate check to pro-ductive industry, and, in a short time, not only the nation would be poorer, but the lower classes themselves would be much more distressed than when they received only eighteen pence a day.

A collection from the rich of eighteen shillings in the pound, even if distributed in the most judicious manner, would have a little the same effect as that resulting from the supposition I have just made, and no possible contributions or sacrifices of the rich, particularly in money, could for any time prevent the recur-rence of distress among the lower members of society, whoever they were. Great changes might, indeed, be made. The rich might become poor, and some of the poor rich, but a part of the society must necessarily feel a difficulty of living, and this difficulty will naturally fall on the least fortunate members.

It may at first appear strange, but I believe it is true, that I cannot by means of money raise a poor man and enable him to live much better than he did before, without proportionably depressing others in the same class. If I retrench the quantity of food consumed in my house, and give him what I have cut off, I then benefit him, without depressing any but myself and family, who, perhaps, may be well able to bear it. If I turn up a piece of uncultivated land, and give him the produce, I then benefit both him and all the members of the society, because what he before consumed is thrown into the common stock, and probably some of the new produce with it. But if I only give him money, supposing the produce of the country to remain the same, I give him a title to a larger share of that produce than formerly, which share he cannot receive without diminishing the shares of others. It is evident that this effect, in individual instances, must be so small as to be totally imperceptible; but still it must exist, as many other effects do, which, like some of the insects that people the air, elude our grosser perceptions.

Supposing the quantity of food in any country to remain the same for many years together, it is evident that this food must be divided according to the value of each man's patent, or the sum of money that he can afford to spend on this commodity so universally in request. It is a demonstrative truth, therefore, that the patents of one set of men could not be increased in value without diminishing the value of the patents of some other set of men. If the rich were to subscribe and give five shillings a day to five hundred thousand men without retrenching their own tables, no doubt can exist, that as these men would naturally live more at their ease and consume a greater quantity of provisions, there would be less food remaining to divide among the rest, and consequently each man's patent would be diminished in value or the same number of pieces of silver would purchase a smaller quantity of subsistence. (Mr Godwin calls the wealth that a man receives from his ancestors a mouldy patent. It may,

I think, very properly be termed a patent, but I hardly see the propriety of calling it a mouldy one, as it is an article in such constant use.)

An increase of population without a proportional increase of food will evidently have the same effect in lowering the value of each man's patent. The food must necessarily be distributed in smaller quantities, and consequently a day's labour will purchase a smaller quantity of provisions. An increase in the price of provisions would arise either from an increase of population faster than the means of subsistence, or from a different distribution of the money of the society. The food of a country that has been long occupied, if it be increasing, increases slowly and regularly and cannot be made to answer any sudden demands, but variations in the distribution of the money of a society are not infrequently occurring, and are undoubtedly among the causes that occasion the continual variations which we observe in the price of provisions.

The poor laws of England tend to depress the general condition of the poor in these two ways. Their first obvious tendency is to increase population without increasing the food for its support. A poor man may marry with little or no prospect of being able to support a family in independence. They may be said therefore in some measure to create the poor which they maintain, and as the provisions of the country must, in consequence of the increased population, be distributed to every man in smaller proportions, it is evident that the labour of those who are not supported by parish assistance will purchase a smaller quantity of provisions than before and consequently more of them must be driven to ask for support.

Secondly, the quantity of provisions consumed in workhouses upon a part of the society that cannot in general be considered as the most valuable part diminishes the shares that would otherwise belong to more industrious and more worthy members, and thus in the same manner forces more to become dependent. If the poor in the workhouses were to live better than they now do, this new distribution of the money of the society would tend more conspicuously to depress the condition of those out of the workhouses by occasioning a rise in the price of provisions.

Fortunately for England, a spirit of independence still remains among the peasantry. The poor laws are strongly calculated to eradicate this spirit. They have succeeded in part, but had they succeeded as completely as might have been expected their pernicious tendency would not have been so long concealed.

Hard as it may appear in individual instances, dependent poverty ought to be held disgraceful. Such a stimulus seems to be absolutely necessary to promote the happiness of the great mass of mankind, and every general attempt to weaken this stimulus, however benevolent its apparent intention, will always defeat its own purpose. If men are induced to marry from a prospect of parish provision, with little or no chance of maintaining their families in independence, they are not only unjustly tempted to bring unhappiness and dependence upon themselves and children, but they are tempted, without knowing it, to injure all in the same class with themselves. A labourer who marries without being able to support a family may in some respects be considered as an enemy to all his fellow-labourers.

I feel no doubt whatever that the parish laws of England have contributed to raise the price of provisions and to lower the real price of labour. They have therefore contributed to impoverish that class of people whose only possession is their labour. It is also difficult to suppose that they have not powerfully contributed to generate that carelessness and want of frugality observable among the poor, so contrary to the disposition frequently to be remarked among petty tradesmen and small farmers. The labouring poor, to use a vulgar expression, seem always to live from hand to mouth. Their present wants employ their whole attention, and they seldom think of the future. Even when they have an opportunity of saving they seldom exercise it, but all that is beyond their present necessities goes, generally speaking, to the ale-house. The poor laws of England may therefore be said to diminish both the power and the will to save among the common people, and thus to weaken one of the strongest incentives to sobriety and industry, and consequently to happiness.

It is a general complaint among master manufacturers that high wages ruin all their workmen, but it is difficult to conceive that these men would not save a part of their high wages for the future support of their families, instead of spending it in drunkenness and dissipation, if they did not rely on parish assistance for support in case of accidents. And that the poor employed in manufactures consider this assistance as a reason why they may spend all the wages they earn and enjoy themselves while they can appears to be evident from the number of families that, upon the failure of any great manufactory, immediately fall upon the parish, when perhaps the wages earned in this manufactory while it flourished were sufficiently above the price of common country labour to have allowed them to save enough for their support till they could find some other channel for their industry.

A man who might not be deterred from going to the ale-house from the consideration that on his death, or sickness, he should leave his wife and family upon the parish might yet hesitate in thus dissipating his earnings if he were assured that, in either of these cases, his family must starve or be left to the support of casual bounty. In China, where the real as well as nominal price of labour is very low, sons are yet obliged by law to support their aged and helpless parents. Whether such a law would be advisable in this country I will not pretend to determine. But it seems at any rate highly improper, by positive institutions, which render dependent poverty so general, to weaken that disgrace, which for the best and most humane reasons ought to attach to it.

The mass of happiness among the common people cannot but be diminished when one of the strongest checks to idleness and dissipation is thus removed, and when men are thus allured to marry with little or no prospect of being able to maintain a family in independence. Every obstacle in the way of marriage must undoubtedly be considered as a species of unhappiness. But as from the laws of our nature some check to population must exist, it is better that it should be checked from a foresight of the difficulties attending a family and the fear of dependent poverty than that it should be encouraged, only to be repressed afterwards by want and sickness.

It should be remembered always that there is an essential

difference between food and those wrought commodities, the raw materials of which are in great plenty. A demand for these last will not fail to create them in as great a quantity as they are wanted. The demand for food has by no means the same creative power. In a country where all the fertile spots have been seized, high offers are necessary to encourage the farmer to lay his dressing on land from which he cannot expect a profitable return for some years. And before the prospect of advantage is sufficiently great to encourage this sort of agricultural enterprise, and while the new produce is rising, great distresses may be suffered from the want of it. The demand for an increased quantity of subsistence is, with few exceptions, constant everywhere, yet we see how slowly it is answered in all those countries that have been long occupied.

The poor laws of England were undoubtedly instituted for the most benevolent purpose, but there is great reason to think that they have not succeeded in their intention. They certainly mitigate some cases of very severe distress which might otherwise occur, yet the state of the poor who are supported by parishes, considered in all its circumstances, is very far from being free from misery. But one of the principal objections to them is that for this assistance which some of the poor receive, in itself almost a doubtful blessing, the whole class of the common people of England is subjected to a set of grating, inconvenient, and tyrannical laws, totally inconsistent with the genuine spirit of the constitution. The whole business of settlements, even in its present amended state, is utterly contradictory to all ideas of freedom. The parish persecution of men whose families are likely to become chargeable, and of poor women who are near lying-in, is a most disgraceful and disgusting tyranny. And the obstructions continually occasioned in the market of labour by these laws have a constant tendency to add to the difficulties of those who are struggling to support themselves without assistance.

These evils attendant on the poor laws are in some degree irremediable. If assistance be to be distributed to a certain class of people, a power must be given somewhere of discriminating the proper objects and of managing the concerns of the institutions that are necessary, but any great interference with the affairs of other people is a species of tyranny, and in the common course of things the exercise of this power may be expected to become grating to those who are driven to ask for support. The tyranny of Justices, Churchwardens, and Overseers, is a common complaint among the poor, but the fault does not lie so much in these persons, who probably, before they were in power, were not worse than other people, but in the nature of all such institutions.

The evil is perhaps gone too far to be remedied, but I feel little doubt in my own mind that if the poor laws had never existed, though there might have been a few more instances of very severe distress, yet that the aggregate mass of happiness among the common people would have been much greater than it is at present.

Mr Pitt's Poor Bill has the appearance of being framed with benevolent intentions, and the clamour raised against it was in many respects ill directed, and unreasonable.[5] But it must be confessed that it possesses in a high degree the great and radical defect of all systems of the kind, that of tending to increase population without increasing the means for its support, and thus to depress the condition of those that are not supported by parishes, and, consequently, to create more poor.

To remove the wants of the lower classes of society is indeed an arduous task. The truth is that the pressure of distress on this part of a community is an evil so deeply seated that no human ingenuity can reach it. Were I to propose a palliative, and palliatives are all that the nature of the case will admit, it should be, in the first place, the total abolition of all the present parish-laws. This would at any rate give liberty and freedom of action to the peasantry of England, which they can hardly be said to possess at present. They would then be able to settle without interruption, wherever there was a prospect of a greater plenty of work and a higher price for labour. The market of labour would then be free, and those obstacles removed which, as things are now, often for a considerable time prevent the price from rising according to the demand.

Secondly, premiums might be given for turning up fresh

land, and all possible encouragements held out to agriculture above manufactures, and to tillage above grazing. Every endeavour should be used to weaken and destroy all those institutions relating to corporations, apprenticeships, etc., which cause the labours of agriculture to be worse paid than the labours of trade and manufactures. For a country can never produce its proper quantity of food while these distinctions remain in favour of artisans. Such encouragements to agriculture would tend to furnish the market with an increasing quantity of healthy work, and at the same time, by augmenting the produce of the country, would raise the comparative price of labour and ameliorate the condition of the labourer. Being now in better circumstances, and seeing no prospect of parish assistance, he would be more able, as well as more inclined, to enter into associations for providing against the sickness of himself or family.

Lastly, for cases of extreme distress, county workhouses might be established, supported by rates upon the whole kingdom, and free for persons of all counties, and indeed of all nations. The fare should be hard, and those that were able obliged to work. It would be desirable that they should not be considered as comfortable asylums in all difficulties, but merely as places where severe distress might find some alleviation. A part of these houses might be separated, or others built for a most beneficial purpose, which has not been infrequently taken notice of, that of providing a place where any person, whether native or foreigner, might do a day's work at all times and receive the market price for it. Many cases would undoubtedly be left for the exertion of individual benevolence.

A plan of this kind, the preliminary of which should be an abolition of all the present parish laws, seems to be the best calculated to increase the mass of happiness among the common people of England. To prevent the recurrence of misery, is, alas! beyond the power of man. In the vain endeavour to attain what in the nature of things is impossible, we now sacrifice not only possible but certain benefits. We tell the common people that if they will submit to a code of tyrannical regulations, they shall never be in want. They do submit to these regulations.

They perform their part of the contract, but we do not, nay cannot, perform ours, and thus the poor sacrifice the valuable blessing of liberty and receive nothing that can be called an equivalent in return.

Notwithstanding, then, the institution of the poor laws in England, I think it will be allowed that considering the state of the lower classes altogether, both in the towns and in the country, the distresses which they suffer from the want of proper and sufficient food, from hard labour and unwholesome habitations, must operate as a constant check to incipient population.

To these two great checks to population, in all long occupied countries, which I have called the preventive and the positive checks, may be added vicious customs with respect to women, great cities, unwholesome manufactures, luxury, pestilence, and war.

All these checks may be fairly resolved into misery and vice. And that these are the true causes of the slow increase of population in all the states of modern Europe, will appear sufficiently evident from the comparatively rapid increase that has invariably taken place whenever these causes have been in any considerable degree removed.

CHAPTER VI

New colonies – Reasons for their rapid increase – North American Colonies – Extraordinary instance of increase in the back settlements – Rapidity with which even old states recover the ravages of war, pestilence, famine, or the convulsions of nature.

IT has been universally remarked that all new colonies settled in healthy countries, where there was plenty of room and food, have constantly increased with astonishing rapidity in their population. Some of the colonies from ancient Greece, in no very long period, more than equalled their parent states in numbers and strength. And not to dwell on remote instances, the European settlements in the new world bear ample testimony to the truth of a remark, which, indeed, has never, that I know of, been doubted. A plenty of rich land, to be had for little or nothing, is so powerful a cause of population as to overcome all other obstacles. No settlements could well have been worse managed than those of Spain in Mexico, Peru, and Quito. The tyranny, superstition, and vices of the mother-country were introduced in ample quantities among her children. Exorbitant taxes were exacted by the Crown. The most arbitrary restrictions were imposed on their trade. And the governors were not behind hand in rapacity and extortion for themselves as well as their master. Yet, under all these difficulties, the colonies made a quick progress in population. The city of Lima, founded since the conquest, is represented by Ulloa as containing fifty thousand inhabitants near fifty years ago.[6] Quito, which had been but a hamlet of Indians, is represented by the same author as in his time equally populous. Mexico is said to contain a hundred thousand inhabitants, which, notwithstanding the exaggerations of the Spanish writers, is supposed to be five times greater than what it contained in the time of Montezuma.[7]

In the Portuguese colony of Brazil, governed with almost

equal tyranny, there were supposed to be, thirty years since, six hundred thousand inhabitants of European extraction.

The Dutch and French colonies, though under the government of exclusive companies of merchants, which, as Dr Adam Smith says very justly, is the worst of all possible governments, still persisted in thriving under every disadvantage.

But the English North American colonies, now the powerful people of the United States of America, made by far the most rapid progress. To the plenty of good land which they possessed in common with the Spanish and Portuguese settlements, they added a greater degree of liberty and equality. Though not without some restrictions on their foreign commerce, they were allowed a perfect liberty of managing their own internal affairs. The political institutions that prevailed were favourable to the alienation and division of property. Lands that were not cultivated by the proprietor within a limited time were declared grantable to any other person. In Pennsylvania there was no right of primogeniture, and in the provinces of New England the eldest had only a double share. There were no tithes in any of the States, and scarcely any taxes. And on account of the extreme cheapness of good land a capital could not be more advantageously employed than in agriculture, which at the same time that it supplies the greatest quantity of healthy work affords much the most valuable produce to the society.

The consequence of these favourable circumstances united was a rapidity of increase probably without parallel in history. Throughout all the northern colonies, the population was found to double itself in twenty-five years. The original number of persons who had settled in the four provinces of new England in 1643 was 21,200. (I take these figures from Dr Price's two volumes of *Observations*; not having Dr Styles' pamphlet, from which he quotes, by me.[8]) Afterwards, it is supposed that more left them than went to them. In the year 1760, they were increased to half a million. They had therefore all along doubled their own number in twenty-five years. In New Jersey the period of doubling appeared to be twenty-two years; and in Rhode Island still less. In the back settlements, where the inhabitants applied themselves solely to agriculture, and luxury was not known, they were found to double their own number in fifteen years, a most extraordinary instance of increase. Along the sea coast, which would naturally be first inhabited, the period of doubling was about thirty-five years; and in some of the maritime towns, the population was absolutely at a stand.

In instances of this kind the powers of the earth appear to be fully equal to answer all the demands for food that can be made upon it by man. But we should be led into an error if we were thence to suppose that population and food ever really increase in the same ratio. The one is still a geometrical and the other an arithmetical ratio, that is, one increases by multiplication, and the other by addition. Where there are few people, and a great quantity of fertile land, the power of the earth to afford a yearly increase of food may be compared to a great reservoir of water, supplied by a moderate stream. The faster population increases, the more help will be got to draw off the water, and consequently an increasing quantity will be taken every year. But the sooner, undoubtedly, will the reservoir be exhausted, and the streams only remain. When acre has been added to acre, till all the fertile land is occupied, the yearly increase of food will depend upon the amelioration of the land already in possession; and even this moderate stream will be gradually diminishing. But population, could it be supplied with food, would go on with unexhausted vigour, and the increase of one period would furnish the power of a greater increase the next, and this without any limit.

These facts seem to shew that population increases exactly in the proportion that the two great checks to it, misery and vice, are removed, and that there is not a truer criterion of the happiness and innocence of a people than the rapidity of their increase. The unwholesomeness of towns, to which some persons are necessarily driven from the nature of their trades, must be considered as a species of misery, and every the slightest check to marriage, from a prospect of the difficulty of maintaining a family, may be fairly classed under the same head. In short it is difficult to conceive any check to population which does not come under the description of some species of misery or vice.

The population of the thirteen American States before the war was reckoned at about three millions. Nobody imagines that Great Britain is less populous at present for the emigration of the small parent stock that produced these numbers. On the contrary, a certain degree of emigration is known to be favourable to the population of the mother country. It has been particularly remarked that the two Spanish provinces from which the greatest number of people emigrated to America, became in consequence more populous. Whatever was the original number of British emigrants that increased so fast in the North American Colonies, let us ask, why does not an equal number produce an equal increase in the same time in Great Britain? The great and obvious cause to be assigned is the want of room and food, or, in other words, misery, and that this is a much more powerful cause even than vice appears sufficiently evident from the rapidity with which even old states recover the desolations of war, pestilence, or the accidents of nature. They are then for a short time placed a little in the situation of new states, and the effect is always answerable to what might be expected. If the industry of the inhabitants be not destroyed by fear or tyranny, subsistence will soon increase beyond the wants of the reduced numbers, and the invariable consequence will be that population which before, perhaps, was nearly stationary, will begin immediately to increase.

The fertile province of Flanders, which has been so often the seat of the most destructive wars, after a respite of a few years, has appeared always as fruitful and as populous as ever. Even the Palatinate lifted up its head again after the execrable ravages of Louis the Fourteenth.[9] The effects of the dreadful plague in London in 1666 were not perceptible fifteen or twenty years afterwards. The traces of the most destructive famines in China and Indostan are by all accounts very soon obliterated.[10] It may even be doubted whether Turkey and Egypt are upon an average much less populous for the plagues that periodically lay them waste. If the number of people which they contain be less now than formerly, it is, probably, rather to be attributed to the tyranny and oppression of the government under which they groan, and the consequent discouragements to agriculture, than to the loss which they sustain by the plague. The most tremendous convulsions of nature, such as volcanic eruptions and earthquakes, if they do not happen so frequently as to drive away the inhabitants, or to destroy their spirit of industry, have but a trifling effect on the average population of any state. Naples, and the country under Vesuvius, are still very populous, notwithstanding the repeated eruptions of that mountain. And Lisbon and Lima are now, probably, nearly in the same state with regard to population as they were before the last earthquakes.[11]

CHAPTER VII

A probable cause of epidemics – Extracts from Mr Suessmilch's tables – Periodical returns of sickly seasons to be expected in certain cases – Proportion of births to burials for short periods in any country an inadequate criterion of the real average increase of population – Best criterion of a permanent increase of population – Great frugality of living one of the causes of the famines of China and Indostan – Evil tendency of one of the clauses in Mr Pitt's Poor Bill – Only one proper way of encouraging population – Causes of the happiness of nations – Famine, the last and most dreadful mode by which nature represses a redundant population – The three propositions considered as established.

By great attention to cleanliness, the plague seems at length to be completely expelled from London. But it is not improbable that among the secondary causes that produce even sickly seasons and epidemics ought to be ranked a crowded population and unwholesome and insufficient food. I have been led to this remark, by looking over some of the tables of Mr Suessmilch,[12] which Dr Price has extracted in one of his notes to the postscript on the controversy respecting the population of England and Wales. They are considered as very correct, and if such tables were general, they would throw great light on the different ways by which population is repressed and prevented from increasing beyond the means of subsistence in any country. I will extract a part of the tables, with Dr Price's remarks.

IN THE KINGDOM OF PRUSSIA, AND DUKEDOM OF LITHUANIA

Annual Average	Births	Burials	Marriages	Proportion of Births to Marriages	Proportion of Births to Burials
10 Yrs to 1702	21,963	14,718	5,928	37 to 10	150 to 100
5 Yrs to 1716	21,602	11,984	4,968	37 to 10	180 to 100
5 Yrs to 1756	28,392	19,154	5,599	50 to 10	148 to 100

'N.B. In 1709 and 1710, a pestilence carried off 247,733 of the inhabitants of this country, and in 1736 and 1737, epidemics prevailed, which again checked its increase.'

It may be remarked, that the greatest proportion of births to burials, was in the five years after the great pestilence.

DUCHY OF POMERANIA

Annual Average	Births	Burials	Marriages	Proportion of Births to Marriages	Proportion of Births to Burials
6 Yrs to 1702	6,540	4,647	1,810	36 to 10	140 to 100
6 Yrs to 1708	7,455	4,208	1,875	39 to 10	177 to 100
6 Yrs to 1726	8,432	5,627	2,131	39 to 10	150 to 100
4 Yrs to 1756	12,767	9,281	2,957	43 to 10	137 to 100

'In this instance the inhabitants appear to have been almost doubled in fifty-six years, no very bad epidemics having once interrupted the increase, but the three years immediately following the last period (to 1759) were so sickly that the births were sunk to 10,229 and the buriols raised to 15,068.'

Is it not probable that in this case the number of inhabitants had increased faster than the food and the accommodations necessary to preserve them in health? The mass of the people would, upon this supposition, be obliged to live harder, and a greater number would be crowded together in one house, and it is not surely improbable that these were among the natural causes that produced the three sickly years. These causes may produce such an effect, though the country, absolutely considered, may not be extremely crowded and populous. In a country even thinly inhabited, if an increase of population take place, before more food is raised, and more houses are built, the inhabitants must be distressed in some degree for room and subsistence. Were the marriages in England, for the next eight or ten years, to be more prolifick than usual, or even were a greater number of marriages than usual to take place, supposing the number of houses to remain the same, instead of five or six to a cottage, there must be seven or eight, and this, added to the necessity of harder living, would probably have a very unfavourable effect on the health of the common people.

NEUMARK OF BRANDENBURGH

Annual Average	Births	Burials	Marriages	Proportion of Births to Marriages	Proportion of Births to Burials
5 Yrs to 1701	5,433	3,483	1,436	37 to 10	155 to 100
5 Yrs to 1726	7,012	4,254	1,713	40 to 10	164 to 100
5 Yrs to 1756	7,978	5,567	1,891	42 to 10	143 to 100

'Epidemics prevailed for six years, from 1736, to 1741, which checked the increase.'

DUKEDOM OF MAGDEBURGH

Annual Average	Births	Burials	Marriages	Proportion of Births to Marriages	Proportion of Births to Burials
5 Yrs to 1702	6,431	4,103	1,681	38 to 10	156 to 100
5 Yrs to 1717	7,590	5,335	2,076	36 to 10	142 to 100
5 Yrs to 1756	8,850	8,069	2,193	40 to 10	109 to 100

'The years 1738, 1740, 1750, and 1751, were particularly sickly.'
For further information on this subject, I refer the reader to Mr Suessmilch's tables. The extracts that I have made are sufficient to shew the periodical, though irregular, returns of sickly seasons, and it seems highly probable that a scantiness of room and food was one of the principal causes that occasioned them.

It appears from the tables that these countries were increasing rather fast for old states, notwithstanding the occasional sickly seasons that prevailed. Cultivation must have been improving, and marriages, consequently, encouraged. For the checks to population appear to have been rather of the positive, than of the preventive kind. When from a prospect of increasing plenty in any country, the weight that represses population is in some degree removed, it is highly probable that the motion will be continued beyond the operation of the cause that first impelled it. Or, to be more particular, when the increasing produce of a country, and the increasing demand for labour, so far ameliorate the condition of the labourer as greatly to encourage marriage, it is probable that the custom of early marriages will continue till the population of the country has gone beyond the increased produce, and sickly seasons appear to be the natural and necessary consequence. I should expect, therefore, that those countries where subsistence was increasing sufficiently at times to encourage population but not to answer all its demands, would be more subject to periodical epidemics than those where the population could more completely accommodate itself to the average produce.

An observation the converse of this will probably also be found true. In those countries that are subject to periodical sicknesses, the increase of population, or the excess of births above the burials, will be greater in the intervals of these periods than is usual, *caeteris paribus*, in the countries not so much subject to such disorders. If Turkey and Egypt have been nearly stationary in their average population for the last century, in the intervals of their periodical plagues, the births must have exceeded the burials in a greater proportion than in such countries as France and England.

The average proportion of births to burials in any country for a period of five to ten years, will hence appear to be a very inadequate criterion by which to judge of its real progress in population. This proportion certainly shews the rate of increase during those five or ten years; but we can by no means thence infer what had been the increase for the twenty years before, or what would be the increase for the twenty years after. Dr Price observes that Sweden, Norway, Russia, and the kingdom of Naples, are increasing fast; but the extracts from registers that he has given are not for periods of sufficient extent to establish the fact. It is highly probable, however, that Sweden, Norway, and Russia, are really increasing their population, though not at the rate that the proportion of births to burials for the short periods that Dr Price takes would seem to shew. (See Dr Price's *Observations*, Vol. II, postscript to the controversy on the population of England and Wales.) For five years, ending in 1777, the proportion of births to burials in the kingdom of Naples was 144 to 100, but there is reason to suppose that this proportion would indicate an increase much greater than would be really found to have taken place in that kingdom during a period of a hundred years.

Dr Short compared the registers of many villages and market

towns in England for two periods;[13] the first, from Queen Elizabeth to the middle of the last century,[14] and the second, from different years at the end of the last century to the middle of the present. And from a comparison of these extracts, it appears that in the former period the births exceeded the burials in the proportion of 124 to 100, but in the latter, only in the proportion of 111 to 100. Dr Price thinks that the registers in the former period are not to be depended upon, but, probably, in this instance they do not give incorrect proportions. At least there are many reasons for expecting to find a greater excess of births above the burials in the former period than in the latter. In the natural progress of the population of any country, more good land will, *caeteris paribus*, be taken into cultivation in the earlier stages of it than in the later. (I say *'caeteris paribus'*, because the increase of the produce of any country will always very greatly depend on the spirit of industry that prevails, and the way in which it is directed. The knowledge and habits of the people, and other temporary causes, particularly the degree of civil liberty and equality existing at the time, must always have great influence in exciting and directing this spirit.) And a greater proportional yearly increase of produce will almost invariably be followed by a greater proportional increase of population. But, besides this great cause, which would naturally give the excess of births above burials greater at the end of Queen Elizabeth's reign than in the middle of the present century, I cannot help thinking that the occasional ravages of the plague in the former period must have had some tendency to increase this proportion. If an average of ten years had been taken in the intervals of the returns of this dreadful disorder, or if the years of plague had been rejected as accidental, the registers would certainly give the proportion of births to burials too high for the real average increase of the population. For some few years after the great plague in 1666, it is probable that there was a more than usual excess of births above burials, particularly if Dr Price's opinion be founded, that England was more populous at the revolution (which happened only twenty-two years afterwards) than it is at present.

Mr King, in 1693, stated the proportion of the births to the burials throughout the Kingdom, exclusive of London, as 115 to 100.[15] Dr Short makes it, in the middle of the present century, 111 to 100, including London. The proportion in France for five years, ending in 1774, was 117 to 100. If these statements are near the truth; and if there are no very great variations at particular periods in the proportions, it would appear that the population of France and England has accommodated itself very nearly to the average produce of each country. The discouragements to marriage, the consequent vicious habits, war, luxury, the silent though certain depopulation of large towns, and the close habitations, and insufficient food of many of the poor, prevent population from increasing beyond the means of subsistence; and, if I may use an expression which certainly at first appears strange, supercede the necessity of great and ravaging epidemics to repress what is redundant. Were a wasting plague to sweep off two millions in England, and six millions in France, there can be no doubt whatever that, after the inhabitants had recovered from the dreadful shock, the proportion of births to burials would be much above what it is in either country at present.

In New Jersey, the proportion of births to deaths on an average of seven years, ending in 1743, was as 300 to 100. In France and England, taking the highest proportion, it is as 117 to 100. Great and astonishing as this difference is, we ought not to be so wonder-struck at it as to attribute it to the miraculous interposition of heaven. The causes of it are not remote, latent and mysterious; but near us, round about us, and open to the investigation of every inquiring mind. It accords with the most liberal spirit of philosophy to suppose that not a stone can fall, or a plant rise, without the immediate agency of divine power. But we know from experience that these operations of what we call nature have been conducted almost invariably according to fixed laws. And since the world began, the causes of population and depopulation have probably been as constant as any of the laws of nature with which we are acquainted.

The passion between the sexes has appeared in every age to be so nearly the same that it may always be considered, in algebraic language, as a given quantity. The great law of necessity which prevents population from increasing in any country beyond the food which it can either produce or acquire, is a law so open to our view, so obvious and evident to our understandings, and so completely confirmed by the experience of every age, that we cannot for a moment doubt it. The different modes which nature takes to prevent or repress a redundant population do not appear, indeed, to us so certain and regular, but though we cannot always predict the mode we may with certainty predict the fact. If the proportion of births to deaths for a few years indicate an increase of numbers much beyond the proportional increased or acquired produce of the country, we may be perfectly certain that unless an emigration takes place, the deaths will shortly exceed the births; and that the increase that had taken place for a few years cannot be the real average increase of the population of the country. Were there no other depopulating causes, every country would, without doubt, be subject to periodical pestilences or famine.

The only true criterion of a real and permanent increase in the population of any country is the increase of the means of subsistence. But even this criterion is subject to some slight variations which are, however, completely open to our view and observations. In some countries population appears to have been forced, that is, the people have been habituated by degrees to live almost upon the smallest possible quantity of food. There must have been periods in such countries when population increased permanently, without an increase in the means of subsistence. China seems to answer to this description. If the accounts we have of it are to be trusted, the lower classes of people are in the habit of living almost upon the smallest possible quantity of food and are glad to get any putrid offals that European labourers would rather starve than eat. The law in China which permits parents to expose their children has tended principally thus to force the population. A nation in this state must necessarily be subject to famines. Where a country is so populous in proportion to the means of subsistence that the average produce of it is but barely sufficient to support the lives of the inhabitants, any deficiency from the badness of seasons must be fatal. It is probable that the very frugal manner in which the

Gentoos are in the habit of living contributes in some degree to the famines of Indostan.[16]

In America, where the reward of labour is at present so liberal, the lower classes might retrench very considerably in a year of scarcity without materially distressing themselves. A famine therefore seems to be almost impossible. It may be expected that in the progress of the population of America, the labourers will in time be much less liberally rewarded. The numbers will in this case permanently increase without a proportional increase in the means of subsistence.

In the different states of Europe there must be some variations in the proportion between the number of inhabitants and the quantity of food consumed, arising from the different habits of living that prevail in each state. The labourers of the South of England are so accustomed to eat fine wheaten bread that they will suffer themselves to be half starved before they will submit to live like the Scotch peasants. They might perhaps in time, by the constant operation of the hard law of necessity, be reduced to live even like the lower Chinese, and the country would then, with the same quantity of food, support a greater population. But to effect this must always be a most difficult, and, every friend to humanity will hope, an abortive attempt. Nothing is so common as to hear of encouragements that ought to be given to population. If the tendency of mankind to increase be so great as I have represented it to be, it may appear strange that this increase does not come when it is thus repeatedly called for. The true reason is that the demand for a greater population is made without preparing the funds necessary to support it. Increase the demand for agricultural labour by promoting cultivation, and with it consequently increase the produce of the country, and ameliorate the condition of the labourer, and no apprehensions whatever need be entertained of the proportional increase of population. An attempt to effect this purpose in any other way is vicious, cruel, and tyrannical, and in any state of tolerable freedom cannot therefore succeed. It may appear to be the interest of the rulers, and the rich of a state, to force population, and thereby lower the price of labour, and consequently the expense of fleets and armies, and the cost of manufactures for foreign sale; but every attempt of the kind should be carefully watched and strenuously resisted by the friends of the poor, particularly when it comes under the deceitful garb of benevolence, and is likely, on that account, to be cheerfully and cordially received by the common people.

I entirely acquit Mr Pitt of any sinister intention in that clause of his Poor Bill which allows a shilling a week to every labourer for each child he has above three. I confess, that before the bill was brought into Parliament, and for some time after, I thought that such a regulation would be highly beneficial, but further reflection on the subject has convinced me that if its object be to better the condition of the poor, it is calculated to defeat the very purpose which it has in view. It has no tendency that I can discover to increase the produce of the country, and if it tend to increase the population, without increasing the produce, the necessary and inevitable consequence appears to be that the same produce must be divided among a greater number, and consequently that a day's labour will purchase a smaller quantity of provisions, and the poor therefore in general must be more distressed.

I have mentioned some cases where population may permanently increase without a proportional increase in the means of subsistence. But it is evident that the variation in different states, between the food and the numbers supported by it, is restricted to a limit beyond which it cannot pass. In every country, the population of which is not absolutely decreasing, the food must be necessarily sufficient to support, and to continue, the race of labourers.

Other circumstances being the same, it may be affirmed that countries are populous according to the quantity of human food which they produce, and happy according to the liberality with which that food is divided, or the quantity which a day's labour will purchase. Corn countries are more populous than pasture countries, and rice countries more populous than corn countries. The lands in England are not suited to rice, but they would all bear potatoes; and Dr Adam Smith observes that if potatoes were to become the favourite vegetable food of the common people, and if the same quantity of land was employed in their culture as is now employed in the culture of corn, the country would be able to support a much greater population, and would consequently in a very short time have it.[17]

The happiness of a country does not depend, absolutely, upon its poverty or its riches, upon its youth or its age, upon its being thinly or fully inhabited, but upon the rapidity with which it is increasing, upon the degree in which the yearly increase of food approaches to the yearly increase of an unrestricted population. This approximation is always the nearest in new colonies, where the knowledge and industry of an old state operate on the fertile unappropriated land of a new one. In other cases, the youth or the age of a state is not in this respect of very great importance. It is probable that the food of Great Britain is divided in as great plenty to the inhabitants, at the present period, as it was two thousand, three thousand, or four thousand years ago. And there is reason to believe that the poor and thinly inhabited tracts of the Scotch Highlands are as much distressed by an overcharged population as the rich and populous province of Flanders.

Were a country never to be overrun by a people more advanced in arts, but left to its own natural progress in civilization; from the time that its produce might be considered as an unit, to the time that it might be considered as a million, during the lapse of many hundred years, there would not be a single period when the mass of the people could be said to be free from distress, either directly or indirectly, for want of food. In every state in Europe, since we have first had accounts of it, millions and millions of human existences have been repressed from this simple cause; though perhaps in some of these states an absolute famine has never been known.

Famine seems to be the last, the most dreadful resource of nature. The power of population is so superior to the power in the earth to produce subsistence for man, that premature death must in some shape or other visit the human race. The vices of mankind are active and able ministers of depopulation. They are the precursors in the great army of destruction; and often finish the dreadful work themselves. But should they fail in this war of extermination, sickly seasons, epidemics, pestilence, and plague, advance in terrific array, and sweep off their thousands and ten thousands. Should success be still incomplete, gigantic inevitable famine stalks in the rear, and with one mighty blow levels the population with the food of the world.

Must it not then be acknowledged by an attentive examiner of the histories of mankind, that in every age and in every state in which man has existed, or does now exist.

That the increase of population is necessarily limited by the means of subsistence.

That population does invariably increase when the means of subsistence increase. And that the superior power of population it repressed, and the actual population kept equal to the means of subsistence, by misery and vice?

CHAPTER VIII

Mr Wallace – Error of supposing that the difficulty arising from population is at a great distance – Mr Condorcet's sketch of the progress of the human mind – Period when the oscillation, mentioned by Mr Condorcet, ought to be applied to the human race.

To a person who draws the preceding obvious inferences, from a view of the past and present state of mankind, it cannot but be a matter of astonishment that all the writers on the perfectibility of man and of society who have noticed the argument of an overcharged population, treat it always very slightly and invariably represent the difficulties arising from it as at a great and almost immeasurable distance. Even Mr Wallace, who thought the argument itself of so much weight as to destroy his whole system of equality, did not seem to be aware that any difficulty would occur from this cause till the whole earth had been cultivated like a garden and was incapable of any further increase of produce. Were this really the case, and were a beautiful system of equality in other respects practicable, I cannot think that our ardour in the pursuit of such a scheme ought to be damped by the contemplation of so remote a difficulty. An event at such a distance might fairly be left to providence, but the truth is that if the view of the argument given in this *Essay* be just the difficulty, so far from being remote, would be imminent and immediate. At every period during the progress of cultivation, from the present moment to the time when the whole earth was become like a garden, the distress for want of food would be constantly pressing on all mankind, if they were equal. Though the produce of the earth might be increasing every year, population would be increasing much faster, and the redundancy must necessarily be repressed by the periodical or constant action of misery or vice.

Mr Condorcet's *Esquisse d'un Tableau Historique des Progrès de l'Esprit Humain*, was written, it is said, under the pressure of that cruel proscription which terminated in his death. If he had no hopes of its being seen during his life and of its interesting France in his favour, it is a singular instance of the attachment of a man to principles, which every day's experience was so fatally for himself contradicting. To see the human mind in one of the most enlightened nations of the world, and after a lapse of some thousand years, debased by such a fermentation of disgusting passions, of fear, cruelty, malice, revenge, ambition, madness, and folly as would have disgraced the most savage nation in the most barbarous age must have been such a tremendous shock to his ideas of the necessary and inevitable progress of the human mind that nothing but the firmest conviction of the truth of his principles, in spite of all appearances, could have withstood.

This posthumous publication is only a sketch of a much larger work, which he proposed should be executed. It necessarily, therefore, wants that detail and application which can alone prove the truth of any theory. A few observations will be sufficient to shew how completely the theory is contradicted when it is applied to the real, and not to an imaginary, state of things.

In the last division of the work, which treats of the future progress of man towards perfection, he says, that comparing, in the different civilized nations of Europe, the actual population with the extent of territory, and observing their cultivation, their industry, their divisions of labour, and their means of subsistence, we shall see that it would be impossible to preserve the same means of subsistence, and, consequently, the same population, without a number of individuals who have no other means of supplying their wants than their industry. Having allowed the necessity of such a class of men, and adverting afterwards to the precarious revenue of those families that would depend so entirely on the life and health of their chief, he says, very justly: 'There exists then, a necessary cause of inequality, of dependence, and even of misery, which menaces, without ceasing, the most numerous and active class of our societies.' (To save time and long quotations, I shall here give the substance of some of Mr Condorcet's sentiments, and hope I shall not misrepresent them. But I refer the reader to the work itself, which will amuse, if it does not convince him.) The difficulty is just and well stated, and I am afraid that the mode by which he proposes it should be removed will be found inefficacious. By the application of calculations to the probabilities of life and the interest of money, he proposes that a fund should be established which should assure to the old an assistance, produced, in part, by their own former savings, and, in part, by the savings of individuals who in making the same sacrifice die before they reap the benefit of it. The same, or a similar fund, should give assistance to women and children who lose their husbands, or fathers, and afford a capital to those who were of an age to found a new family, sufficient for the proper development of their industry. These establishments, he observes, might be made in the name and under the protection of the society. Going still further, he says that, by the just application of calculations, means might be found of more completely preserving a state of equality, by preventing credit from being the exclusive privilege of great fortunes, and yet giving it a basis equally solid, and by rendering the progress of industry, and the activity of commerce, less dependent on great capitalists.

Such establishments and calculations may appear very promising upon paper, but when applied to real life they will be found to be absolutely nugatory. Mr Condorcet allows that a class of people which maintains itself entirely by industry is necessary to every state. Why does he allow this? No other reason can well be assigned than that he conceives that the labour necessary to procure subsistence for an extended population will not be performed without the goad of necessity. If by establishments of this kind of spur to industry be removed, if the idle and the negligent are placed upon the same footing with regard to their credit, and the future support of their wives and families, as the active and industrious, can we expect to see men exert that animated activity in bettering their condition which now forms the master spring of public prosperity? If an inquisition were to be established to examine the claims of each individual and to determine whether he had or had not exerted himself to the utmost, and to grant or refuse assistance accordingly, this would be little else than a repetition upon a larger scale of the English poor laws and would be completely destructive of the true principles of liberty and equality.

But independent of this great objection to these establishments, and supposing for a moment that they would give no check to productive industry, by far the greatest difficulty remains yet behind.

Were every man sure of a comfortable provision for his family, almost every man would have one, and were the rising generation free from the 'killing frost' of misery,[18] population must rapidly increase. Of this Mr Condorcet seems to be fully aware himself, and after having described further improvements, he says:

But in this progress of industry and happiness, each generation will be called to more extended enjoyments, and in consequence, by the physical constitution of the human frame, to an increase in the number of individuals. Must not there arrive a period then, when these laws, equally necessary, shall counteract each other? When the increase of the number of men surpassing their means of subsistence, the necessary result must be either a continual diminution of happiness and population, a movement truly retrograde, or, at least, a kind of oscillation between good and evil? In societies arrived at this term, will not this oscillation be a constantly subsisting cause of periodical misery? Will it not mark the limit when all further amelioration will become impossible, and point out that term to the perfectibility of the human race which it may reach in the course of ages, but can never pass?

He then adds,

There is no person who does not see how very distant such a period is from us, but shall we ever arrive at it? It is equally impossible to pronounce for or against the future realization of an event which cannot take place but at an era when the human race will have attained improvements, of which we can at present scarcely form a conception.

Mr Condorcet's picture of what may be expected to happen when the number of men shall surpass the means of their subsistence is justly drawn. The oscillation which he describes will certainly take place and will without doubt be a constantly subsisting cause of periodical misery. The only point in which I differ from Mr Condorcet with regard to this picture is the period when it may be applied to the human race. Mr Condorcet thinks that it cannot possibly be applicable but at an era extremely distant. If the proportion between the natural increase of population and food which I have given be in any degree near the truth, it will appear, on the contrary, that the period when the number of men surpass their means of subsistence has long since arrived, and that this necessary oscillation, this constantly subsisting cause of periodical misery, has existed ever since we have had any histories of mankind, does exist at present, and will for ever continue to exist, unless some decided change take place in the physical constitution of our nature.

Mr Condorcet, however, goes on to say that should the period, which he conceives to be so distant, ever arrive, the human race, and the advocates for the perfectibility of man, need not be alarmed at it. He then proceeds to remove the difficulty in a manner which I profess not to understand. Having observed, that the ridiculous prejudices of superstition would by that time have ceased to throw over morals a corrupt and degrading austerity, he alludes, either to a promiscuous concubinage, which would prevent breeding, or to something else as unnatural. To remove the difficulty in this way will, surely, in the opinion of most men, be to destroy that virtue and purity of manners, which the advocates of equality, and of the perfectibility of man, profess to be the end and object of their views.

CHAPTER IX

Mr Condorcet's conjecture concerning the organic perfectibility of man, and the indefinite prolongation of human life –
Fallacy of the argument, which infers an unlimited progress
from a partial improvement, the limit of which cannot be
ascertained, illustrated in the breeding of animals, and the
cultivation of plants.

THE last question which Mr Condorcet proposes for examination is the organic perfectibility of man. He observes that if the
proofs which have been already given and which, in their development will receive greater force in the work itself, are sufficient
to establish the indefinite perfectibility of man upon the supposition of the same natural faculties and the same organization
which he has at present, what will be the certainty, what the
extent of our hope, if this organization, these natural faculties
themselves, are susceptible of amelioration?

From the improvement of medicine, from the use of more
wholesome food and habitations, from a manner of living which
will improve the strength of the body by exercise without im-
pairing it by excess, from the destruction of the two great causes
of the degradation of man, misery, and too great riches, from
the gradual removal of transmissible and contagious disorders by
the improvement of physical knowledge, rendered more effica-
cious by the progress of reason and of social order, he infers that
though man will not absolutely become immortal, yet that the
duration between his birth and natural death will increase without ceasing, will have no assignable term, and may properly be
expressed by the word 'indefinite'. He then defines this word to
mean either a constant approach to an unlimited extent, without
ever reaching it, or an increase in the immensity of ages to an
extent greater than any assignable quantity.

But surely the application of this term in either of these senses
to the duration of human life is in the highest degree unphilosophical and totally unwarranted by any appearances in the

laws of nature. Variations from different causes are essentially distinct from a regular and unretrograde increase. The average duration of human life will to a certain degree vary from healthy or unhealthy climates, from wholesome or unwholesome food, from virtuous or vicious manners, and other causes, but it may be fairly doubted whether there is really the smallest perceptible advance in the natural duration of human life since first we have had any authentic history of man. The prejudices of all ages have indeed been directly contrary to this supposition, and though I would not lay much stress upon these prejudices, they will in some measure tend to prove that there has been no marked advance in an opposite direction.

It may perhaps be said that the world is yet so young, so completely in its infancy, that it ought not to be expected that any difference should appear so soon.

If this be the case, there is at once an end of all human science. The whole train of reasonings from effects to causes will be destroyed. We may shut our eyes to the book of nature, as it will no longer be of any use to read it. The wildest and most improbable conjectures may be advanced with as much certainty as the most just and sublime theories, founded on careful and reiterated experiments. We may return again to the old mode of philosophising and make facts bend to systems, instead of establishing systems upon facts. The grand and consistent theory of Newton will be placed upon the same footing as the wild and eccentric hypotheses of Descartes.[19] In short, if the laws of nature are thus fickle and inconstant, if it can be affirmed and be believed that they will change, when for ages and ages they have appeared immutable, the human mind will no longer have any incitements to inquiry, but must remain fixed in inactive torpor, or amuse itself only in bewildering dreams and extravagant fancies.

The constancy of the laws of nature and of effects and causes is the foundation of all human knowledge, though far be it from me to say that the same power which framed and executes the laws of nature may not change them all 'in a moment, in the twinkling of an eye'.[20] Such a change may undoubtedly happen. All that I mean to say is that it is impossible to infer it from reasoning. If without any previous observable symptoms or indications of a change, we can infer that a change will take place, we may as well make any assertion whatever and think it as unreasonable to be contradicted in affirming that the moon will come in contact with the earth tomorrow, as in saying that the sun will rise at its usual time.

With regard to the duration of human life, there does not appear to have existed from the earliest ages of the world to the present moment the smallest permanent symptom or indication of increasing prolongation. The observable effects of climate, habit, diet, and other causes, on length of life have furnished the pretext for asserting its indefinite extension; and the sandy foundation on which the argument rests is that because the limit of human life is undefined; because you cannot mark its precise term, and say so far exactly shall it go and no further; that therefore its extent may increase for ever, and be properly termed indefinite or unlimited. But the fallacy and absurdity of this argument will sufficiently appear from a slight examination of what Mr Condorcet calls the organic perfectibility, or degeneration, of the race of plants and animals, which he says may be regarded as one of the general laws of nature.

I am told that it is a maxim among the improvers of cattle that you may breed to any degree of nicety you please, and they found this maxim upon another, which is that some of the offspring will possess the desirable qualities of the parents in a greater degree. In the famous Leicestershire breed of sheep, the object is to procure them with small heads and small legs.[21] Proceeding upon these breeding maxims, it is evident that we might go on till the heads and legs were evanescent quantities, but this is so palpable an absurdity that we may be quite sure that the premises are not just and that there really is a limit, though we cannot see it or say exactly where it is. In this case, the point of the greatest degree of improvement, or the smallest size of the head and legs, may be said to be undefined, but this is very different from unlimited, or from indefinite, in Mr Condorcet's acceptation of the term. Though I may not be able in the present instance to mark the limit at which further improvement will stop, I can very easily mention a point at which it will not arrive. I should not scruple to assert that were the breeding to continue for ever, the head and legs of these sheep would never be so small as the head and legs of a rat.

It cannot be true, therefore, that among animals, some of the offspring will possess the desirable qualities of the parents in a greater degree, or that animals are indefinitely perfectible.

The progress of a wild plant to a beautiful garden flower is perhaps more marked and striking than anything that takes place among animals, yet even here it would be the height of absurdity to assert that the progress was unlimited or indefinite. One of the most obvious features of the improvement is the increase of size. The flower has grown gradually larger by cultivation. If the progress were really unlimited it might be increased *ad infinitum*, but this is so gross an absurdity that we may be quite sure that among plants as well as among animals there is a limit to improvement, though we do not exactly know where it is. It is probable that the gardeners who contend for flower prizes have often applied stronger dressing without success. At the same time it would be highly presumptuous in any man to say that he had seen the finest carnation or anemone that could ever be made to grow. He might however assert without the smallest chance of being contradicted by a future fact, that no carnation or anemone could ever by cultivation be increased to the size of a large cabbage; and yet there are assignable quantities much greater than a cabbage. No man can say that he has seen the largest ear of wheat, or the largest oak that could ever grow; but he might easily, and with perfect certainty, name a point of magnitude at which they would not arrive. In all these cases therefore, a careful distinction should be made, between an unlimited progress, and a progress where the limit is merely undefined.

It will be said, perhaps, that the reason why plants and animals cannot increase indefinitely in size is, that they would fall by their own weight. I answer, how do we know this but from experience? – from experience of the degree of strength with which these bodies are formed. I know that a carnation, long before it reached the size of a cabbage, would not be supported by its stalk, but I only know this from my experience of the weakness and want of tenacity in the materials of a carnation stalk. There are many substances in nature of the same size that would support as large a head as a cabbage.

The reasons of the mortality of plants are at present perfectly unknown to us. No man can say why such a plant is annual, another biennial, and another endures for ages. The whole affair in all these cases, in plants, animals, and in the human race, is an affair of experience, and I only conclude that man is mortal because the invariable experience of all ages has proved the mortality of those materials of which his visible body is made:

What can we reason, but from what we know?[22]

Sound philosophy will not authorize me to alter this opinion of the mortality of man on earth, till it can be clearly proved that the human race has made, and is making, a decided progress towards an illimitable extent of life. And the chief reason why I adduced the two particular instances from animals and plants was to expose and illustrate, if I could, the fallacy of that argument which infers an unlimited progress, merely because some partial improvement has taken place, and that the limit of this improvement cannot be precisely ascertained.

The capacity of improvement in plants and animals, to a certain degree, no person can possibly doubt. A clear and decided progress has already been made, and yet, I think, it appears that it would be highly absurd to say that this progress has no limits. In human life, though there are great variations from different causes, it may be doubted whether, since the world began, any organic improvement whatever in the human frame can be clearly ascertained. The foundations, therefore, on which the arguments for the organic perfectibility of man rest, are unusually weak, and can only be considered as mere conjectures. It does not, however, by any means seem impossible that by an attention to breed, a certain degree of improvement, similar to that among animals, might take place among men. Whether intellect could be communicated may be a matter of doubt: but size, strength, beauty, complexion, and perhaps even longevity are in a degree transmissible. The error does not seem to lie in supposing a small degree of improvement possible, but in not discriminating between a small improvement, the limit of which is undefined, and an improvement really unlimited. As the human race, however, could not be improved in this way, without condemning all the bad specimens to celibacy, it is not probable that an attention to breed should ever become general; indeed, I know of no well-directed attempts of this kind, except in the ancient family of the Bickerstaffs, who are said to have been very successful in whitening the skins and increasing the height of their race by prudent marriages, particularly by that very judicious cross with Maud, the milk-maid, by which some capital defects in the constitutions of the family were corrected.[23]

It will not be necessary, I think, in order more completely to shew the improbability of any approach in man towards immortality on earth, to urge the very great additional weight that an increase in the duration of life would give to the argument of population.

Many, I doubt not, will think that the attempting gravely to controvert so absurd a paradox as the immortality of man on earth, or indeed, even the perfectibility of man and society, is a waste of time and words, and that such unfounded conjectures are best answered by neglect. I profess, however, to be of a different opinion. When paradoxes of this kind are advanced by ingenious and able men, neglect has no tendency to convince them of their mistakes. Priding themselves on what they conceive to be a mark of the reach and size of their own understandings, of the extent and comprehensiveness of their views, they will look upon this neglect merely as an indication of poverty, and narrowness, in the mental exertions of their contemporaries, and only think that the world is not yet prepared to receive their sublime truths.

On the contrary, a candid investigation of these subjects, accompanied with a perfect readiness to adopt any theory warranted by sound philosophy, may have a tendency to convince them that in forming improbable and unfounded hypotheses, so far from enlarging the bounds of human science, they are contracting it, so far from promoting the improvement of the human mind, they are obstructing it; they are throwing us back again almost into the infancy of knowledge and weakening the foundations of that mode of philosophising, under the auspices of which science has of late made such rapid advances. The present rage for wide and unrestrained speculation seems to be a kind of mental intoxication, arising, perhaps, from the great and unexpected discoveries which have been made of late years, in various branches of science. To men elate and giddy with such successes, every thing appeared to be within the grasp of human powers; and, under this illusion, they confounded subjects where no real progress could be proved with those where the progress had been marked, certain, and acknowledged. Could they be persuaded to sober themselves with a little severe and chastised thinking, they would see, that the cause of truth, and of sound philosophy, cannot but suffer by substituting wild flights and unsupported assertions for patient investigation, and well authenticated proofs.

Mr Condorcet's book may be considered not only as a sketch of the opinions of a celebrated individual, but of many of the literary men in France at the beginning of the Revolution. As such, though merely a sketch, it seems worthy of attention.

CHAPTER X

Mr Godwin's system of equality – Error of attributing all the vices of mankind to human institutions – Mr Godwin's first answer to the difficulty arising from population totally insufficient – Mr Godwin's beautiful system of equality supposed to be realized – Its utter destruction simply from the principle of population in so short a time as thirty years.

In reading Mr Godwin's ingenious and able work on *Political Justice*, it is impossible not to be struck with the spirit and energy of his style, the force and precision of some of his reasonings, the ardent tone of his thoughts, and particularly with that impressive earnestness of manner which gives an air of truth to the whole. At the same time, it must be confessed that he has not proceeded in his inquiries with the caution that sound philosophy seems to require. His conclusions are often unwarranted by his premises. He fails sometimes in removing the objections which he himself brings forward. He relies too much on general and abstract propositions which will not admit of application. And his conjectures certainly far outstrip the modesty of nature.

The system of equality which Mr Godwin proposes is, without doubt, by far the most beautiful and engaging of any that has yet appeared. An amelioration of society to be produced merely by reason and conviction wears much more the promise of permanence than any change effected and maintained by force. The unlimited exercise of private judgement is a doctrine inexpressibly grand and captivating and has a vast superiority over those systems where every individual is in a manner the slave of the public. The substitution of benevolence as the master-spring and moving principle of society, instead of self-love, is a consummation devoutly to be wished. In short, it is impossible to contemplate the whole of this fair structure without emotions of delight and admiration, accompanied with ardent longing for the period of its accomplishment. But, alas!

that moment can never arrive. The whole is little better than a dream, a beautiful phantom of the imagination. These 'gorgeous palaces' of happiness and immortality, these 'solemn temples' of truth and virtue will dissolve, 'like the baseless fabric of a vision', when we awaken to real life and contemplate the true and genuine situation of man on earth.[24]

Mr Godwin, at the conclusion of the third chapter of his eighth book, speaking of population, says:

There is a principle in human society, by which population is perpetually kept down to the level of the means of subsistence. Thus among the wandering tribes of America and Asia, we never find through the lapse of ages that population has so increased as to render necessary the cultivation of the earth.

This principle, which Mr Godwin thus mentions as some mysterious and occult cause and which he does not attempt to investigate, will be found to be the grinding law of necessity, misery, and the fear of misery.

The great error under which Mr Godwin labours throughout his whole work is the attributing almost all the vices and misery that are seen in civil society to human institutions. Political regulations and the established administration of property are with him the fruitful sources of all evil, the hotbeds of all the crimes that degrade mankind. Were this really a true state of the case, it would not seem a hopeless task to remove evil completely from the world, and reason seems to be the proper and adequate instrument for effecting so great a purpose. But the truth is, that though human institutions appear to be the obvious and obtrusive causes of much mischief to mankind, yet in reality they are light and superficial, they are mere feathers that float on the surface, in comparison with those deeper seated causes of impurity that corrupt the springs and render turbid the whole stream of human life.

Mr Godwin, in his chapter on the benefits attendant on a system of equality, says:

The spirit of oppression, the spirit of servility, and the spirit of fraud, these are the immediate growth of the established administration of property. They are alike hostile to intellectual improvement.

The other vices of envy, malice, and revenge are their inseparable companions. In a state of society where men lived in the midst of plenty and where all shared alike the bounties of nature, these sentiments would inevitably expire. The narrow principle of selfishness would vanish. No man being obliged to guard his little store or provide with anxiety and pain for his restless wants, each would lose his individual existence in the thought of the general good. No man would be an enemy to his neighbour, for they would have no subject of contention, and, of consequence, philanthropy would resume the empire which reason assigns her. Mind would be delivered from her perpetual anxiety about corporal support, and free to expatiate in the field of thought, which is congenial to her. Each would assist the inquiries of all.[25]

This would, indeed, be a happy state. But that it is merely an imaginary picture, with scarcely a feature near the truth, the reader, I am afraid, is already too well convinced.

Man cannot live in the midst of plenty. All cannot share alike the bounties of nature. Were there no established administration of property, every man would be obliged to guard with force his little store. Selfishness would be triumphant. The subjects of contention would be perpetual. Every individual mind would be under a constant anxiety about corporal support, and not a single intellect would be left free to expatiate in the field of thought.

How little Mr Godwin has turned the attention of his penetrating mind to the real state of man on earth will sufficiently appear from the manner in which he endeavours to remove the difficulty of an overcharged population. He says:

The obvious answer to this objection, is, that to reason thus is to foresee difficulties at a great distance. Three fourths of the habitable globe is now uncultivated. The parts already cultivated are capable of immeasurable improvement. Myriads of centuries of still increasing population may pass away, and the earth be still found sufficient for the subsistence of its inhabitants.

I have already pointed out the error of supposing that no distress and difficulty would arise from an overcharged population before the earth absolutely refused to produce any more. But let us imagine for a moment Mr Godwin's beautiful system of equality realized in its utmost purity, and see how soon this difficulty might be expected to press under so perfect a form of society. A theory that will not admit of application cannot possibly be just.

Let us suppose all the causes of misery and vice in this island removed. War and contention cease. Unwholesome trades and manufactories do not exist. Crowds no longer collect together in great and pestilent cities for purposes of court intrigue, of commerce, and vicious gratifications. Simple, healthy, and rational amusements take place of drinking, gaming, and debauchery. There are no towns sufficiently large to have any prejudicial effects on the human constitution. The greater part of the happy inhabitants of this terrestrial paradise live in hamlets and farmhouses scattered over the face of the country. Every house is clean, airy, sufficiently roomy, and in a healthy situation. All men are equal. The labours of luxury are at end. And the necessary labours of agriculture are shared amicably among all. The number of persons, and the produce of the island, we suppose to be the same as at present. The spirit of benevolence, guided by impartial justice, will divide this produce among all the members of the society according to their wants. Though it would be impossible that they should all have animal food every day, yet vegetable food, with meat occasionally, would satisfy the desires of a frugal people and would be sufficient to preserve them in health, strength, and spirits.

Mr Godwin considers marriage as a fraud and a monopoly. Let us suppose the commerce of the sexes established upon principles of the most perfect freedom. Mr Godwin does not think himself that this freedom would lead to a promiscuous intercourse, and in this I perfectly agree with him. The love of variety is a vicious, corrupt, and unnatural taste and could not prevail in any great degree in a simple and virtuous state of society. Each man would probably select himself a partner, to whom he would adhere as long as that adherence continued to be the choice of both parties. It would be of little consequence, according to Mr Godwin, how many children a woman had or to whom they belonged. Provisions and assistance would spontaneously flow from the quarter in which they abounded, to the quarter that was deficient. (See Bk VIII, ch. 8; in the third edition, Vol II, p. 512.) And every man would be ready to furnish instruction to the rising generation according to his capacity.

I cannot conceive a form of society so favourable upon the whole to population. The irremediableness of marriage, as it is at present constituted, undoubtedly deters many from entering into that state. An unshackled intercourse on the contrary would be a most powerful incitement to early attachments, and as we are supposing no anxiety about the future support of children to exist, I do not conceive that there would be one woman in a hundred, of twenty-three, without a family.

With these extraordinary encouragements to population, and every cause of depopulation, as we have supposed, removed, the numbers would necessarily increase faster than in any society that has ever yet been known. I have mentioned, on the authority of a pamphlet published by a Dr Styles and referred to by Dr Price, that the inhabitants of the back settlements of America doubled their numbers in fifteen years. England is certainly a more healthy country than the back settlements of America, and as we have supposed every house in the island to be airy and wholesome, and the encouragements to have a family greater even than with the back settlers, no probable reason can be assigned why the population should not double itself in less, if possible, than fifteen years. But to be quite sure that we do not go beyond the truth, we will only suppose the period of doubling to be twenty-five years, a ratio of increase which is well known to have taken place throughout all the Northern States of America.

There can be little doubt that the equalization of property which we have supposed, added to the circumstance of the labour of the whole community being directed chiefly to agriculture, would tend greatly to augment the produce of the country. But to answer the demands of a population increasing so rapidly, Mr Godwin's calculation of half an hour a day for each man would certainly not be sufficient. It is probable that the half of every man's time must be employed for this purpose. Yet with such, or much greater exertions, a person who is acquainted with the nature of the soil in this country, and who reflects on the fertility of the lands already in cultivation, and the barrenness of those that are not cultivated, will be very much disposed to doubt whether the whole average produce could possibly be doubled in twenty-five years from the present period. The only chance of success would be the ploughing up all the grazing countries and putting an end almost entirely to the use of animal food. Yet a part of this scheme might defeat itself. The soil of England will not produce much without dressing, and cattle seem to be necessary to make that species of manure which best suits the land. In China it is said that the soil in some of the provinces is so fertile as to produce two crops of rice in the year without dressing. None of the lands in England will answer to this description.

Difficult, however, as it might be to double the average produce of the island in twenty-five years, let us suppose it effected. At the expiration of the first period therefore, the food, though almost entirely vegetable, would be sufficient to support in health the doubled population of fourteen millions.

During the next period of doubling, where will the food be found to satisfy the importunate demands of the increasing numbers? Where is the fresh land to turn up? Where is the dressing necessary to improve that which is already in cultivation? There is no person with the smallest knowledge of land but would say that it was impossible that the average produce of the country could be increased during the second twenty-five years by a quantity equal to what it at present yields. Yet we will suppose this increase, however improbable, to take place. The exuberant strength of the argument allows of almost any concession. Even with this concession, however, there would be seven millions at the expiration of the second term unprovided for. A quantity of food equal to the frugal support of twenty-one millions, would be to be divided among twenty-eight millions.

Alas! what becomes of the picture where men lived in the midst of plenty, where no man was obliged to provide with anxiety and pain for his restless wants, where the narrow principle of selfishness did not exist, where Mind was delivered from her perpetual anxiety about corporal support and free to expatiate in the field of thought which is congenial to her. This beautiful fabric of imagination vanishes at the severe touch of truth. The spirit of benevolence, cherished and invigorated by plenty, is repressed by the chilling breath of want. The hateful passions that had vanished reappear. The mighty law of self-preservation expels all the softer and more exalted emotions of the soul. The temptations to evil are too strong for human nature to resist. The corn is plucked before it is ripe, or secreted in unfair proportions, and the whole black train of vices that belong to falsehood are immediately generated. Provisions no longer flow in for the support of the mother with a large family. The children are sickly from insufficient food. The rosy flush of health gives place to the pallid cheek and hollow eye of misery. Benevolence, yet lingering in a few bosoms, makes some faint expiring struggles, till at length self-love resumes his wonted empire and lords it triumphant over the world.

No human institutions here existed, to the perverseness of which Mr Godwin ascribes the original sin of the worst men. (Bk VIII, ch. 3; in the third edition, Vol. II, p. 462.) No opposition had been produced by them between public and private good. No monopoly had been created of those advantages which reason directs to be left in common. No man had been goaded to the breach of order by unjust laws. Benevolence had established her reign in all hearts: and yet in so short a period as within fifty years, violence, oppression, falsehood, misery, every hateful vice, and every form of distress, which degrade and sadden the present state of society, seem to have been generated by the most imperious circumstances, by laws inherent in the nature of man, and absolutely independent of all human regulations.

If we are not yet too well convinced of the reality of this melancholy picture, let us but look for a moment into the next period of twenty-five years; and we shall see twenty-eight millions of human beings without the means of support; and before the conclusion of the first century, the population would be one hundred and twelve millions, and the food only sufficient for thirty-five millions, leaving seventy-seven millions unprovided for. In these ages want would be indeed triumphant, and rapine and murder must reign at large: and yet all this time we are supposing the produce of the earth absolutely unlimited, and the yearly increase greater than the boldest speculator can imagine.

This is undoubtedly a very different view of the difficulty arising from population from that which Mr Godwin gives, when he says, 'Myriads of centuries of still increasing population may pass away, and the earth be still found sufficient for the subsistence of its inhabitants.'

I am sufficiently aware that the redundant twenty-eight millions, or seventy-seven millions, that I have mentioned, could never have existed. It is a perfectly just observation of Mr Godwin, that, 'There is a principle in human society, by which population is perpetually kept down to the level of the means of subsistence.' The sole question is, what is this principle? Is it some obscure and occult cause? Is it some mysterious interference of heaven which, at a certain period, strikes the men with impotence, and the women with barrenness? Or is it a cause, open to our researches, within our view, a cause, which has constantly been observed to operate, though with varied force, in every state in which man has been placed? Is it not a degree of misery, the necessary and inevitable result of the laws of nature, which human institutions, so far from aggravating, have tended considerably to mitigate, though they never can remove?

It may be curious to observe, in the case that we have been supposing, how some of the laws which at present govern civilized society, would be successively dictated by the most imperious necessity. As man, according to Mr Godwin, is the creature of the impressions to which he is subject, the goadings of want could not continue long, before some violations of public or private stock would necessarily take place. As these violations increased in number and extent, the more active and comprehensive intellects of the society would soon perceive, that while population was fast increasing, the yearly produce of the country would shortly begin to diminish. The urgency of the case would suggest the necessity of some immediate measures to be taken for the general safety. Some kind of convention would then be called, and the dangerous situation of the country stated in the strongest terms. It would be observed, that while they lived in the midst of plenty, it was of little consequence who laboured the least, or who possessed the least, as every man was perfectly willing and ready to supply the wants of his neighbour. But that the question was no longer whether one man should give to another that which he did not use himself, but whether he should give to his neighbour the food which was absolutely necessary to his own existence. It would be represented, that the number of those that were in want very greatly exceeded the number and means of those who should supply them; that these pressing wants, which from the state of the produce of the country could not all be gratified, had occasioned some flagrant violations of justice; that these violations had already checked the increase of food, and would, if they were not by some means or other prevented, throw the whole community in confusion; that imperious necessity seemed to dictate that a yearly increase of produce should, if possible, be obtained at all events; that in order to effect this first, great, and indispensable purpose, it would be advisable to make a more complete division of land, and to secure every man's stock against violation by the most powerful sanctions, even by death itself.

It might be urged perhaps by some objectors that, as the fertility of the land increased, and various accidents occurred, the share of some men might be much more than sufficient for their support, and that when the reign of self-love was once established, they would not distribute their surplus produce without some compensation in return. It would be observed, in answer, that this was an inconvenience greatly to be lamented; but that it was an evil which bore no comparison to the black train of distresses that would inevitably be occasioned by the insecurity of property; that the quantity of food which one man could consume was necessarily limited by the narrow capacity of the human stomach; that it was not certainly probable that he should throw away the rest; but that even if he exchanged his surplus food for the labour of others, and made them in some degree dependent on him, this would still be better than that these others should absolutely starve.

It seems highly probable, therefore, that an administration of property, not very different from that which prevails in civilized states at present, would be established, as the best, though inadequate, remedy for the evils which were pressing on the society.

The next subject that would come under discussion, intimately connected with the preceding, is the commerce between the sexes. It would be urged by those who had turned their attention to the true cause of the difficulties under which the community laboured, that while every man felt secure that all his children would be well provided for by general benevolence, the powers of the earth would be absolutely inadequate to produce food for the population which would inevitably ensue; that even if the whole attention and labour of the society were directed to this sole point, and if, by the most perfect security of property, and every other encouragement that could be thought of, the greatest possible increase of produce were yearly obtained; yet still, that the increase of food would by no means keep pace with the much more rapid increase of population; that some check to population therefore was imperiously called for; that the most natural and obvious check seemed to be to make every man provide for his own children; that this would operate in some respect as a measure and guide in the increase of population, as it might be expected that no man would bring beings into the world, for whom he could not find the means of support; that where this notwithstanding was the case, it seemed necessary, for the example of others, that the disgrace and inconvenience attending such a conduct should fall upon the individual, who had thus inconsiderately plunged himself and innocent children in misery and want.

The institution of marriage, or at least, of some express or implied obligation on every man to support his own children, seems to be the natural result of these reasonings in a community under the difficulties that we have supposed.

The view of these difficulties presents us with a very natural origin of the superior disgrace which attends a breach of chastity in the woman than in the man. It could not be expected that women should have resources sufficient to support their own children. When therefore a woman was connected with a man, who had entered into no compact to maintain her children, and, aware of the inconveniences that he might bring upon himself, had deserted her, these children must necessarily fall for support upon the society, or starve. And to prevent the frequent recurrence of such an inconvenience, as it would be highly unjust to punish so natural a fault by personal restraint or infliction, the men might agree to punish it with disgrace. The offence is besides more obvious and conspicuous in the woman, and less liable to any mistake. The father of a child may not always be known, but the same uncertainty cannot easily exist with regard to the mother. Where the evidence of the offence was most complete, and the inconvenience to the society at the same time the greatest, there it was agreed that the large share of blame should fall. The obligation on every man to maintain his children, the society would enforce, if there were occasion; and the greater degree of inconvenience or labour, to which a family would necessarily subject him, added to some portion of disgrace which every human being must incur who leads another into unhappiness, might be considered as a sufficient punishment for the man.

That a woman should at present be almost driven from society for an offence which men commit nearly with impunity, seems to be undoubtedly a breach of natural justice. But the origin of the custom, as the most obvious and effectual method of preventing the frequent recurrence of a serious inconvenience to a community, appears to be natural, though not perhaps perfectly justifiable. This origin, however, is now lost in the new train of ideas which the custom has since generated. What at first might be dictated by state necessity is now supported by female delicacy, and operates with the greatest force on that part of society where, if the original intention of the custom were preserved, there is the least real occasion for it.

When these two fundamental laws of society, the security of property, and the institution of marriage, were once established, inequality of conditions must necessarily follow. Those who were born after the division of property would come into a world already possessed. If their parents, from having too large a family, could not give them sufficient for their support, what are they to do in a world where everything is appropriated? We have seen the fatal effects that would result to a society, if every man had a valid claim to an equal share of the produce of the earth. The members of a family which was grown too large for the original division of land appropriated to it could not then demand a part of the surplus produce of others, as a debt of justice. It has appeared, that from the inevitable laws of our nature some human beings must suffer from want. These are the unhappy persons who, in the great lottery of life, have drawn a blank. The number of these claimants would soon exceed the ability of the surplus produce to supply. Moral merit is a very difficult distinguishing criterion, except in extreme cases. The owners of surplus produce would in general seek some more obvious mark of distinction. And it seems both natural and just that, except upon particular occasions, their choice should fall upon those who were able, and professed themselves willing, to exert their strength in procuring a further surplus produce; and thus at once benefiting the community, and enabling these proprietors to afford assistance to greater numbers. All who were in want of food would be urged by imperious necessity to offer their labour in exchange for this article so absolutely essential to existence. The fund appropriated to the maintenance of labour would be the aggregate quantity of food possessed by the owners of land beyond their own consumption. When the demands upon this fund were great and numerous, it would naturally be divided in very small shares. Labour would be ill paid. Men would offer to work for a bare subsistence, and the rearing of families would be checked by sickness and misery. On the contrary, when this fund was increasing fast, when it was great in proportion to the number of claimants, it would be divided in much larger shares. No man would exchange his labour without receiving an ample quantity of food in return. Labourers would live in ease and comfort, and would consequently be able to rear a numerous and vigorous offspring.

On the state of this fund, the happiness, or the degree of misery, prevailing among the lower classes of people in every known state at present chiefly depends. And on this happiness, or degree of misery, depends the increase, stationariness, or decrease of population.

And thus it appears, that a society constituted according to the most beautiful form that imagination can conceive, with benevolence for its moving principle, instead of self-love, and with every evil disposition in all its members corrected by reason and not force, would, from the inevitable laws of nature, and not from any original depravity of man, in a very short period degenerate into a society constructed upon a plan not essentially different from that which prevails in every known state at present; I mean, a society divided into a class of proprietors, and a class of labourers, and with self-love the main-spring of the great machine.

In the supposition I have made, I have undoubtedly taken the increase of population smaller, and the increase of produce greater, than they really would be. No reason can be assigned why, under the circumstances I have supposed, population should not increase faster than in any known instance. If then we were to take the period of doubling at fifteen years, instead of twenty-five years, and reflect upon the labour necessary to double the produce in so short a time, even if we allow it possible, we may venture to pronounce with certainty that if Mr Godwin's system of society was established in its utmost perfection, instead of myriads of centuries, not thirty years could elapse before its utter destruction from the simple principle of population.

I have taken no notice of emigration for obvious reasons. If such societies were instituted in other parts of Europe, these countries would be under the same difficulties with regard to population, and could admit no fresh members into their bosoms. If this beautiful society were confined to this Island, it must have degenerated strangely from its original purity, and administer but a very small portion of the happiness it proposed; in short, its essential principle must be completely destroyed, before any of its members would voluntarily consent to leave it, and live under such governments as at present exist in Europe, or submit to the extreme hardships of first settlers in new regions. We well know, from repeated experience, how much misery and hardship men will undergo in their own country, before they can determine to desert it; and how often the most tempting proposals of embarking for new settlements have been rejected by people who appeared to be almost starving.

CHAPTER XI

Mr Godwin's conjecture concerning the future extinction
of the passion between the sexes – Little apparent grounds
for such a conjecture – Passion of love not inconsistent either
with reason or virtue.

WE have supported Mr Godwin's system of society once completely established. But it is supposing an impossibility. The
same causes in nature which would destroy it so rapidly, were it
once established, would prevent the possibility of its establishment. And upon what grounds we can presume a change in
these natural causes, I am utterly at a loss to conjecture. No
move towards the extinction of the passion between the sexes
has taken place in the five or six thousand years that the
world has existed. Men in the decline of life have in all ages de-
claimed against a passion which they have ceased to feel, but with
as little reason as success. Those who from coldness of constitu-
tional temperament have never felt what love is, will surely be
allowed to be very incompetent judges with regard to the power
of this passion to contribute to the sum of pleasurable sensations
in life. Those who have spent their youth in criminal excesses
and have prepared for themselves, as the comforts of their age,
corporeal debility and mental remorse may well inveigh against
such pleasures as vain and futile, and unproductive of lasting
satisfaction. But the pleasures of pure love will bear the contemplation of the most improved reason, and the most exalted
virtue. Perhaps there is scarcely a man who has once experienced
the genuine delight of virtuous love, however great his intellectual pleasure may have been, that does not look back to the
period as the sunny spot in his whole life, where his imagination
loves to bask, which he recollects and contemplates with the
fondest regrets, and which he would most wish to live over
again. The superiority of intellectual to sensual pleasures consists rather in their filling up more time, in their having a larger

range, and in their being less liable to satiety, than in their being more real and essential.

Intemperance in every enjoyment defeats its own purpose. A walk in the finest day through the most beautiful country, if pursued too far, ends in pain and fatigue. The most wholesome and invigorating food, eaten with an unrestrained appetite, produces weakness instead of strength. Even intellectual pleasures, though certainly less liable than others to satiety, pursued with too little intermission, debilitate the body, and impair the vigour of the mind. To argue against the reality of these pleasures from their abuse seems to be hardly just. Morality, according to Mr Godwin, is a calculation of consequences, or, as Archdeacon Paley very justly expresses it, the will of God, as collected from general expediency.[26] According to either of these definitions, a sensual pleasure not attended with the probability of unhappy consequences does not offend against the laws of morality, and if it be pursued with such a degree of temperance as to leave the most ample room for intellectual attainments, it must undoubtedly add to the sum of pleasurable sensations in life. Virtuous love, exalted by friendship, seems to be that sort of mixture of sensual and intellectual enjoyment particularly suited to the nature of man, and most powerfully calculated to awaken the sympathies of the soul, and produce the most exquisite gratifications.

Mr Godwin says, in order to shew the evident inferiority of the pleasures of sense, 'Strip the commerce of the sexes of all its attendant circumstances, and it would be generally despised' (Bk. I, ch. 5; in the third edition, Vol. I, pp. 71–72). He might as well say to a man who admired trees: strip them of their spreading branches and lovely foliage, and what beauty can you see in a bare pole? But it was the tree with the branches and foliage, and not without them, that excited admiration. One feature of an object may be as distinct, and excite as different emotions, from the aggregate as any two things the most remote, as a beautiful woman, and a map of Madagascar. It is 'the symmetry of person, the vivacity, the voluptuous softness of temper, the affectionate kindness of feelings, the imagination and the wit' of a woman that excite the passion of love, and not the mere distinction of her being female. Urged by the passion of love, men have been driven into acts highly prejudicial to the general interests of society, but probably they would have found no difficulty in resisting the temptation, had it appeared in the form of a woman with no other attractions whatever but her sex. To strip sensual pleasures of all their adjuncts, in order to prove their inferiority, is to deprive a magnet of some of its most essential causes of attraction, and then to say that it is weak and inefficient.

In the pursuit of every enjoyment, whether sensual or intellectual, reason, that faculty which enables us to calculate consequences, is the proper corrective and guide. It is probable therefore that improved reason will always tend to prevent the abuse of sensual pleasures, though it by no means follows that it will extinguish them.

I have endeavoured to expose the fallacy of that argument which infers an unlimited progress from a partial improvement, the limits of which cannot be exactly ascertained. It has appeared, I think, that there are many instances in which a decided progress has been observed, where yet it would be a gross absurdity to suppose that progress indefinite. But towards the extinction of the passion between the sexes, no observable progress whatever has hitherto been made. To suppose such an extinction, therefore, is merely to offer an unfounded conjecture, unsupported by any philosophical probabilities.

It is a truth, which history I am afraid makes too clear, that some men of the highest mental powers have been addicted not only to a moderate, but even to an immoderate indulgence in the pleasures of sensual love. But allowing, as I should be inclined to do, notwithstanding numerous instances to the contrary, that great intellectual exertions tend to diminish the empire of this passion over man, it is evident that the mass of mankind must be improved more highly than the brightest ornaments of the species at present before any difference can take place sufficient sensibly to affect population. I would by no means suppose that the mass of mankind has reached its term of improvement, but the principal argument of this essay tends to place in a strong point of view the improbability that the lower classes of people in any country should ever be sufficiently free from want and labour to obtain any high degree of intellectual improvement.

CHAPTER XII

Mr Godwin's conjecture concerning the indefinite prolongation of human life – Improper inference drawn from the effects of mental stimulants on the human frame, illustrated in various instances – Conjectures not founded on any indications in the past, not to be considered as philosophical conjectures – Mr Godwin's and Mr Condorcet's conjecture respecting the approach of man towards immortality on earth, a curious instance of the inconsistency of scepticism.

MR GODWIN'S conjecture respecting the future approach of man towards immortality on earth seems to be rather oddly placed in a chapter which professes to remove the objection to his system of equality from the principle of population. Unless he supposes the passion between the sexes to decrease faster than the duration of life increases, the earth would be more encumbered than ever. But leaving this difficulty to Mr Godwin, let us examine a few of the appearances from which the probable immortality of man is inferred.

To prove the power of the mind over the body, Mr Godwin observes:

How often do we find a piece of good news dissipating a distemper? How common is the remark that those accidents which are to the indolent a source of disease are forgotten and extirpated in the busy and active? I walk twenty miles in an indolent and half determined temper and am extremely fatigued. I walk twenty miles full of ardour, and with a motive that engrosses my soul, and I come in as fresh and as alert as when I began my journey. Emotion excited by some unexpected word, by a letter that is delivered to us, occasions the most extraordinary revolutions in our frame, accelerates the circulation, causes the heart to palpitate, the tongue to refuse its office, and has been known to occasion death by extreme anguish or extreme joy. There is nothing indeed of which the physician is more aware than of the power of the mind in assisting or retarding convalescence.

The instances here mentioned are chiefly instances of the effects of mental stimulants on the bodily frame. No person has ever for a moment doubted the near, though mysterious, connection of mind and body. But it is arguing totally without knowledge of the nature of stimulants to suppose, either that they can be applied continually with equal strength, or if they could be so applied, for a time, that they would not exhaust and wear out the subject. In some of the cases here noticed, the strength of the stimulus depends upon its novelty and unexpectedness. Such a stimulus cannot, from its nature, be repeated often with the same effect, as it would by repetition lose that property which gives it its strength.

In the other cases, the argument is from a small and partial effect, to a great and general effect, which will in numberless instances be found to be a very fallacious mode of reasoning. The busy and active man may in some degree counteract, or what is perhaps nearer the truth, may disregard those slight disorders of frame which fix the attention of a man who has nothing else to think of; but this does not tend to prove that activity of mind will enable a man to disregard a high fever, the smallpox, or the plague.

The man who walks twenty miles with a motive that engrosses his soul does not attend to his slight fatigue of body when he comes in; but double his motive, and set him to walk another twenty miles, quadruple it, and let him start a third time, and so on; and the length of his walk will ultimately depend upon muscle and not mind. Powell,[27] for a motive of ten guineas, would have walked further probably than Mr Godwin, for a motive of half a million. A motive of uncommon power acting upon a frame of moderate strength would, perhaps, make the man kill himself by his exertions, but it would not make him walk a hundred miles in twenty-four hours. This statement of the case shews the fallacy of supposing that the person was really not at all tired in his first walk of twenty miles, because he did not appear to be so, or, perhaps, scarcely felt any fatigue himself. The mind cannot fix its attention strongly on more than one object at once. The twenty thousand pounds so engrossed his thoughts that he did not attend to any slight soreness of foot, or stiffness of limb. But had he been really as fresh and as alert, as when he first set off, he would be able to go the second twenty miles with as much ease as the first, and so on, the third, &c. Which leads to a palpable absurdity. When a horse of spirit is nearly half tired, by the stimulus of the spur, added to the proper management of the bit, he may be put so much upon his mettle, that he would appear to a stander-by, as fresh and as high spirited as if he had not gone a mile. Nay, probably, the horse himself, while in the heat and passion occasioned by this stimulus, would not feel any fatigue; but it would be strangely contrary to all reason and experience, to argue from such an appearance that, if the stimulus were continued, the horse would never be tired. The cry of a pack of hounds will make some horses, after a journey of forty miles on the road, appear as fresh, and as lively, as when they first set out. Were they then to be hunted, no perceptible abatement would at first be felt by their riders in their strength and spirits, but towards the end of a hard day, the previous fatigue would have its full weight and effect, and make them tire sooner. When I have taken a long walk with my gun, and met with no success, I have frequently returned home feeling a considerable degree of uncomfortableness from fatigue. Another day, perhaps, going over nearly the same extent of ground with a good deal of sport, I have come home fresh, and alert. The difference in the sensation of fatigue upon coming in, on the different days, may have been very striking, but on the following mornings I have found no such difference. I have not perceived that I was less stiff in my limbs, or less footsore, on the morning after the day of the sport, than on the other morning.

In all these cases, stimulants upon the mind seem to act rather by taking off the attention from the bodily fatigue, than by really and truly counteracting it. If the energy of my mind had really counteracted the fatigue of my body, why should I feel tired the next morning? If the stimulus of the hounds had as completely overcome the fatigue of the journey in reality, as it did in appearance, why should the horse be tired sooner than if he had not gone the forty miles? I happen to have a very bad fit of the toothache at the time I am writing this. In the eagerness of composition, I every now and then, for a moment or two, forget it. Yet I cannot help thinking that the process, which causes the pain, is still going forwards, and that the nerves which carry the information of it to the brain are even during these moments demanding attention and room for their appropriate vibrations. The multiplicity of vibrations of another kind may perhaps prevent their admission, or overcome them for a time when admitted, till a shoot of extraordinary energy puts all other vibration to the rout, destroys the vividness of my argumentative conceptions, and rides triumphant in the brain. In this case, as in the others, the mind seems to have little or no power in counteracting or curing the disorder, but merely possesses a power, if strongly excited, of fixing its attention on other subjects.

I do not, however, mean to say that a sound and vigorous mind has no tendency whatever to keep the body in a similar state. So close and intimate is the union of mind and body that it would be highly extraordinary if they did not mutually assist each other's functions. But, perhaps, upon a comparison, the body has more effect upon the mind than the mind upon the body. The first object of the mind is to act as purveyor to the wants of the body. When these wants are completely satisfied, an active mind is indeed apt to wander further, to range over the fields of science, or sport in the regions of imagination, to fancy that it has 'shuffled off this mortal coil', and is seeking its kindred element. But all these efforts are like the vain exertions of the hare in the fable. The slowly moving tortoise, the body, never fails to overtake the mind, however widely and extensively it may have ranged, and the brightest and most energetic intellects, unwillingly as they may attend to the first or second summons, must ultimately yield the empire of the brain to the calls of hunger, or sink with the exhausted body in sleep.

It seems as if one might say with certainty that if a medicine could be found to immortalize the body there would be no fear of its [not] being accompanied by the immortality of the mind. But the immortality of the mind by no means seems to infer the immortality of the body. On the contrary, the greatest conceivable energy of mind would probably exhaust and destroy the strength of the body. A temperate vigour of mind appears to be favourable to health, but very great intellectual exertions tend rather, as has been often observed, to wear out the scabbard. Most of the instances which Mr Godwin has brought to prove the power of the mind over the body, and the consequent probability of the immortality of man, are of this latter description, and could such stimulants be continually applied, instead of tending to immortalize, they would tend very rapidly to destroy the human frame.

The probable increase of the voluntary power of man over his animal frame comes next under Mr Godwin's consideration, and he concludes by saying, that the voluntary power of some men, in this respect, is found to extend to various articles in which other men are impotent. But this is reasoning against an almost universal rule from a few exceptions; and these exceptions seem to be rather tricks, than powers that may be exerted to any good purpose. I have never heard of any man who could regulate his pulse in a fever, and doubt much, if any of the persons here alluded to have made the smallest perceptible progress in the regular correction of the disorders of their frames and the consequent prolongation of their lives.

Mr Godwin says, 'Nothing can be more unphilosophical than to conclude, that, because a certain species of power is beyond the train of our present observation, that it is beyond the limits of the human mind.' I own my ideas of philosophy are in this respect widely different from Mr Godwin's. The only distinction that I see, between a philosophical conjecture, and the assertions of the Prophet Mr Brothers,[28] is, that one is founded upon indications arising from the train of our present observations, and the other has no foundation at all. I expect that great discoveries are yet to take place in all the branches of human science, particularly in physics; but the moment we leave past experience as the foundation of our conjectures concerning the future, and, still more, if our conjectures absolutely contradict past experience, we are thrown upon a wide field of uncertainty, and any one supposition is then just as good as another. If a person were to tell me that men would ultimately have eyes and hands behind them as well as before them, I should admit the usefulness of the addition, but should give as a reason for my disbelief of it, that I saw no indications whatever in the past from which I could infer the smallest probability of such a change. If this be not allowed a valid objection, all conjectures are alike, and all equally philosophical. I own it appears to me that in the train of our present observations, there are no more genuine indications that man will become immortal upon earth than that he will have four eyes and four hands, or that trees will grow horizontally instead of perpendicularly.

It will be said, perhaps, that many discoveries have already taken place in the world that were totally unforeseen and unexpected. This I grant to be true; but if a person had predicted these discoveries without being guided by any analogies or indications from past facts, he would deserve the name of seer or prophet, but not of philosopher. The wonder that some of our modern discoveries would excite in the savage inhabitants of Europe in the times of Theseus and Achilles,[29] proves but little. Persons almost entirely unacquainted with the powers of a machine cannot be expected to guess at its effects. I am far from saying, that we are at present by any means fully acquainted with the powers of the human mind; but we certainly know more of this instrument than was known four thousand years ago; and therefore, though not to be called competent judges, we are certainly much better able than savages to say what is, or is not, within its grasp. A watch would strike a savage with as much surprise as a perpetual motion; yet one is to us a most familiar piece of mechanism, and the other has constantly eluded the efforts of the most acute intellects. In many instances we are now able to perceive the causes, which prevent an unlimited improvement in those inventions, which seemed to promise fairly for it at first. The original improvers of telescopes would probably think, that as long as the size of the specula and the length of the tubes could be increased, the powers and advantages of the instrument would increase; but experience has since taught us, that the smallness of the field, the deficiency of light, and the circumstance of the atmosphere being magnified, prevent the beneficial results that were to be expected from telescopes of extraordinary size and power. In many parts of knowledge, man has been almost constantly making some progress; in other parts, his efforts have been invariably baffled. The savage would not probably be able to guess at the causes of this mighty difference. Our further experience has given us some little insight into these causes, and has therefore enabled us better to judge, if not of what we are to expect in future, at least of what we are not to expect, which, though negative, is a very useful piece of information.

As the necessity of sleep seems rather to depend upon the body than the mind, it does not appear how the improvement of the mind can tend very greatly to supersede this 'conspicuous infirmity'.[30] A man who by great excitements on his mind is able to pass two or three nights without sleep, proportionably exhausts the vigour of his body, and this diminution of health and strength will soon disturb the operations of his understanding, so that by these great efforts he appears to have made no real progress whatever in superseding the necessity of this species of rest.

There is certainly a sufficiently marked difference in the various characters of which we have some knowledge, relative to the energies of their minds, their benevolent pursuits, etc., to enable us to judge whether the operations of intellect have any decided effect in prolonging the duration of human life. It is certain that no decided effect of this kind has yet been observed. Though no attention of any kind has ever produced such an effect as could be construed into the smallest semblance of an approach towards immortality, yet of the two, a certain attention to the body seems to have more effect in this respect than an attention to the mind. The man who takes his temperate meals and his bodily exercise, with scrupulous regularity, will generally be found more healthy than the man who, very deeply engaged in intellectual pursuits, often forgets for a time these bodily cravings. The citizen who has retired, and whose ideas, perhaps, scarcely soar above or extend beyond his little garden, puddling all the morning about his borders of box,[31] will, perhaps, live as long as the philosopher whose range of intellect is the most extensive, and whose views are the clearest of any of his contemporaries. It has been positively observed by those who have attended to the bills of mortality that women live longer upon an average than men, and, though I would not by any means say that their intellectual faculties are inferior, yet, I think, it must be allowed that, from their different education, there are not so many women as men, who are excited to vigorous mental exertion.

As in these and similar instances, or to take a larger range, as in the great diversity of characters that have existed during some thousand years, no decided difference has been observed in the duration of human life from the operation of intellect, the mortality of man on earth seems to be as completely established, and exactly upon the same grounds, as any one, the most constant, of the laws of nature. An immediate act of power in the Creator of the Universe might, indeed, change one or all of these laws, either suddenly or gradually, but without some indications of such a change, and such indications do not exist, it is just as unphilosophical to suppose that the life of man may be prolonged beyond any assignable limits, as to suppose that the attraction of the earth will gradually be changed into repulsion and that stones will ultimately rise instead of fall or that the earth will fly off at a certain period to some more genial and warmer sun.

The conclusion of this chapter presents us,[32] undoubtedly, with a very beautiful and desirable picture, but like some of the landscapes drawn from fancy and not imagined with truth, it fails of that interest in the heart which nature and probability can alone give.

I cannot quit this subject without taking notice of these conjectures of Mr Godwin and Mr Condorcet concerning the indefinite prolongation of human life, as a very curious instance of the longing of the soul after immortality. Both these gentlemen have rejected the light of revelation which absolutely promises eternal life in another state. They have also rejected the light of natural religion, which to the ablest intellects in all ages has indicated the future existence of the soul. Yet so congenial is the idea of immortality to the mind of man that they cannot consent entirely to throw it out of their systems. After all their fastidious scepticisms concerning the only probable mode of immortality, they introduce a species of immortality of their own, not only completely contradictory to every law of philosophical probability, but in itself in the highest degree narrow, partial, and unjust. They suppose that all the great, virtuous, and exalted minds that have ever existed or that may exist for some thousands, perhaps millions of years, will be sunk in annihilation, and that only a few beings, not greater in number than can exist at once upon the earth, will be ultimately crowned with immortality. Had such a tenet been advanced as a tenet of revelation I am very sure that all the enemies of religion, and probably Mr Godwin and Mr Condorcet among the rest, would have exhausted the whole force of their ridicule upon it, as the most puerile, the most absurd, the poorest, the most pitiful, the most iniquitously unjust, and, consequently, the most unworthy of the Deity that the superstitious folly of man could invent.

What a strange and curious proof do these conjectures exhibit of the inconsistency of scepticism! For it should be observed, that there is a very striking and essential difference between believing an assertion which absolutely contradicts the most uniform experience, and an assertion which contradicts nothing, but is merely beyond the power of our present observation and knowledge. So diversified are the natural objects around us, so many instances of mighty power daily offer themselves to our view, that we may fairly presume, that there are many forms and operations of nature which we have not yet observed, or which, perhaps, we are not capable of observing with our present confined inlets of knowledge. The resurrection of a spiritual body from a natural body does not appear in itself a more wonderful instance of power than the germination of a blade of wheat from the grain, or of an oak from an acorn. Could we conceive an intelligent being, so placed as to be conversant only with inanimate or full grown objects, and never to have witnessed the process of vegetation and growth; and were another being to shew him two little pieces of matter, a grain of wheat, and an acorn, to desire him to examine them, to analyse them if he pleased, and endeavour to find out their properties and essences; and then to tell him, that however trifling these little bits of matter might appear to him, that they possessed such curious powers of selection, combination, arrangement, and almost of creation, that upon being put into the ground, they would choose, amongst all the dirt and moisture that surrounded them, those parts which best suited their purpose, that they would collect and arrange these parts with wonderful taste, judgement, and execution, and would rise up into beautiful forms, scarcely in any respect analogous to the little bits of matter which were first placed in the earth. I feel very little doubt that the imaginary being which I have supposed would hesitate more, would require better authority, and stronger proofs, before he believed these strange assertions, than if he had been told, that a being of mighty power, who had been the cause of all that he saw around him, and of that existence of which he himself was conscious, would, by a great act of power upon the death and corruption of human creatures, raise up the essence of thought in an incorporeal, or at least invisible form, to give it a happier existence in another state.

The only difference, with regard to our own apprehensions, that is not in favour of the latter assertion is that the first miracle we have repeatedly seen, and the last miracle we have not seen. I admit the full weight of this prodigious difference, but surely no man can hesitate a moment in saying that, putting Revelation out of the question, the resurrection of a spiritual body from a natural body, which may be merely one among the many operations of nature which we cannot see, is an event indefinitely more probable than the immortality of man on earth, which is not only an event of which no symptoms or indications have yet appeared, but is a positive contradiction to one of the most constant of the laws of nature that has ever come within the observation of man.

When we extend our view beyond this life, it is evident that we can have no other guides than authority, or conjecture, and perhaps, indeed, an obscure and undefined feeling. What I say here, therefore, does not appear to me in any respect to contradict what I said before, when I observed that it was unphilosophical to expect any specifick event that was not indicated by some kind of analogy in the past. In ranging beyond the bourne from which no traveller returns, we must necessarily quit this rule; but with regard to events that may be expected to happen on earth, we can seldom quit it consistently with true philosophy. Analogy has, however, as I conceive, great latitude. For instance, man has discovered many of the laws of nature: analogy seems to indicate that he will discover many more; but no analogy seems to indicate that he will discover a sixth sense, or a new species of power in the human mind, entirely beyond the train of our present observations.

The powers of selection, combination, and transmutation, which every seed shews, are truly miraculous. Who can imagine that these wonderful faculties are contained in these little bits of matter? To me it appears much more philosophical to suppose that the mighty God of nature is present in full energy in all these operations. To this all powerful Being, it would be equally easy to raise an oak without an acorn as with one. The preparatory process of putting seeds into the ground is merely ordained for the use of man, as one among the various other excitements necessary to awaken matter into mind. It is an idea that will be found consistent, equally with the natural phenomena around us, with the various events of human life, and with the successive revelations of God to man, to suppose that the world is a mighty process for the creation and formation of mind. Many vessels will necessarily come out of this great furnace in wrong shapes. These will be broken and thrown aside as useless; while those vessels whose forms are full of truth, grace, and loveliness, will be wafted into happier situations, nearer the presence of the mighty maker.

I ought perhaps again to make an apology to my readers for dwelling so long upon a conjecture which many, I know, will think too absurd and improbable to require the least discussion. But if it be as improbable and as contrary to the genuine spirit of philosophy as I own I think it is, why should it not be shewn to be so in a candid examination? A conjecture, however improbable on the first view of it, advanced by able and ingenious men, seems at least to deserve investigation. For my own part I feel no disinclination whatever to give that degree of credit to the opinion of the probable immortality of man on earth, which the appearances that can be brought in support of it deserve. Before we decide upon the utter improbability of such an event, it is but fair impartially to examine these appearances; and from such an examination I think we may conclude, that we have rather less reason for supposing that the life of man may be indefinitely prolonged, than that trees may be made to grow indefinitely high, or potatoes indefinitely large. Though Mr Godwin advances the idea of the indefinite prolongation of human life merely as a conjecture, yet as he has produced some appearances, which in his conception favour the supposition, he must certainly intend that these appearances should be examined and this is all that I have meant to do.

CHAPTER XIII

Error of Mr Godwin in considering man too much in the light of a being merely rational – In the compound being, man, the passions will always act as disturbing forces in the decisions of the understanding – Reasonings of Mr Godwin on the subject of coercion – Some truths of a nature not to be communicated from one man to another.

IN the chapter which I have been examining, Mr Godwin professes to consider the objection to his system of equality from the principle of population. It has appeared, I think clearly, that he is greatly erroneous in his statement of the distance of this difficulty, and that instead of myriads of centuries, it is really not thirty years, or even thirty days, distant from us. The supposition of the approach of man to immortality on earth is certainly not of a kind to soften the difficulty. The only argument, therefore, in the chapter which has any tendency to remove the objection is the conjecture concerning the extinction of the passion between the sexes, but as this is a mere conjecture, unsupported by the smallest shadow of proof, the force of the objection may be fairly said to remain unimpaired, and it is undoubtedly of sufficient weight of itself completely to overturn Mr Godwin's whole system of equality. I will, however, make one or two observations on a few of the prominent parts of Mr Godwin's reasonings which will contribute to place in a still clearer point of view the little hope that we can reasonably entertain of those vast improvements in the nature of man and of society which he holds up to our admiring gaze in his *Political Justice*.

Mr Godwin considers man too much in the light of a being merely intellectual. This error, at least such I conceive it to be, pervades his whole work and mixes itself with all his reasonings. The voluntary actions of men may originate in their opinions, but these opinions will be very differently modified in creatures compounded of a rational faculty and corporal propensities from what they would be in beings wholly intellectual. Mr Godwin, in proving that sound reasoning and truth are capable of being adequately communicated, examines the proposition first practically, and then adds, 'Such is the appearance which this proposition assumes, when examined in a loose and practical view. In strict consideration it will not admit of debate. Man is a rational being, etc.' (Bk. I, ch. 5; in the third edition Vol. I, p. 88). So far from calling this a strict consideration of the subject, I own I should call it the loosest, and most erroneous, way possible, of considering it. It is the calculating the velocity of a falling body in vacuo, and persisting in it, that it would be the same through whatever resisting mediums it might fall. This was not Newton's mode of philosophizing. Very few general propositions are just in application to a particular subject. The moon is not kept in her orbit round the earth, nor the earth in her orbit round the sun, by a force that varies merely in the inverse ratio of the squares of the distances. To make the general theory just in application to the revolutions of these bodies, it was necessary to calculate accurately the disturbing force of the sun upon the moon, and of the moon upon the earth; and till these disturbing forces were properly estimated, actual observations on the motions of these bodies would have proved that the theory was not accurately true.

I am willing to allow that every voluntary act is preceded by a decision of the mind, but it is strangely opposite to what I should conceive to be the just theory upon the subject, and a palpable contradiction to all experience, to say that the corporal propensities of man do not act very powerfully, as disturbing forces, in these decisions. The question, therefore, does not merely depend upon whether a man may be made to understand a distinct proposition or be convinced by an unanswerable argument. A truth may be brought home to his conviction as a rational being, though he may determine to act contrary to it, as a compound being. The cravings of hunger, the love of liquor, the desire of possessing a beautiful woman, will urge men to actions, of the fatal consequences of which, to the general interests of society, they are prefectly well convinced, even at the very time they commit them. Remove their bodily cravings, and they would not hesitate a moment in determining against such actions. Ask them their opinion of the same conduct in another person, and they would immediately reprobate it. But in their own case, and under all the circumstances of their situation with these bodily cravings, the decision of the compound being is different from the conviction of the rational being.

If this be the just view of the subject, and both theory and experience unite to prove that it is, almost all Mr Godwin's reasonings on the subject of coercion in his seventh chapter, will appear to be founded on error. He spends some time in placing in a ridiculous point of view the attempt to convince a man's understanding and to clear up a doubtful proposition in his mind, by blows. Undoubtedly it is both ridiculous and barbarous, and so is cock-fighting, but one has little more to do with the real object of human punishments than the other. One frequent (indeed much too frequent) mode of punishment is death. Mr Godwin will hardly think this intended for conviction, at least it does not appear how the individual or the society could reap much future benefit from an understanding enlightened in this manner.

The principal objects which human punishments have in view are undoubtedly restraint and example; restraint, or removal, of an individual member whose vicious habits are likely to be prejudicial to the society; and example, which by expressing the sense of the community with regard to a particular crime, and by associating more nearly and visibly crime and punishment, holds out a moral motive to dissuade others from the commission of it.

Restraint, Mr Godwin thinks, may be permitted as a temporary expedient, though he reprobates solitary imprisonment, which has certainly been the most successful, and, indeed, almost the only attempt towards the moral amelioration of offenders. He talks of the selfish passions that are fostered by solitude and of the virtues generated in society. But surely these virtues are not generated in the society of a prison. Were the offender confined to the society of able and virtuous men he would probably be more improved than in solitude. But is this practicable? Mr Godwin's ingenuity is more frequently employed in finding out evils than in suggesting practical remedies.

Punishment, for example, is totally reprobated. By endeavouring to make examples too impressive and terrible, nations have, indeed, been led into the most barbarous cruelties, but the abuse of any practice is not a good argument against its use. The indefatigable pains taken in this country to find out a murder, and the certainty of its punishment, has powerfully contributed to generate that sentiment which is frequent in the mouths of the common people, that a murder will sooner or later come to light; and the habitual horror in which murder is in consequence held will make a man, in the agony of passion, throw down his knife for fear he should be tempted to use it in the gratification of his revenge. In Italy, where murderers, by flying to a sanctuary, are allowed more frequently to escape, the crime has never been held in the same detestation and has consequently been more frequent. No man, who is at all aware of the operation of moral motives, can doubt for a moment, that if every murder in Italy had been invariably punished, the use of the stiletto in transports of passion would have been comparatively but little known.

That human laws either do, or can, proportion the punishment accurately to the offence, no person will have the folly to assert. From the inscrutability of motives the thing is absolutely impossible, but this imperfection, though it may be called a species of injustice, is no valid argument against human laws. It is the lot of man, that he will frequently have to choose between two evils; and it is a sufficient reason for the adoption of any institution, that it is the best mode that suggests itself of preventing greater evils. A continual endeavour should undoubtedly prevail to make these institutions as perfect as the nature of them will admit. But nothing is so easy as to find fault with human institutions; nothing so difficult as to suggest adequate practical improvements. It is to be lamented, that more men of talents employ their time in the former occupation than in the latter.

The frequency of crime among men, who, as the common saying is, know better, sufficiently proves, that some truths may be brought home to the conviction of the mind without always producing the proper effect upon the conduct. There are other truths of a nature that perhaps never can be adequately communicated from one man to another. The superiority of the pleasures of intellect to those of sense, Mr Godwin considers as a fundamental truth. Taking all circumstances into consideration, I should be disposed to agree with him; but how am I to communicate this truth to a person who has scarcely ever felt intellectual pleasure? I may as well attempt to explain the nature and beauty of colours to a blind man. If I am ever so laborious, patient, and clear, and have the most repeated opportunities of expostulation, any real progress toward the accomplishment of my purpose seems absolutely hopeless. There is no common measure between us. I cannot proceed step by step: it is a truth of a nature absolutely incapable of demonstration. All that I can say is, that the wisest and best men in all ages had agreed in giving the preference, very greatly, to the pleasures of intellect; and that my own experience completely confirmed the truth of their decisions; that I had found sensual pleasures vain, transient, and continually attended with tedium and disgust; but that intellectual pleasures appeared to me ever fresh and young, filled up all my hours satisfactorily, gave a new zest to life, and diffused a lasting serenity over my mind. If he believe me, it can only be from respect and veneration for my authority: it is credulity, and not conviction. I have not said any thing, nor can any thing be said, of a nature to produce real conviction. The affair is not an affair of reasoning, but of experience. He would probably observe in reply, what you say may be very true with regard to yourself and many other good men, but for my own part I feel very differently upon the subject. I have very frequently taken up a book and almost as frequently gone to sleep over it; but when I pass an evening with a gay party, or a pretty woman, I feel alive, and in spirits, and truly enjoy my existence.

Under such circumstances, reasoning and arguments are not instruments from which success can be expected. At some future time perhaps, real satiety of sensual pleasures, or some accidental impressions that awakened the energies of his mind, might effect that, in a month, which the most patient and able expostulations might be incapable of effecting in forty years.

CHAPTER XIV

Mr Godwin's five propositions respecting political truth, on which his whole work hinges, not established – Reasons we have for supposing, from the distress occasionad by the principle of population, that the vices and moral weakness of man can never be wholly eradicated – Perfectibility, in the sense in which Mr Godwin uses the term, not applicable to man – Nature of the real perfectibility of man illustrated.

I F the reasonings of the preceding chapter are just, the corollaries respecting political truth, which Mr Godwin draws from the proposition that the voluntary actions of men originate in their opinions, will not appear to be clearly established. These corollaries are, 'Sound reasoning and truth, when adequately communicated, must always be victorious over error: Sound reasoning and truth are capable of being so communicated: Truth is omnipotent: The vices and moral weakness of man are not invincible: Man is perfectible, or in other words, susceptible of perpetual improvement.'[33]

The first three propositions may be considered a complete syllogism. If by adequately communicated, be meant such a conviction as to produce an adequate effect upon the conduct, the major may be allowed and the minor denied. The consequent, or the omnipotence of truth, of course falls to the ground. If by 'adequately communicated' be meant merely the conviction of the rational faculty, the major must be denied, the minor will be only true in cases capable of demonstration, and the consequent equally falls. The fourth proposition Mr Godwin calls the preceding proposition, with a slight variation in the statement. If so, it must accompany the preceding proposition in its fall. But it may be worth while to inquire, with reference to the principal argument of this essay, into the particular reasons which we have for supposing that the vices and moral weakness of man can never be wholly overcome in this world.

Man, according to Mr Godwin, is a creature formed what he

is by the successive impressions which he has received, from the first moment that the germ from which he sprung was animated. Could he be placed in a situation, where he was subject to no evil impressions whatever, though it might be doubted whether in such a situation virtue could exist, vice would certainly be banished. The great bent of Mr Godwin's work on *Political Justice*, if I understand it rightly, is to shew that the greater part of the vices and weaknesses of men proceed from the injustice of their political and social institutions, and that if these were removed and the understandings of men more enlightened, there would be little or no temptation in the world to evil. As it has been clearly proved, however, (at least as I think) that this is entirely a false conception, and that, independent of any political or social institutions whatever, the greater part of mankind, from the fixed and unalterable laws of nature, must ever be subject to the evil temptations arising from want, besides other passions, it follows from Mr Godwin's definition of man that such impressions, and combinations of impressions, cannot be afloat in the world without generating a variety of bad men. According to Mr Godwin's own conception of the formation of character, it is surely as improbable that under such circumstances all men will be virtuous as that sixes will come up a hundred times following upon the dice. The great variety of combinations upon the dice in a repeated succession of throws appears to me not inaptly to represent the great variety of character that must necessarily exist in the world, supposing every individual to be formed what he is by that combination of impressions which he has received since his first existence. And this comparision will, in some measure, shew the absurdity of supposing, that exceptions will ever become general rules; that extraordinary and unusual combinations will be frequent; or that the individual instances of great virtue which had appeared in all ages of the world will ever prevail universally.

I am aware that Mr Godwin might say that the comparison is in one respect inaccurate, that in the case of the dice, the preceding causes, or rather the chances respecting the preceding causes, were always the same, and that, therefore, I could have no good reason for supposing that a greater number of sixes would come up in the next hundred times of throwing than in the preceding same number of throws. But, that man had in some sort a power of influencing those causes that formed character, and that every good and virtuous man that was produced, by the influence which he must necessarily have, rather increased the probability that another such virtuous character would be generated, whereas the coming up of sixes upon the dice once, would certainly not increase the probability of their coming up a second time. I admit this objection to the accuracy of the comparison, but it is only partially valid. Repeated experience has assured us, that the influence of the most virtuous character will rarely prevail against very strong temptations to evil. It will undoubtedly affect some, but it will fail with a much greater number. Had Mr Godwin succeeded in his attempt to prove that these temptations to evil could by the exertions of man be removed, I would give up the comparison; or at least allow, that a man might be so far enlightened with regard to the mode of shaking his elbow, that he would be able to throw sixes every time. But as long as a great number of those impressions which form character, like the nice motions of the arm, remain absolutely independent of the will of man, though it would be the height of folly and presumption to attempt to calculate the relative proportions of virtue and vice at the future periods of the world, it may be safely asserted that the vices and moral weakness of mankind, taken in the mass, are invincible.

The fifth proposition is the general deduction from the four former and will consequently fall, as the foundations which support it have given way. In the sense in which Mr Godwin understands the term 'perfectible', the perfectibility of man cannot be asserted, unless the preceding propositions could have been clearly established. There is, however, one sense, which the term will bear, in which it is, perhaps, just. It may be said with truth that man is always susceptible of improvement, or that there never has been, or will be, a period of his history, in which he can be said to have reached his possible acme of perfection. Yet it does not by any means follow from this, that our efforts to improve man will always succeed, or even that he will ever make, in the greatest number of ages, any extraordinary strides towards perfection. The only inference that can be drawn is that the precise limit of his improvement cannot possibly be known. And I cannot help again reminding the reader of a distinction which, it appears to me, ought particularly to be attended to in the present question: I mean, the essential difference there is between an unlimited improvement and an improvement the limit of which cannot be ascertained. The former is an improvement not applicable to man under the present laws of his nature. The latter, undoubtedly, is applicable.

The real perfectibility of man may be illustrated, as I have mentioned before, by the perfectibility of a plant. The object of the enterprising florist is, as I conceive, to unite size, symmetry, and beauty of colour. It would surely be presumptuous in the most successful improver to affirm, that he possessed a carnation in which these qualities existed in the greatest possible state of perfection. However beautiful his flower may be, other care, other soil, or other suns, might produce one still more beautiful. Yet, although he may be aware of the absurdity of supposing that he has reached perfection, and though he may know by what means he attained that degree of beauty in the flower which he at present possesses, yet he cannot be sure that by pursuing similar means, rather increased in strength, he will obtain a more beautiful blossom. By endeavouring to improve one quality, he may impair the beauty of another. The richer mould which he would employ to increase the size of his plant would probably burst the calyx, and destroy at once its symmetry. In a similar manner, the forcing manure used to bring about the French Revolution, and to give a greater freedom and energy to the human mind, has burst the calyx of humanity, the restraining bond of all society; and, however large the separate petals have grown, however strongly, or even beautifully, a few of them have been marked, the whole is at present a loose, deformed, disjointed mass, without union, symmetry, or harmony of colouring.

Were it of consequence to improve pinks and carnations, though we could have no hope of raising them as large as cabbages, we might undoubtedly expect, by successive efforts, to obtain more beautiful specimens than we at present possess. No person can deny the importance of improving the happiness of the human species. Every the least advance in this respect is highly valuable. But an experiment with the human race is not like an experiment upon inanimate objects. The bursting of a flower may be a trifle. Another will soon succeed it. But the bursting of the bonds of society is such a separation of parts as cannot take place without giving the most acute pain to thousands: and a long time may elapse, and much misery may be endured, before the wound grows up again.

As the five propositions which I have been examining may be considered as the corner stones of Mr Godwin's fanciful structure, and, indeed, as expressing the aim and bent of his whole work, however excellent much of his detached reasoning may be, he must be considered as having failed in the great object of his undertaking. Besides the difficulties arising from the compound nature of man, which he has by no means sufficiently smoothed, the principal argument against the perfectibility of man and society remains whole and unimpaired from any thing that he has advanced. And as far as I can trust my own judgement, this argument appears to be conclusive, not only against the perfectibility of man, in the enlarged sense in which Mr Godwin understands the term, but against any very marked and striking change for the better, in the form and structure of general society; by which I mean any great and decided amelioration of the condition of the lower classes of mankind, the most numerous, and, consequently, in a general view of the subject, the most important part of the human race. Were I to live a thousand years, and the laws of nature to remain the same, I should little fear, or rather little hope, a contradiction from experience in asserting that no possible sacrifices or exertions of the rich, in a country which had been long inhabited, could for any time place the lower classes of the community in a situation equal, with regard to circumstances, to the situation of the common people about thirty years ago in the northern States of America.

The lower classes of people in Europe may at some future period be much better instructed than they are at present; they may be taught to employ the little spare time they have in many better ways than at the ale-house; they may live under better and more equal laws than they have ever hitherto done, perhaps, in any country; and I even conceive it possible, though not probable that they may have more leisure; but it is not in the nature of things that they can be awarded such a quantity of money or subsistence as will allow them all to marry early, in the full confidence that they shall be able to provide with ease for a numerous family.

CHAPTER XV

Models too perfect may sometimes rather impede than promote improvement – Mr Godwin's essay on 'Avarice and Profusion' – Impossibility of dividing the necessary labour of a society amicably among all – Invectives against labour may produce present evil, with little or no chance of producing future good – An accession to the mass of agricultural labour must always be an advantage to the labourer.

MR GODWIN in the preface to his *Enquirer*, drops a few expressions which seem to hint at some change in his opinions since he wrote the *Political Justice*; and as this is a work now of some years standing, I should certainly think that I had been arguing against opinions which the author had himself seen reason to alter, but that in some of the essays of the *Enquirer*, Mr Godwin's peculiar mode of thinking appears in as striking a light as ever.

It has been frequently observed that though we cannot hope to reach perfection in any thing, yet that it must always be advantageous to us to place before our eyes the most perfect models. This observation has a plausible appearance, but is very far from being generally true. I even doubt its truth in one of the most obvious exemplifications that would occur. I doubt whether a very young painter would receive so much benefit, from an attempt to copy a highly finished and perfect picture, as from copying one where the outlines were more strongly marked and the manner of laying on the colours was more easily discoverable. But in cases where the perfection of the model is a perfection of a different and superior nature from that towards which we should naturally advance, we shall not always fail in making any progress towards it, but we shall in all probability impede the progress which we might have expected to make had we not fixed our eyes upon so perfect a model. A highly intellectual being, exempt from the infirm calls of hunger or sleep, is undoubtedly a much more perfect

174

existence than man, but were man to attempt to copy such a model, he would not only fail in making any advances towards it; but by unwisely straining to imitate what was inimitable, he would probably destroy the little intellect which he was endeavouring to improve.

The form and structure of society which Mr Godwin describes is as essentially distinct from any forms of society which have hitherto prevailed in the world as a being that can live without food or sleep is from a man. By improving society in its present form, we are making no more advances towards such a state of things as he pictures than we should make approaches towards a line, with regard to which we were walking parallel. The question, therefore, is whether, by looking to such a form of society as our polar star, we are likely to advance or retard the improvement of the human species? Mr Godwin appears to me to have decided this question against himself in his essay on 'Avarice and Profusion' in the *Enquirer*.

Dr Adam Smith has very justly observed that nations as well as individuals grow rich by parsimony and poor by profusion, and that, therefore, every frugal man was a friend and every spendthrift an enemy to his country. The reason he gives is that what is saved from revenue is always added to stock, and is therefore taken from the maintenance of labour that is generally unproductive and employed in the maintenance of labour that realizes itself in valuable commodities. No observation can be more evidently just. The subject of Mr Godwin's essay is a little similar in its first appearance, but in essence is as distinct as possible. He considers the mischief of profusion as an acknowledged truth, and therefore makes his comparison between the avaricious man, and the man who spends his income. But the avaricious man of Mr Godwin is totally a distinct character, at least with regard to his effect upon the prosperity of the state, from the frugal man of Dr Adam Smith. The frugal man in order to make more money saves from his income and adds to his capital, and this capital he either employs himself in the maintenance of productive labour, or he lends it to some other person who will probably employ it in this way. He benefits the state because he adds to its general capital, and because wealth employed as capital not only sets in motion more labour than when spent as income, but the labour is besides of a more valuable kind. But the avaricious man of Mr Godwin locks up his wealth in a chest and sets in motion no labour of any kind, either productive or unproductive. This is so essential a difference that Mr Godwin's decision in his essay appears at once as evidently false as Dr Adam Smith's position is evidently true. It could not, indeed, but occur to Mr Godwin that some present inconvenience might arise to the poor from thus locking up the funds destined for the maintenance of labour. The only way, therefore, he had of weakening this objection was to compare the two characters chiefly with regard to their tendency to accelerate the approach of that happy state of cultivated equality, on which he says we ought always to fix our eyes as our polar star.

I think it has been proved in the former parts of this essay that such a state of society is absolutely impracticable. What consequences then are we to expect from looking to such a point as our guide and polar star in the great sea of political discovery? Reason would teach us to expect no other than winds perpetually adverse, constant but fruitless toil, frequent shipwreck, and certain misery. We shall not only fail in making the smallest real approach towards such a perfect form of society; but by wasting our strength of mind and body, in a direction in which it is impossible to proceed, and by the frequent distress which we must necessarily occasion by our repeated failures, we shall evidently impede that degree of improvement in society, which is really attainable.

It has appeared that a society constituted according to Mr Godwin's system must, from the inevitable laws of our nature, degenerate into a class of proprietors and a class of labourers, and that the substitution of benevolence for self-love as the moving principle of society, instead of producing the happy effects that might be expected from so fair a name, would cause the same pressure of want to be felt by the whole of society, which is now felt only by a part. It is to the established administration of property and to the apparently narrow principle of self-love that we are indebted for all the noblest exertions of human genius, all the finer and more delicate emotions of the soul, for everything, indeed, that distinguishes the civilized from the savage state; and no sufficient change has as yet taken place in the nature of civilized man to enable us to say that he either is, or ever will be, in a state when he may safely throw down the ladder by which he has risen to this eminence.

If in every society that has advanced beyond the savage state, a class of proprietors and a class of labourers must necessarily exist, it is evident that, as labour is the only property of the class of labourers, every thing that tends to diminish the value of this property must tend to diminish the possession of this part of society. The only way that a poor man has of supporting himself in independence is by the exertion of his bodily strength. This is the only commodity he has to give in exchange for the necessaries of life. It would hardly appear then that you benefit him by narrowing the market for this commodity, by decreasing the demand for labour, and lessening the value of the only property that he possesses.

It should be observed that the principal argument of this *Essay* only goes to prove the necessity of a class of proprietors, and a class of labourers, but by no means infers that the present great inequality of property is either necessary or useful to society. On the contrary, it must certainly be considered as an evil, and every institution that promotes it is essentially bad and impolitic. But whether a government could with advantage to society actively interfere to repress inequality of fortunes may be a matter of doubt. Perhaps the generous system of perfect liberty adopted by Dr Adam Smith and the French economists would be ill exchanged for any system of restraint.

Mr Godwin would perhaps say that the whole system of barter and exchange is a vile and iniquitous traffic. If you would essentially relieve the poor man, you should take a part of his labour upon yourself, or give him your money, without exacting so severe a return for it. In answer to the first method proposed, it may be observed, that even if the rich could be persuaded to assist the poor in this way, the value of the assistance would be comparatively trifling. The rich, though they think themselves of great importance, bear but a small proportion in point of numbers to the poor, and would, therefore, relieve them but of a small part of their burdens by taking a share. Were all those that are employed in the labours of luxuries added to the number of those employed in producing necessaries, and could these necessary labours be amicably divided among all, each man's share might indeed be comparatively light; but desirable as such an amicable division would undoubtedly be, I cannot conceive any practical principle according to which it could take place. It has been shewn, that the spirit of benevolence, guided by the strict impartial justice that Mr Godwin describes, would, if vigorously acted upon, depress in want and misery the whole human race. Let us examine what would be the consequence, if the proprietor were to retain a decent share for himself, but to give the rest away to the poor, without exacting a task from them in return. Not to mention the idleness and the vice that such a proceeding, if general, would probably create in the present state of society, and the great risk there would be, of diminishing the produce of land, as well as the labours of luxury, another objection yet remains.

Mr Godwin seems to have but little respect for practical principles; but I own it appears to me, that he is a much greater benefactor to mankind, who points out how an inferior good may be attained, than he who merely expatiates on the deformity of the present state of society, and the beauty of a different state, without pointing out a practical method, that might be immediately applied, of accelerating our advances from the one, to the other.

It has appeared that from the principle of population more will always be in want than can be adequately supplied. The surplus of the rich man might be sufficient for three, but four will be desirous to obtain it. He cannot make this selection of three out of the four without conferring a great favour on those that are the objects of his choice. These persons must consider themselves as under a great obligation to him and as dependent upon him for their support. The rich man would feel his power and the poor man his dependence, and the evil effects of these two impressions on the human heart are well known. Though I perfectly agree with Mr Godwin therefore in the evil of hard labour, yet I still think it a less evil, and less calculated to debase the human mind, than dependence, and every history of man that we have ever read places in a strong point of view the danger to which that mind is exposed which is entrusted with constant power.

In the present state of things, and particularly when labour is in request, the man who does a day's work for me confers full as great an obligation upon me as I do upon him. I possess what he wants, he possesses what I want. We make an amicable exchange. The poor man walks erect in conscious independence; and the mind of his employer is not vitiated by a sense of power.

Three or four hundred years ago there was undoubtedly much less labour in England, in proportion to the population, than at present, but there was much more dependence, and we probably should not now enjoy our present degree of civil liberty if the poor, by the introduction of manufactures, had not been enabled to give something in exchange for the provisions of the great Lords, instead of being dependent upon their bounty. Even the greatest enemies of trade and manufactures, and I do not reckon myself a very determined friend to them, must allow that when they were introduced into England, liberty came in their train.

Nothing that has been said tends in the most remote degree to undervalue the principle of benevolence. It is one of the noblest and most godlike qualities of the human heart, generated, perhaps, slowly and gradually from self-love, and afterwards intended to act as a general law, whose kind office it should be, to soften the partial deformities, to correct the asperities, and to smooth the wrinkles of its parent: and this seems to be the analogy of all nature. Perhaps there is no one general law of nature that will not appear, to us at least, to produce partial evil; and we frequently observe at the same time, some bountiful provision which, acting as another general law, corrects the inequalities of the first.

The proper office of benevolence is to soften the partial evils arising from self-love, but it can never be substituted in its place. If no man were to allow himself to act till he had completely determined that the action he was about to perform was more conducive than any other to the general good, the most enlightened minds would hesitate in perplexity and amazement; and the unenlightened would be continually committing the grossest mistakes.

As Mr Godwin, therefore, has not laid down any practical principle according to which the necessary labours of agriculture might be amicably shared among the whole class of labourers, by general invectives against employing the poor he appears to pursue an unattainable good through much present evil. For if every man who employs the poor ought to be considered as their enemy, and as adding to the weight of their oppressions, and if the miser is for this reason to be preferred to the man who spends his income, it follows that any number of men who now spend their incomes might, to the advantage of society, be converted into misers. Suppose then that a hundred thousand persons who now employ ten men each were to lock up their wealth from general use, it is evident, that a million of working men of different kinds would be completely thrown out of all employment. The extensive misery that such an event would produce in the present state of society Mr Godwin himself could hardly refuse to acknowledge, and I question whether he might not find some difficulty in proving that a conduct of this kind tended more than the conduct of those who spend their incomes to 'place human beings in the condition in which they ought to be placed.'

But Mr Godwin says that the miser really locks up nothing, that the point has not been rightly understood, and that the true development and definition of the nature of wealth have not been applied to illustrate it. Having defined therefore wealth, very justly, to be the commodities raised and fostered by human labour, he observes that the miser locks up neither corn, nor oxen, nor clothes, nor houses. Undoubtedly he does not really lock up these articles, but he locks up the power of producing them, which is virtually the same. These things are certainly used and consumed by his contemporaries, as truly, and to as great an extent, as if he were a beggar; but not to as great an extent as if he had employed his wealth in turning up more land, in breeding more oxen, in employing more tailors, and in building more houses. But supposing, for a moment, that the conduct of the miser did not tend to check any really useful produce, how are all those who are thrown out of employment to obtain patents which they may shew in order to be awarded a proper share of the food and raiment produced by the society? This is the unconquerable difficulty.

I am perfectly willing to concede to Mr Godwin that there is much more labour in the world than is really necessary, and that, if the lower classes of society could agree among themselves never to work more than six or seven hours in the day, the commodities essential to human happiness might still be produced in as great abundance as at present. But it is almost impossible to conceive that such an agreement could be adhered to. From the principle of population, some would necessarily be more in want than others. Those that had large families would naturally be desirous of exchanging two hours more of their labour for an ampler quantity of subsistence. How are they to be prevented from making this exchange? It would be a violation of the first and most sacred property that a man possesses to attempt, by positive institutions, to interfere with his command over his own labour.

Till Mr Godwin, therefore, can point out some practical plan according to which the necessary labour in a society might be equitably divided, his invectives against labour, if they were attended to, would certainly produce much present evil without approximating us to that state of cultivated equality to which he looks forward as his polar star, and which, he seems to think, should at present be our guide in determining the nature and tendency of human actions. A mariner guided by such a polar star is in danger of shipwreck.

Perhaps there is no possible way in which wealth could in general be employed so beneficially to a state, and particularly to the lower orders of it, as by improving and rendering productive that land which to a farmer would not answer the expense of cultivation. Had Mr Godwin exerted his energetic eloquence in painting the superior worth and usefulness of the character who employed the poor in this way, to him who employed them in narrow luxuries, every enlightened man must have applauded his efforts. The increasing demand for agricultural labour must always tend to better the condition of the poor; and if the accession of work be of this kind, so far is it from being true that the poor would be obliged to work ten hours for the same price that they before worked eight, that the very reverse would be the fact; and a labourer might then support his wife and family as well by the labour of six hours as he could before by the labour of eight.

The labour created by luxuries, though useful in distributing the produce of the country, without vitiating the proprietor by power, or debasing the labourer by dependence, has not, indeed, the same beneficial effects on the state of the poor. A great accession of work from manufacturers, though it may raise the price of labour even more than an increasing demand for agricultural labour, yet, as in this case the quantity of food in the country may not be proportionably increasing, the advantage to the poor will be but temporary, as the price of provisions must necessarily rise in proportion to the price of labour. Relative to this subject, I cannot avoid venturing a few remarks on a part of Dr Adam Smith's *Wealth of Nations*, speaking at the same time with that diffidence which I ought certainly to feel in differing from a person so justly celebrated in the political world.

CHAPTER XVI

Probable error of Dr Adam Smith in representing every increase of the revenue or stock of a society as an increase in the funds for the maintenance of labour – Instances where an increase of wealth can have no tendency to better the condition of the labouring poor – England has increased in riches without a proportional increase in the funds for the maintenance of labour – The state of the poor in China would not be improved by an increase of wealth from manufactures.

THE professed object of Dr Adam Smith's inquiry is the nature and causes of the wealth of nations. There is another inquiry, however, perhaps still more interesting, which he occasionally mixes with it, I mean an inquiry into the causes which affect the happiness of nations or the happiness and comfort of the lower orders of society, which is the most numerous class in every nation. I am sufficiently aware of the near connection of these two subjects, and that the causes which tend to increase the wealth of a state tend also, generally speaking, to increase the happiness of the lower classes of the people. But perhaps Dr Adam Smith has considered these two inquiries as still more nearly connected than they really are; at least, he has not stopped to take notice of those instances where the wealth of a society may increase (according to his definition of 'wealth') without having any tendency to increase the comforts of the labouring part of it. I do not mean to enter into a philosophical discussion of what constitutes the proper happiness of man, but shall merely consider two universally acknowledged ingredients, health, and the command of the necessaries and conveniences of life.

Little or no doubt can exist that the comforts of the labouring poor depend upon the increase of the funds destined for the maintenance of labour, and will be very exactly in proportion to the rapidity of this increase. The demand for labour which such increase would occasion, by creating a competition in the market, must necessarily raise the value of labour, and, till the additional number of hands required were reared, the increased funds would be distributed to the same number of persons as before the increase, and therefore every labourer would live comparatively at his ease. But perhaps Dr Adam Smith errs in representing every increase of the revenue or stock of a society as an increase of these funds. Such surplus stock or revenue will, indeed, always be considered by the individual possessing it as an additional fund from which he may maintain more labour : but it will not be a real and effectual fund for the maintenance of an additional number of labourers, unless the whole, or at least a great part of this increase of the stock or revenue of the society, be convertible into a proportional quantity of provisions; and it will not be so convertible where the increase has arisen merely from the produce of labour, and not from the produce of land. A distinction will in this case occur, between the number of hands which the stock of the society could employ, and the number which its territory can maintain.

To explain myself by an instance. Dr Adam Smith defines the wealth of a nation to consist in the annual produce of its land and labour. This definition evidently includes manufactured produce, as well as the produce of the land. Now supposing a nation for a course of years was to add what it saved from its yearly revenue to its manufacturing capital solely, and not to its capital employed upon land, it is evident that it might grow richer according to the above definition, without a power of supporting a greater number of labourers, and, therefore, without an increase in the real funds for the maintenance of labour. There would, notwithstanding, be a demand for labour from the power which each manufacturer would possess, or at least think he possessed, of extending his old stock in trade or of setting up fresh works. This demand would of course raise the price of labour, but if the yearly stock of provisions in the country was not increasing, this rise would soon turn out to be merely nominal, as the price of provisions must necessarily rise with it. The demand for manufacturing labourers might, indeed, entice many from agriculture and thus tend to diminish the annual produce of the land, but we will suppose any effect of this kind to be compensated by improvements in the instruments of agriculture, and the quantity of provisions therefore to remain the same. Improvements in manufacturing machinery would of course take place, and this circumstance, added to the greater number of hands employed in manufactures, would cause the annual produce of the labour of the country to be upon the whole greatly increased. The wealth therefore of the country would be increasing annually, according to the definition, and might not, perhaps, be increasing very slowly.

The question is whether wealth, increasing in this way, has any tendency to better the condition of the labouring poor. It is a self-evident proposition that any general rise in the price of labour, the stock of provisions remaining the same, can only be a nominal rise, as it must very shortly be followed by a proportional rise in the price of provisions. The increase in the price of labour, therefore, which we have supposed, would have little or no effect in giving the labouring poor a greater command over the necessaries and conveniences of life. In this respect they would be nearly in the same state as before. In one other respect they would be in a worse state. A greater proportion of them would be employed in manufactures, and fewer, consequently, in agriculture. And this exchange of professions will be allowed, I think, by all, to be very unfavourable in respect of health, one essential ingredient of happiness, besides the greater uncertainty of manufacturing labour, arising from the capricious taste of man, the accidents of war, and other causes.

It may be said, perhaps, that such an instance as I have supposed could not occur, because the rise in the price of provisions would immediately turn some additional capital into the channel of agriculture. But this is an event which may take place very slowly, as it should be remarked that a rise in the price of labour had preceded the rise of provisions, and would, therefore, impede the good effects upon agriculture, which the increased value of the produce of the land might otherwise have occasioned.

It might also be said, that the additional capital of the nation would enable it to import provisions sufficient for the maintenance of those whom its stock could employ. A small country with a large navy, and great inland accommodations for carriage, such as Holland, may, indeed, import and distribute an effectual quantity of provisions; but the price of provisions must be very high to make such an importation and distribution answer in large countries less advantageously circumstanced in this respect.

An instance, accurately such as I have supposed, may not, perhaps, ever have occurred, but I have little doubt that instances nearly approximating to it may be found without any very laborious search. Indeed I am strongly inclined to think that England herself, since the Revolution,[34] affords a very striking elucidation of the argument in question.

The commerce of this country, internal as well as external, has certainly been rapidly advancing during the last century. The exchangeable value in the market of Europe of the annual produce of its land and labour has, without doubt, increased very considerably. But, upon examination, it will be found that the increase has been chiefly in the produce of labour and not in the produce of land, and therefore, though the wealth of the nation has been advancing with a quick pace, the effectual funds for the maintenance of labour have been increasing very slowly, and the result is such as might be expected. The increasing wealth of the nation has had little or no tendency to better the condition of the labouring poor. They have not, I believe, a greater command of the necessaries and conveniences of life, and a much greater proportion of them than at the period of the Revolution is employed in manufactures and crowded together in close and unwholesome rooms.

Could we believe the statement of Dr Price that the population of England has decreased since the Revolution, it would even appear that the effectual funds for the maintenance of labour had been declining during the progress of wealth in other respects. For I conceive that it may be laid down as a general rule that if the effectual funds for the maintenance of labour are increasing, that is, if the territory can maintain as well as the stock employ a greater number of labourers, this additional number will quickly spring up, even in spite of such wars as

Dr Price enumerates. And, consequently, if the population of any country has been stationary, or declining, we may safely infer, that, however it may have advanced in manufacturing wealth, its effectual funds for the maintenance of labour cannot have increased.

It is difficult, however, to conceive that the population of England has been declining since the Revolution, though every testimony concurs to prove that its increase, if it has increased, has been very slow. In the controversy which the question has occasioned, Dr Price undoubtedly appears to be much more completely master of his subject, and to possess more accurate information, than his opponents. Judging simply from this controversy, I think one should say that Dr Price's point is nearer being proved than Mr Howlett's.[35] Truth, probably, lies between the two statements, but this supposition makes the increase of population since the Revolution to have been very slow in comparison with the increase of wealth.

That the produce of the land has been decreasing, or even that it has been absolutely stationary during the last century, few will be disposed to believe. The enclosure of commons and waste lands certainly tends to increase the food of the country, but it has been asserted with confidence that the enclosure of common fields has frequently had a contrary effect, and that large tracts of land which formerly produced great quantities of corn, by being converted into pasture both employ fewer hands and feed fewer mouths than before their enclosure. It is, indeed, an acknowledged truth, that pasture land produces a smaller quantity of human subsistence than corn land of the same natural fertility, and could it be clearly ascertained that from the increased demand for butchers' meat of the best quality, and its increased price in consequence, a greater quantity of good land has annually been employed in grazing, the diminution of human subsistence, which this circumstance would occasion, might have counterbalanced the advantages derived from the enclosure of waste lands, and the general improvements in husbandry.

It scarcely need be remarked that the high price of butchers' meat at present, and its low price formerly, were not caused by the scarcity in the one case or the plenty in the other, but by the different expense sustained at the different periods, in preparing cattle for the market. It is, however, possible, that there might have been more cattle a hundred years ago in the country than at present; but no doubt can be entertained, that there is much more meat of a superior quality brought to market at present than ever there was. When the price of butchers' meat was very low, cattle were reared chiefly upon waste lands; and except for some of the principal markets, were probably killed with but little other fatting. The veal that is sold so cheap in some distant counties at present bears little other resemblance than the name, to that which is bought in London. Formerly, the price of butchers' meat would not pay for rearing, and scarcely for feeding, cattle on land that would answer in tillage; but the present price will not only pay for fatting cattle on the very best land, but will even allow of the rearing many, on land that would bear good crops of corn. The same number of cattle, or even the same weight of cattle at the different periods when killed, will have consumed (if I may be allowed the expression) very different quantities of human substance. A fatted beast may in some respects be considered, in the language of the French economists,[36] as an unproductive labourer: he has added nothing to the value of the raw produce that he has consumed. The present system of grazing, undoubtedly tends more than the former system to diminish the quantity of human subsistence in the country, in proportion to the general fertility of the land.

I would not by any means be understood to say that the former system either could or ought to have continued. The increasing price of butchers' meat is a natural and inevitable consequence of the general progress of cultivation; but I cannot help thinking, that the present great demand for butchers' meat of the best quality, and the quantity of good land that is in consequence annually employed to produce it, together with the great number of horses at present kept for pleasure, are the chief causes that have prevented the quantity of human food in the country from keeping pace with the generally increased fertility of the soil; and a change of custom in these respects would, I have little doubt, have a very sensible effect on the quantity of subsistence in the country, and consequently on its population.

The employment of much of the most fertile land in grazing, the improvements in agricultural instruments, the increase of large farms, and particularly the diminution of the number of cottages throughout the kingdom, all concur to prove, that there are not probably so many persons employed in agricultural labour now as at the period of the Revolution. Whatever increase of population, therefore, has taken place, must be employed almost wholly in manufactures, and it is well known that the failure of some of these manufactures, merely from the caprice of fashion, such as the adoption of muslins instead of silks, or of shoe-strings and covered buttons, instead of buckles and metal buttons, combined with the restraints in the market of labour arising from corporation and parish laws, have frequently driven thousands on charity for support. The great increase of the poor rates is, indeed, of itself a strong evidence that the poor have not a greater command of the necessaries and conveniences of life, and if to the consideration, that their condition in this respect is rather worse than better, be added the circumstance, that a much greater proportion of them is employed in large manufactories, unfavourable both to health and virtue, it must be acknowledged, that the increase of wealth of late years has had no tendency to increase the happiness of the labouring poor.

That every increase of the stock or revenue of a nation cannot be considered as an increase of the real funds for the maintenance of labour and, therefore, cannot have the same good effect upon the condition of the poor, will appear in a strong light if the argument be applied to China.

Dr Adam Smith observes that China has probably long been as rich as the nature of her laws and institutions will admit, but that with other laws and institutions, and if foreign commerce were had in honour, she might still be much richer. The question is, would such an increase of wealth be an increase of the real funds for the maintenance of labour, and consequently tend to place the lower classes of people in China in a state of greater plenty?

It is evident, that if trade and foreign commerce were held in great honour in China, from the plenty of labourers, and the cheapness of labour, she might work up manufactures for foreign sale to an immense amount. It is equally evident that from the great bulk of provisions and the amazing extent of her inland territory she could not in return import such a quantity as would be any sensible addition to the annual stock of subsistence in the country. Her immense amount of manufactures, therefore, she would exchange, chiefly, for luxuries collected from all parts of the world. At present, it appears, that no labour whatever is spared in the production of food. The country is rather over-people in proportion to what its stock can employ, and labour is, therefore, so abundant, that no pains are taken to abridge it. The consequence of this is, probably, the greatest production of food that the soil can possibly afford, for it will be generally observed, that processes for abridging labour, though they may enable a farmer to bring a certain quantity of grain cheaper to market, tend rather to diminish than increase the whole produce; and in agriculture, therefore, may, in some respects, be considered rather as private than public advantages.

An immense capital could not be employed in China in preparing manufactures for foreign trade without taking off so many labourers from agriculture as to alter this state of things, and in some degree to diminish the produce of the country. The demand for manufacturing labourers would naturally raise the price of labour, but as the quantity of subsistence would not be increased, the price of provisions would keep pace with it, or even more than keep pace with it if the quantity of provisions were really decreasing. The country would be evidently advancing in wealth, the exchangeable value of the annual produce of its land and labour would be annually augmented, yet the real funds for the maintenance of labour would be stationary, or even declining, and, consequently, the increasing wealth of the nation would rather tend to depress than to raise the condition of the poor. With regard to the command over the necessaries and comforts of life, they would be in the same or rather worse state than before; and a great part of them would have exchanged the healthy labours of agriculture for the unhealthy occupations of manufacturing industry.

The argument, perhaps, appears clearer when applied to China, because it is generally allowed that the wealth of China has been long stationary. With regard to any other country it might be always a matter of dispute at which of the two periods, compared, wealth was increasing the fastest, as it is upon the rapidity of the increase of wealth at any particular period that Dr Adam Smith says the condition of the poor depends. It is evident, however, that two nations might increase exactly with the same rapidity in the exchangeable value of the annual produce of their land and labour, yet if one had applied itself chiefly to agriculture, and the other chiefly to commerce, the funds for the maintenance of labour, and consequently the effect of the increase of wealth in each nation, would be extremely different. In that which had applied itself chiefly to agriculture, the poor would live in great plenty, and population would rapidly increase. In that which had applied itself chiefly to commerce, the poor would be comparatively but little benefited and consequently population would increase slowly.

CHAPTER XVII

Question of the proper definition of the wealth of a state –
Reason given by the French economists for considering all
manufacturers as unproductive labourers, not the true reason
– The labour of artificers and manufacturers sufficiently
productive to individuals, though not to the state – A remarkable passage in Dr Price's two volumes of *Observations* –
Error of Dr Price in attributing the happiness and rapid
population of America, chiefly, to its peculiar state of civilization – No advantage can be expected from shutting our eyes
to the difficulties in the way to the improvement of society.

A QUESTION seems naturally to arise here whether the exchangeable value of the annual produce of the land and labour be the
proper definition of the wealth of a country, or whether
the gross produce of the land, according to the French economists, may not be a more accurate definition. Certain it is that
every increase of wealth, according to the definition of the
economists, will be an increase of the funds for the maintenance of labour, and consequently will always tend to ameliorate the condition of the labouring poor, though an increase of
wealth, according to Dr Adam Smith's definition, will by no
means invariably have the same tendency. And yet it may not
follow from this consideration that Dr Adam Smith's definition
is not just. It seems in many respects improper to exclude the
clothing and lodging of a whole people from any part of their
revenue. Much of it may, indeed, be of very trivial and un-
important value in comparison with the food of the country, yet
still it may be fairly considered as a part of its revenue; and,
therefore, the only point in which I should differ from Dr
Adam Smith is where he seems to consider every increase of the
revenue or stock of a society as an increase of the funds for the
maintenance of labour, and consequently as tending always to
ameliorate the condition of the poor.

The fine silks and cottons, the laces, and other ornamental

luxuries of a rich country, may contribute very considerably to augment the exchangeable value of its annual produce; yet they contribute but in a very small degree to augment the mass of happiness in the society, and it appears to me that it is with some view to the real utility of the produce that we ought to estimate the productiveness or unproductiveness of different sorts of labour. The French economists consider all labour employed in manufactures as unproductive. Comparing it with the labour employed upon land, I should be perfectly disposed to agree with them, but not exactly for the reasons which they give. They say that labour employed upon land is productive because the produce, over and above completely paying the labourer and the farmer, affords a clear rent to the landlord, and that the labour employed upon a piece of lace is unproductive because it merely replaces the provisions that the workman had consumed, and the stock of his employer, without affording any clear rent whatever. But supposing the value of the wrought lace to be such as that, besides paying in the most complete manner the workman and his employer, it could afford a clear rent to a third person, it appears to me that, in comparison with the labour employed upon land, it would be still as unproductive as ever. Though, according to the reasoning used by the French economists, the man employed in the manufacture of lace would, in this case, seem to be a productive labourer; yet according to their definition of the wealth of a state, he ought not to be considered in that light. He will have added nothing to the gross produce of the land : he has consumed a portion of this gross produce, and has left a bit of lace in return; and though he may sell this bit of lace for three times the quantity of provisions that he consumed whilst he was making it, and thus be a very productive labourer with regard to himself, yet he cannot be considered as having added by his labour to any essential part of the riches of the state. The clear rent, therefore, that a certain produce can afford, after paying the expenses of procuring it, does not appear to be the sole criterion, by which to judge of the productiveness or unproductiveness to a state of any particular species of labour.

Suppose that two hundred thousand men, who are now

employed in producing manufactures that only tend to gratify the vanity of a few rich people, were to be employed upon some barren and uncultivated lands, and to produce only half the quantity of food that they themselves consumed; they would be still more productive labourers with regard to the state than they were before, though their labour, so far from affording a rent to a third person, would but half replace the provisions used in obtaining the produce. In their former employment they consumed a certain portion of the food of the country and left in return some silks and laces. In their latter employment they consumed the same quantity of food and left in return provision for a hundred thousand men. There can be little doubt which of the two legacies would be the most really beneficial to the country, and it will, I think, be allowed that the wealth which supported the two hundred thousand men while they were producing silks and laces would have been more usefully employed in supporting them while they were producing the additional quantity of food.

A capital employed upon land may be unproductive to the individual that employs it and yet be highly productive to the society. A capital employed in trade, on the contrary, may be highly productive to the individual, and yet be almost totally unproductive to the society: and this is the reason why I should call manufacturing labour unproductive, in comparison of that which is employed in agriculture, and not for the reason given by the French economists. It is, indeed, almost impossible to see the great fortunes that are made in trade, and the liberality with which so many merchants live, and yet agree in the statement of the economists, that manufacturers can only grow rich by depriving themselves of the funds destined for their support. In many branches of trade the profits are so great as would allow of a clear rent to a third person; but as there is no third person in the case, and as all the profits centre in the master manufacturer, or merchant, he seems to have a fair chance of growing rich,without much privation; and we consequently see large fortunes acquired in trade by persons who have not been remarked for their parsimony.

Daily experience proves that the labour employed in trade

and manufactures is sufficiently productive to individuals, but it certainly is not productive in the same degree to the state. Every accession to the food of a country tends to the immediate benefit of the whole society; but the fortunes made in trade tend but in a remote and uncertain manner to the same end, and in some respects have even a contrary tendency. The home trade of consumption is by far the most important trade of every nation. China is the richest country in the world, without any other. Putting then, for a moment, foreign trade out of the question, the man who, by an ingenious manufacture, obtains a double portion out of the old stock of provisions, will certainly not to be so useful to the state as the man who, by his labour, adds a single share to the former stock. The consumable commodities of silks, laces, trinkets, and expensive furniture, are undoubtedly a part of the revenue of the society; but they are the revenue only of the rich, and not of the society in general. An increase in this part of the revenue of a state, cannot, therefore, be considered of the same importance as an increase of food, which forms the principal revenue of the great mass of the people.

Foreign commerce adds to the wealth of a state, according to Dr Adam Smith's definition, though not according to the definition of the economists. Its principal use, and the reason, probably, that it has in general been held in such high estimation is that it adds greatly to the external power of a nation or to its power of commanding the labour of other countries; but it will be found, upon a near examination, to contribute but little to the increase of the internal funds for the maintenance of labour, and consequently but little to the happiness of the greatest part of society. In the natural progress of a state towards riches, manufactures, and foreign commerce would follow, in their order, the high cultivation of the soil. In Europe, this natural order of things has been inverted, and the soil has been cultivated from the redundancy of manufacturing capital, instead of manufactures rising from the redundancy of capital employed upon land. The superior encouragement that has been given to the industry of the towns, and the consequent higher price that is paid for the labour of artificers than for the labour of those employed in husbandry, are probably the reasons why so much soil in Europe remains uncultivated. Had a different policy been pursued throughout Europe, it might undoubtedly have been much more populous than at present, and yet not be more incumbered by its population.

I cannot quit this curious subject of the difficulty arising from population, a subject that appears to me to deserve a minute investigation and able discussion much beyond my power to give it, without taking notice of an extraordinary passage in Dr Price's two volumes of *Observations*. Having given some tables on the probabilities of life, in towns and in the country, he says (Vol. II, p. 243, italics supplied):

From this comparison, it appears with how much truth great cities have been called the graves of mankind. It must also convince all who consider it, that according to the observation, at the end of the fourth essay, in the former volume, it is by no means strictly proper to consider our diseases as the original intention of nature. They are, without doubt, in general our own creation. *Were there a country where the inhabitants led lives entirely natural and virtuous, few of them would die without measuring out the whole period of present existence allotted to them; pain and distemper would be unknown among them, and death would come upon them like a sleep, in consequence of no other cause than gradual and unavoidable decay.*

I own that I felt myself obliged to draw a very opposite conclusion from the facts advanced in Dr Price's two volumes. I had for some time been aware that population and food increased in different ratios, and a vague opinion had been floating in my mind that they could only be kept equal by some species of misery or vice, but the perusal of Dr Price's two volumes of *Observations*, after that opinion had been conceived, raised it at once to conviction. With so many facts in his view to prove the extraordinary rapidity with which population increases when unchecked, and with such a body of evidence before him to elucidate even the manner by which the general laws of nature repress a redundant population, it is perfectly inconceivable to me how he could write the passage that I have quoted. He was a strenuous advocate for early marriages, as the best preservative against vicious manners. He had no fanciful conceptions about

the extinction of the passion between the sexes, like Mr Godwin, nor did he ever think of eluding the difficulty in the ways
hinted at by Mr Condorcet. He frequently talks of giving the
prolifick powers of nature room to exert themselves. Yet with
these ideas, that his understanding could escape from the
obvious and necessary inference that an unchecked population
would increase, beyond comparison, faster than the earth, by the
best directed exertions of man, could produce food for its support, appears to me as astonishing as if he had resisted the
conclusion of one of the plainest propositions of Euclid.[37]

Dr Price, speaking of the different stages of the civilized
state, says, 'The first, or simple stages of civilization, are those
which favour most the increase and the happiness of mankind.'
He then instances the American colonies, as being at that time
in the first and happiest of the states that he had described, and
as affording a very striking proof of the effects of the different
stages of civilization on population. But he does not seem to
be aware that the happiness of the Americans depended much
less upon their peculiar degree of civilization than upon the
peculiarity of their situation, as new colonies, upon their having
a great plenty of fertile uncultivated land. In parts of Norway,
Denmark, or Sweden, or in this country, two or three hundred
years ago, he might have found perhaps nearly the same degree
of civilization, but by no means the same happiness or the same
increase of population. He quotes himself a statute of Henry
the Eighth,[38] complaining of the decay of tillage, and the
enhanced price of provisions, 'whereby a marvellous number of
people were rendered incapable of maintaining themselves and
families.' The superior degree of civil liberty which prevailed in
America contributed, without doubt, its share to promote the
industry, happiness, and population of these states, but even
civil liberty, all powerful as it is, will not create fresh land. The
Americans may be said, perhaps, to enjoy a greater degree of
civil liberty, now they are an independent people, than while
they were in subjection in England, but we may be perfectly
sure that population will not long continue to increase with the
same rapidity as it did then.

A person who contemplated the happy state of the lower

classes of people in America twenty years ago would naturally wish to retain them for ever in that state, and might think, perhaps, that by preventing the introduction of manufactures and luxury he might effect his purpose, but he might as reasonably expect to prevent a wife or mistress from growing old by never exposing her to the sun or air. The situation of new colonies, well governed, is a bloom of youth that no efforts can arrest. There are, indeed, many modes of treatment in the political, as well as animal, body, that contribute to accelerate or retard the approaches of age, but there can be no chance of success, in any mode that could be devised, for keeping either of them in perpetual youth. By encouraging the industry of the towns more than the industry of the country, Europe may be said, perhaps, to have brought on a premature old age. A different policy in this respect would infuse fresh life and vigour into every state. While from the law of primogeniture, and other European customs, land bears a monopoly price, a capital can never be employed in it with much advantage to the individual; and, therefore, it is not probable that the soil should be properly cultivated. And, though in every civilized state a class of proprietors and a class of labourers must exist, yet one permanent advantage would always result from a nearer equalization of property. The greater the number of proprietors, the smaller must be the number of labourers: a greater part of society would be in the happy state of possessing property: and a smaller part in the unhappy state of possessing no other property than their labour. But the best directed exertions, though they may alleviate, can never remove the pressure of want, and it will be difficult for any person who contemplates the genuine situation of man on earth, and the general laws of nature, to suppose it possible that any, the most enlightened, efforts could place mankind in a state where 'few would die without measuring out the whole period of present existence allotted to them; where pain and distemper would be unknown among them; and death would come upon them like a sleep, in consequence of no other cause than gradual and unavoidable decay.'

It is, undoubtedly, a most disheartening reflection that the great obstacle in the way to any extraordinary improvement in society is of a nature that we can never hope to overcome. The perpetual tendency in the race of man to increase beyond the means of subsistence is one of the general laws of animated nature which we can have no reason to expect will change. Yet, discouraging as the contemplation of this difficulty must be to those whose exertions are laudably directed to the improvement of the human species, it is evident that no possible good can arise from any endeavours to slur it over or keep it in the background. On the contrary, the most baleful mischiefs may be expected from the unmanly conduct of not daring to face truth because it is unpleasing. Independently of what relates to this great obstacle, sufficient yet remains to be done for mankind to animate us to the most unremitted exertion. But if we proceed without a thorough knowledge and accurate comprehension of the nature, extent, and magnitude of the difficulties we have to encounter, or if we unwisely direct our efforts towards an object in which we cannot hope for success, we shall not only exhaust our strength in fruitless exertions and remain at as great a distance as ever from the summit of our wishes, but we shall be perpetually crushed by the recoil of this rock of Sisyphus.[39]

CHAPTER XVIII

The constant pressure of distress on man, from the principle of population, seems to direct our hopes to the future – State of trial inconsistent with our ideas of the foreknowledge of God – The world, probably, a mighty process for awakening matter into mind – Theory of the formation of mind – Excitements from the wants of the body – Excitements from the operation of general laws – Excitements from the difficulties of life arising from the principle of population.

THE view of human life which results from the contemplation of the constant pressure of distress on man from the difficulty of subsistence, by shewing the little expectation that he can reasonably entertain of perfectibility on earth, seems strongly to point his hopes to the future. And the temptations to which he must necessarily be exposed, from the operation of those laws of nature which we have been examining, would seem to represent the world in the light in which it has been frequently considered, as a state of trial and school of virtue preparatory to a superior state of happiness. But I hope I shall be pardoned if I attempt to give a view in some degree different of the situation of man on earth, which appears to me to be more consistent with the various phenomena of nature which we observe around us and more consonant to our ideas of the power, goodness, and foreknowledge of the Deity.

It cannot be considered as an unimproving exercise of the human mind to endeavour to 'vindicate the ways of God to man' if we proceed with a proper distrust of our own understandings and a just sense of our insufficiency to comprehend the reason of all we see,[40] if we hail every ray of light with gratitude, and, when no light appears, think that the darkness is from within and not from without, and bow with humble deference to the supreme wisdom of him whose 'thoughts are above our thoughts' 'as the heavens are high above the earth.'[41]

In all our feeble attempts, however, to 'find out the Almighty to perfection', it seems absolutely necessary that we should reason from nature up to nature's God and not presume to reason from God to nature. The moment we allow ourselves to ask why some things are not otherwise, instead of endeavouring to account for them as they are, we shall never know where to stop, we shall be led into the grossest and most childish absurdities, all progress in the knowledge of the ways of Providence must necessarily be at an end, and the study will even cease to be an improving exercise of the human mind. Infinite power is so vast and incomprehensible an idea that the mind of man must necessarily be bewildered in the contemplation of it. With the crude and puerile conceptions which we sometimes form of this attribute of the Deity, we might imagine that God could call into being myriads and myriads of existences, all free from pain and imperfection, all eminent in goodness and wisdom, all capable of the highest enjoyments, and unnumbered as the points throughout infinite space. But when from these vain and extravagant dreams of fancy, we turn our eyes to the book of nature, where alone we can read God as he is, we see a constant succession of sentient beings, rising apparently from so many specks of matter, going through a long and sometimes painful process in this world, but many of them attaining, ere the termination of it, such high qualities and powers as seem to indicate their fitness for some superior state. Ought we not then to correct our crude and puerile ideas of Infinite Power from the contemplation of what we actually see existing? Can we judge of the Creator but from his creation? And, unless we wish to exalt the power of God at the expense of his goodness, ought we not to conclude that even to the great Creator, almighty as he is, a certain process may be necessary, a certain time (or at least what appears to us as time) may be requisite, in order to form beings with those exalted qualities of mind which will fit them for his high purposes?

A state of trial seems to imply a previously formed existence that does not agree with the appearance of man in infancy and indicates something like suspicion and want of foreknowledge, inconsistent with those ideas which we wish to cherish of the Supreme Being. I should be inclined, therefore, as I have hinted before, to consider the world and this life as the mighty process of God, not for the trial, but for the creation and formation of mind, a process necessary to awaken inert, chaotic matter into spirit, to sublimate the dust of the earth into soul, to elicit an ethereal spark from the clod of clay. And in this view of the subject, the various impressions and excitements which man receives through life may be considered as the forming hand of his Creator, acting by general laws, and awakening his sluggish existence, by the animating touches of the Divinity, into a capacity of superior enjoyment. The original sin of man is the torpor and corruption of the chaotic matter in which he may be said to be born.[42]

It could answer no good purpose to enter into the question whether mind be a distinct substance from matter, or only a finer form of it. The question is, perhaps, after all, a question merely of words. Mind is as essentially mind, whether formed from matter or any other substance. We know from experience that soul and body are most intimately united, and every appearance seems to indicate that they grow from infancy together. It would be a supposition attended with very little probability to believe that a complete and full formed spirit existed in every infant, but that it was clogged and impeded in its operations during the first twenty years of life by the weakness, or hebetude, of the organs in which it was enclosed. As we shall all be disposed to agree that God is the creator of mind as well as of body, and as they both seem to be forming and unfolding themselves at the same time, it cannot appear inconsistent either with reason or revelation, if it appear to be consistent with phenomena of nature, to suppose that God is constantly occupied in forming mind out of matter and that the various impressions that man receives through life is the process for that purpose. The employment is surely worthy of the highest attributes of the Deity.

This view of the state of man on earth will not seem to be unattended with probability, if, judging from the little experience we have of the nature of mind, it shall appear upon investigation that the phenomena around us, and the various events of human life, seem peculiarly calculated to promote this great end, and especially if, upon this supposition, we can account, even to our own narrow understandings, for many of those roughnesses and inequalities in life which querulous man too frequently makes the subject of his complaint against the God of nature.

The first great awakeners of the mind seem to be the wants of the body. (It was my intention to have entered at some length into this subject as a kind of second part to the *Essay*. A long interruption, from particular business, has obliged me to lay aside this intention, at least for the present. I shall now, therefore, only give a sketch of a few of the leading circumstances that appear to me to favour the general supposition that I have advanced.) They are the first stimulants that rouse the brain of infant man into sentient activity, and such seems to be the sluggishness of original matter that unless by a peculiar course of excitements other wants, equally powerful, are generated, these stimulants seem, even afterwards, to be necessary to continue that activity which they first awakened. The savage would slumber for ever under his tree unless he were roused from his torpor by the cravings of hunger or the pinchings of cold, and the exertions that he makes to avoid these evils, by procuring food, and building himself a covering, are the exercises which form and keep in motion his faculties, which otherwise would sink into listless inactivity. From all that experience has taught us concerning the structure of the human mind, if those stimulants to exertion which arise from the wants of the body were removed from the mass of mankind, we have much more reason to think that they would be sunk to the level of brutes, from a deficiency of excitements, than that they would be raised to the rank of philosophers by the possession of leisure. In those countries where nature is the most redundant in spontaneous produce the inhabitants will not be found the most remarkable for acuteness of intellect. Necessity has been with great truth called the mother of invention. Some of the noblest exertions of the human mind have been set in motion by the necessity of satisfying the wants of the body. Want has not unfrequently given wings to the imagination of the poet, pointed the flowing periods of the historian, and added acuteness to the researches of the philosopher, and though there are undoubtedly many minds at present so far improved by the various excitements of knowledge, or of social sympathy, that they would not relapse into listlessness if their bodily stimulants were removed, yet it can scarcely be doubted that these stimulants could not be withdrawn from the mass of mankind without producing a general and fatal torpor, destructive of all the germs of future improvement.

Locke, if I recollect, says that the endeavour to avoid pain rather than the pursuit of pleasure is the great stimulus to action in life: and that in looking to any particular pleasure, we shall not be roused into action in order to obtain it, till the contemplation of it has continued so long as to amount to a sensation of pain or uneasiness under the absence of it.[43] To avoid evil and to pursue good seem to be the great duty and business of man, and this world appears to be peculiarly calculated to afford opportunity of the most unremitted exertion of this kind, and it is by this exertion, by these stimulants, that mind is formed. If Locke's idea be just, and there is great reason to think that it is, evil seems to be necessary to create exertion, and exertion seems evidently necessary to create mind.

The necessity of food for the support of life gives rise, probably, to a greater quantity of exertion than any other want, bodily or mental. The Supreme Being has ordained that the earth shall not produce good in great quantities till much preparatory labour and ingenuity has been exercised upon its surface. There is no conceivable connection to our comprehensions, between the seed and the plant or tree that rises from it. The Supreme Creator might, undoubtedly, raise up plants of all kinds, for the use of his creatures, without the assistance of those little bits of matter, which we call seed, or even without the assisting labour and attention of man. The processes of ploughing and clearing the ground, of collecting and sowing seeds, are not surely for the assistance of God in his creation, but are made previously necessary to the enjoyment of the blessings of life, in order to rouse man into action, and form his mind to reason.

To furnish the most unremitted excitements of this kind, and to urge man to further the gracious designs of Providence by the full cultivation of the earth, it has been ordained that population should increase much faster than food. This general law (as it has appeared in the former parts of this *Essay*) undoubtedly produces much partial evil, but a little reflection may, perhaps, satisfy us, that it produces a great overbalance of good. Strong excitements seem necessary to create exertion, and to direct this exertion, and form the reasoning faculty, it seems absolutely necessary, that the Supreme Being should act always according to general laws. The constancy of the laws of nature, or the certainty with which we may expect the same effects from the same causes, is the foundation of the faculty of reason. If in the ordinary course of things, the finger of God were frequently visible, or to speak more correctly, if God were frequently to change his purpose (for the finger of God is, indeed, visible in every blade of grass that we see), a general and fatal torpor of the human faculties would probably ensue; even the bodily wants of mankind would cease to stimulate them to exertion, could they not reasonably expect that if their efforts were well directed they would be crowned with success. The constancy of the laws of nature is the foundation of the industry and foresight of the husbandman, the indefatigable ingenuity of the artificer, the skilful researches of the physician and anatomist, and the watchful observation and patient investigation of the natural philosopher. To this constancy we owe all the greatest and noblest efforts of intellect. To this constancy we owe the immortal mind of a Newton.

As the reasons, therefore, for the constancy of the laws of nature seem, even to our understandings, obvious and striking; if we return to the principle of population and consider man as he really is, inert, sluggish, and averse from labour, unless compelled by necessity (and it is surely the height of folly to talk of man, according to our crude fancies of what he might be), we may pronounce with certainty that the world would not have been peopled, but for the superiority of the power of population to the means of subsistence. Strong and constantly operative as this stimulus is on man to urge him to the cultivation of the earth, if we still see that cultivation proceeds very slowly, we may fairly conclude that a less stimulus would have been insufficient. Even under the operation of this constant excitement, savages will inhabit countries of the greatest natural fertility for a long period before they betake themselves to pasturage or agriculture. Had population and food increased in the same ratio, it is probable that man might never have emerged from the savage state. But supposing the earth once well peopled, an Alexander, a Julius Caesar, a Tamberlane,[44] or a bloody revolution might irrecoverably thin the human race, and defeat the great designs of the Creator. The ravages of a contagious disorder would be felt for ages; and an earthquake might unpeople a region for ever. The principle, according to which population increases, prevents the vices of mankind, or the accidents of nature, the partial evils arising from general laws, from obstructing the high purpose of the creation. It keeps the inhabitants of the earth always fully up to the level of the means of subsistence; and is constantly acting upon man as a powerful stumulus, urging him to the further cultivation of the earth, and to enable it, consequently, to support a more extended population. But it is impossible that this law can operate, and produce the effects apparently intended by the Supreme Being, without occasioning partial evil. Unless the principle of population were to be altered according to the circumstances of each separate country (which would not only be contrary to our universal experience, with regard to the laws of nature, but would contradict even our own reason, which sees the absolute necessity of general laws for the formation of intellect), it is evident that the same principle which, seconded by industry, will people a fertile region in a few years must produce distress in countries that have been long inhabited.

It seems, however, every way probable that even the acknowledged difficulties occasioned by the law of population tend rather to promote than impede the general purpose of Providence. They excite universal exertion and contribute to that infinite variety of situations, and consequently of impressions, which seems upon the whole favourable to the growth of mind. It is probable, that too great or too little excitement, extreme poverty, or too great riches may be alike unfavourable in this respect. The middle regions of society seem to be best suited to intellectual improvement, but it is contrary to the analogy of all nature to expect that the whole of society can be a middle region. The temperate zones of the earth seem to be the most favourable to the mental and corporal energies of man, but all cannot be temperate zones. A world, warmed and enlightened but by one sun, must from the laws of matter have some parts chilled by perpetual frosts and others scorched by perpetual heats. Every piece of matter lying on a surface must have an upper and an under side, all the particles cannot be in the middle. The most valuable parts of an oak, to a timber merchant, are not either the roots or the branches, but these are absolutely necessary to the existence of the middle part, or stem, which is the object in request. The timber merchant could not possibly expect to make an oak grow without roots or branches, but if he could find out a mode of cultivation which would cause more of the substance to go to stem, and less to root and branch, he would be right to exert himself in bringing such a system into general use.

In the same manner, though we cannot possibly expect to exclude riches and poverty from society, yet if we could find out a mode of government by which the numbers in the extreme regions would be lessened and the numbers in the middle regions increased, it would be undoubtedly our duty to adopt it. It is not, however, improbable that as in the oak, the roots and branches could not be diminished very greatly without weakening the vigorous circulation of the sap in the stem, so in society the extreme parts could not be diminished beyond a certain degree without lessening that animated exertion throughout the middle parts, which is the very cause that they are the most favourable to the growth of intellect. If no man could hope to rise or fear to fall, in society, if industry did not bring with it its reward and idleness its punishment, the middle parts would not certainly be what they now are. In reasoning upon this subject, it is evident that we ought to consider chiefly the mass of mankind and not individual instances. There are undoubtedly many minds, and there ought to be many, according to the chances out of so great a mass, that, having been vivified early by a peculiar course of excitements, would not need the constant action of narrow motives to continue them in activity. But if we were to review the various useful discoveries, the valuable writings, and other laudable exertions of mankind, I believe we should find that more were to be attributed to the narrow motives that operate upon the many than to the apparently more enlarged motives that operate upon the few.

Leisure is, without doubt, highly valuable to man, but taking man as he is, the probability seems to be that in the greater number of instances it will produce evil rather than good. It has been not infrequently remarked that talents are more common among younger brothers than among elder brothers, but it can scarcely be imagined that younger brothers are, upon an average, born with a greater original susceptibility of parts. The difference, if there really is any observable difference, can only arise from their different situations. Exertion and activity are in general absolutely necessary in one case and are only optional in the other.

That the difficulties of life contribute to generate talents, every day's experience must convince us. The exertions that men find it necessary to make, in order to support themselves or families, frequently awaken faculties that might otherwise have lain for ever dormant, and it has been commonly remarked that new and extraordinary situations generally create minds adequate to grapple with the difficulties in which they are involved.

CHAPTER XIX

The sorrows of life necessary to soften and humanize the heart – The excitements of social sympathy often produce characters of a higher order than the mere possessors of talents – Moral evil probably necessary to the production of moral excellence – Excitements from intellectual wants continually kept up by the infinite variety of nature, and the obscurity that involves metaphysical subjects – The difficulties in revelation to be accounted for upon this principle – The degree of evidence which the scriptures contain, probably, best suited to the improvement of the human faculties, and the moral amelioration of mankind – The idea that mind is created by excitements seems to account for the existence of natural and moral evil.

THE sorrows and distresses of life form another class of excitements, which seem to be necessary, by a peculiar train of impressions, to soften and humanize the heart, to awaken social sympathy, to generate all the Christian virtues, and to afford scope for the ample exertion of benevolence. The general tendency of an uniform course of prosperity is rather to degrade than exalt the character. The heart that has never known sorrow itself will seldom be feelingly alive to the pains and pleasures, the wants and wishes, of its fellow beings. It will seldom be overflowing with that warmth of brotherly love, those kind and amiable affections, which dignify the human character even more than the possession of the highest talents. Talents, indeed, though undoubtedly a very prominent and fine feature of mind, can by no means be considered as constituting the whole of it. There are many minds which have not been exposed to those excitements that usually form talents, that have yet been vivified to a high degree by the excitements of social sympathy. In every rank of life, in the lowest as frequently as in the highest, characters are to be found overflowing with the milk of human kindness, breathing love towards God and man, and, though without those peculiar powers of mind called talents, evidently holding a higher rank in the scale of beings than many who possess them. Evangelical charity, meekness, piety, and all that class of virtues distinguished particularly by the name of Christian virtues do not seem necessarily to include abilities; yet a soul possessed of these amiable qualities, a soul awakened and vivified by these delightful sympathies, seems to hold a nearer commerce with the skies than mere acuteness of intellect.

The greatest talents have been frequently misapplied and have produced evil proportionate to the extent of their powers. Both reason and revelation seem to assure us that such minds will be condemned to eternal death, but while on earth, these vicious instruments performed their part in the great mass of impressions, by the disgust and abhorrence which they excited. It seems highly probable that moral evil is absolutely necessary to the production of moral excellence. A being with only good placed in view may be justly said to be impelled by a blind necessity. The pursuit of good in this case can be no indication of virtuous propensities. It might be said, perhaps, that Infinite Wisdom cannot want such an indication as outward action, but would foreknow with certainly whether the being would choose good or evil. This might be a plausible argument against a state of trial, but will not hold against the supposition that mind in this world is in a state of formation. Upon this idea, the being that has seen moral evil and has felt disapprobation and disgust at it is essentially different from the being that has seen only good. They are pieces of clay that have received distinct impressions: they must, therefore, necessarily be in different shapes; or, even if we allow them both to have the same lovely form of virtue, it must be acknowledged that one has undergone the further process, necessary to give firmness and durability to its substance, while the other is still exposed to injury, and liable to be broken by every accidental impulse. An ardent love and admiration of virtue seems to imply the existence of something opposite to it, and it seems highly probable that the same beauty of form and substance, the same perfection of character, could not be generated without the impressions of disapprobation which arise from the spectacle of moral evil.

When the mind has been awakened into activity by the passions, and the wants of the body, intellectual wants arise; and the desire of knowledge, and the impatience under ignorance, form a new and important class of excitements. Every part of nature seems peculiarly calculated to furnish stimulants to mental exertion of this kind, and to offer inexhaustible food for the most unremitted inquiry. Our immortal Bard says of Cleopatra:

> Custom cannot stale
> Her infinite variety.[45]

The expression, when applied to any one object, may be considered as a poetical amplification, but it is accurately true when applied to nature. Infinite variety seems, indeed, eminently her characteristic feature. The shades that are here and there blended in the picture give spirit, life, and prominence to her exuberant beauties, and those roughnesses and inequalities, those inferior parts that support the superior, though they sometimes offend the fastidious microscopic eye of short-sighted man, contribute to the symmetry, grace, and fair proportion of the whole.

The infinite variety of the forms and operations of nature, besides tending immediately to awaken and improve the mind by the variety of impressions that it creates, opens other fertile sources of improvement by offering so wide and extensive a field for investigation and research. Uniform, undiversified perfection could not possess the same awakening powers. When we endeavour then to contemplate the system of the universe, when we think of the stars as the suns of other systems scattered throughout infinite space, when we reflect that we do not probably see a millionth part of those bright orbs that are beaming light and life to unnumbered worlds, when our minds, unable to grasp the immeasurable conception, sink, lost and confounded, in admiration at the mighty incomprehensible power of the Creator, let us not querulously complain that all climates are not equally genial, that perpetual spring does not reign throughout the year, that all God's creatures do not possess the same advantages, that clouds and tempests sometimes darken the natural world and vice and misery the moral world, and that all the works of the creation are not formed with equal perfection. Both reason and experience seem to indicate to us that the infinite variety of nature (and variety cannot exist without inferior parts, or apparent blemishes) is admirably adapted to further the high purpose of the creation and to produce the greatest possible quantity of good.

The obscurity that involves all metaphysical subjects appears to me, in the same manner, peculiarly calculated to add to that class of excitements which arise from the thirst of knowledge. It is probable that man, while on earth, will never be able to attain complete satisfaction on these subjects; but this is by no means a reason that he should not engage in them. The darkness that surrounds these interesting topics of human curiosity may be intended to furnish endless motives to intellectual activity and exertion. The constant effort to dispel this darkness, even if it fail of success, invigorates and improves the thinking faculty. If the subjects of human inquiry were once exhausted, mind would probably stagnate; but the infinitely diversified forms and operations of nature, together with the endless food for speculation which metaphysical subjects offer, prevent the possibility that such a period should ever arrive.

It is by no means one of the wisest sayings of Solomon that 'there is no new thing under the sun.' [46] On the contrary, it is probable that were the present system to continue for millions of years, continual additions would be making to the mass of human knowledge, and yet, perhaps, it may be a matter of doubt whether what may be called the capacity of mind be in any marked and decided manner increasing. A Socrates, a Plato, or an Aristotle, however confessedly inferior in knowledge to the philosophers of the present day, do not appear to have been much below them in intellectual capacity. Intellect rises from a speck, continues in vigour only for a certain period, and will not perhaps admit while on earth of above a certain number of impressions. These impressions may, indeed, be infinitely modified, and from these various modifications, added probably to a difference in the susceptibility of the original germs, arise the endless diversity of character that we see in the world; but reason and experience seem both to assure us that the capacity of individual minds does not increase in proportion to the mass of existing knowledge. (It is probable that no two grains of wheat are exactly alike. Soil undoubtedly makes the principal difference in the blades that spring up, but probably not all. It seems natural to suppose some sort of difference in the original germs that are afterwards awakened into thought, and the extraordinary difference of susceptibility in very young children seems to confirm the supposition.)

The finest minds seem to be formed rather by efforts at original thinking, by endeavours to form new combinations, and to discover new truths, than by passively receiving the impressions of other men's ideas. Could we suppose the period arrived, when there was not further hope of future discoveries, and the only employment of mind was to acquire pre-existing knowledge, without any efforts to form new and original combinations, though the mass of human knowledge were a thousand times greater than it is at present, yet it is evident that one of the noblest stimulants to mental exertion would have ceased; the finest feature of intellect would be lost; everything allied to genius would be at an end; and it appears to be impossible, that, under such circumstances, any individuals could possess the same intellectual energies as were possessed by a Locke, a Newton, or a Shakespeare, or even by a Socrates, a Plato, an Aristotle or a Homer.

If a revelation from heaven of which no person could feel the smallest doubt were to dispel the mists that now hang over metaphysical subjects, were to explain the nature and structure of mind, the affections and essences of all substances, the mode in which the Supreme Being operates in the works of the creation, and the whole plan and scheme of the Universe, such an accession of knowledge so obtained, instead of giving additional vigour and activity to the human mind, would in all probability tend to repress future exertion and to damp the soaring wings of intellect.

For this reason I have never considered the doubts and difficulties that involve some parts of the sacred writings as any argument against their divine original. The Supreme Being might, undoubtedly, have accompanied his revelations to man by such a succession of miracles, and of such a nature, as would have produced universal overpowering conviction and have put an end at once to all hesitation and discussion. But weak as our reason is to comprehend the plans of the great Creator, it is yet sufficiently strong to see the most striking objections to such a revelation. From the little we know of the structure of the human understanding, we must be convinced that an over-powering conviction of this kind, instead of tending to the improvement and moral amelioration of man, would act like the touch of a torpedo on all intellectual exertion and would almost put an end to the existence of virtue. If the scriptural denunciations of eternal punishment were brought home with the same certainty to every man's mind as that the night will follow the day, this one vast and gloomy idea would take such full possession of the human faculties as to leave no room for any other conceptions, the external actions of men would be all nearly alike, virtuous conduct would be no indication of virtuous disposition, vice and virtue would be blended together in one common mass, and though the all-seeing eye of God might distinguish them they must necessarily make the same impressions on man, who can judge only from external appearances. Under such a dispensation, it is difficult to conceive how human beings could be formed to a detestation of moral evil, and a love and admiration of God, and of moral excellence.

Our ideas of virtue and vice are not, perhaps, very accurate and well-defined; but few, I think, would call an action really virtuous which was performed simply and solely from the dread of a very great punishment or the expectation of a very great reward. The fear of the Lord is very justly said to be the beginning of wisdom, but the end of wisdom is the love of the Lord and the admiration of moral good. The denunciations of future punishment contained in the scriptures seem to be well calculated to arrest the progress of the vicious and awaken the attention of the careless, but we see from repeated experience that they are not accompanied with evidence of such a nature as to overpower the human will and to make men lead virtuous lives with vicious dispositions, merely from a dread of hereafter. A genuine faith, by which I mean a faith that shews itself in all the virtues of a truly Christian life, may generally be considered as an indication of an amiable and virtuous disposition, operated upon more by love than by pure unmixed fear.

When we reflect on the temptations to which man must necessarily be exposed in this world, from the structure of his frame, and the operation of the laws of nature, and the consequent moral certainty that many vessels will come out of this mighty creative furnace in wrong shapes, it is perfectly impossible to conceive that any of these creatures of God's hand can be condemned to eternal suffering. Could we once admit such an idea, all our natural conceptions of goodness and justice would be completely overthrown, and we could no longer look up to God as a merciful and righteous Being. But the doctrine of life and immortality which was brought to light by the gospel, the doctrine that the end of righteousness is everlasting life, but that the wages of sin are death, is in every respect just and merciful, and worthy of the great Creator. Nothing can appear more consonant to our reason than that those beings which come out of the creative process of the world in lovely and beautiful forms should be crowned with immortality, while those which come out misshapen, those whose minds are not suited to a purer and happier state of existence, should perish and be condemned to mix again with their original clay. Eternal condemnation of this kind may be considered as a species of eternal punishment, and it is not wonderful that it should be represented, sometimes, under images of suffering. But life and death, salvation and destruction, are more frequently opposed to each other in the New Testament than happiness and misery. The Supreme Being would appear to us in a very different view if we were to consider him as pursuing the creatures that had offended him with eternal hate and torture, instead of merely condemning to their original insensibility those beings that, by the operation of general laws, had not been formed with qualities suited to a purer state of happiness. [47]

Life is, generally speaking, a blessing independent of a future state. It is a gift which the vicious would not always be ready to throw away, even if they had no fear of death. The partial pain, therefore, that is inflicted by the supreme Creator, while he is forming numberless beings to a capacity of the highest enjoyments, is but as the dust of the balance in comparison of the happiness that is communicated, and we have every reason to think that there is no more evil in the world than what is absolutely necessary as one of the ingredients in the mighty process.

The striking necessity of general laws for the formation of intellect will not in any respect be contradicted by one or two exceptions, and these evidently not intended for partial purposes, but calculated to operate upon a great part of mankind, and through many ages. Upon the idea that I have given of the formation of mind, the infringement of the general law of nature, by a divine revelation, will appear in the light of the immediate hand of God mixing new ingredients in the mighty mass, suited to the particular state of the process, and calculated to give rise to a new and powerful train of impressions, tending to purify, exalt, and improve the human mind. The miracles that accompanied these revelations when they had once excited the attention of mankind, and rendered it a matter of most interesting discussion, whether the doctrine was from God or man, had performed their part, had answered the purpose of the Creator; and these communications of the divine will were afterwards left to make their way by their own intrinsic excellence; and, by operating as moral motives, gradually to influence and improve, and not to overpower and stagnate the faculties of man.

It would be, undoubtedly, presumptuous to say that the Supreme Being could not possibly have effected his purpose in any other way than that which he has chosen, but as the revelation of the divine will which we possess is attended with some doubts and difficulties, and as our reason points out to us the strongest objections to a revelation which would force immediate, implicit, universal belief, we have surely just cause to think that these doubts and difficulties are no argument against the divine origin of the scriptures, and that the species of evidence which they possess is best suited to the improvement of the human faculties and the moral amelioration of mankind.

The idea that the impressions and excitements of this world

are the instruments with which the Supreme Being forms matter into mind, and that the necessity of constant exertion to avoid evil and to pursue good is the principal spring of these impressions and excitements, seems to smooth many of the difficulties that occur in a contemplation of human life, and appears to me to give a satisfactory reason for the existence of natural and moral evil, and, consequently, for that part of both, and it certainly is not a very small part, which arises from the principle of population. But, though, upon this supposition, it seems highly improbable that evil should ever be removed from the world, yet it is evident that this impression would not answer the apparent purpose of the Creator, it would not act so powerfully as an excitement to exertion, if the quanity of it did not diminish or increase with the activity or the indolence of man. The continual variations in the weight and in the distribution of this pressure keep alive a constant expectation of throwing it off.

> Hope springs eternal in the human breast,
> Man never is, but always to be blest.[48]

Evil exists in the world not to create despair but activity. We are not patiently to submit to it, but to exert ourselves to avoid it. It is not only the interest but the duty of every individual to use his utmost efforts to remove evil from himself and from as large a circle as he can influence, and the more he exercises himself in this duty, the more wisely he directs his efforts, and the more successful these efforts are, the more he will probably improve and exalt his own mind and the more completely does he appear to fulfil the will of his Creator.

A

SUMMARY VIEW

OF THE

PRINCIPLE OF POPULATION.

BY THE

Rev. T. R. MALTHUS, A.M., F.R.S.

LONDON:

JOHN MURRAY, ALBEMARLE-STREET.

MDCCCXXX.

ADVERTISEMENT

I⊤ has been frequently remarked, that no work has been so much talked of by persons who do not seem to have read it as Mr Malthus's *Essay on Population*. Partly from the nature of the subject, and partly from the size of the work, this seems to have taken place from an early period of its publication; nor did the subsequent editions succeed in remedying this partial and uncandid mode of discussing such a subject.

On the publication of the third edition, an Appendix was added in reply to some of the most prominent objections which had been made to the principles of the work. In introducing it, Mr Malthus says:

My object is to correct some of the misrepresentations which have gone abroad respecting two or three of the most important points of the Essay; and I should feel greatly obliged to those who have not had leisure to read the whole work, if they would cast their eyes over the few following pages, that they may not, from the partial and incorrect statements which they have heard, mistake the import of some of my opinions, and attribute to me others which I have never held.

This Appendix was published separately for the use of the purchasers of the quarto edition, and was very soon out of print.

As the discussion of the subject still continues, and the same misrepresentations have been revived, it was in contemplation to republish the Appendix, with the subsequent additions made to it, in a separate and cheap form, in order to enable those woh have any wish to consider the subject fairly to comply with Mr Malthus's request, by a very slight sacrifice of time and expense.

As the whole, however, of this Appendix is to be found in the fifth and sixth editions, and may easily be consulted, it has since been thought, that it would be more useful to publish, separately, a large extract from an article which was contributed by Mr Malthus to the *Supplement* of the *Encyclopaedia Britannica*.

The proprietors have liberally consented to this separate publication; and it is hoped that it will be found to give a useful summary of the *Principle of Population* in a small compass, and best to answer the purpose intended.

I N taking a view of animated nature, we cannot fail to be struck with a prodigious power of increase in plants and animals. Their capacity in this respect is, indeed, almost infinitely various, according with the endless variety of the works of nature, and the different purposes which they seem appointed to fulfil. But, whether they increase slowly or rapidly, if they increase by seed or generation, their natural tendency must be to increase in a geometrical ratio, that is, by multiplication; and at whatever rate they are increasing during any one period, if no further obstacles be opposed to them, they must proceed in a geometrical progression.

In the growth of wheat, a vast quantity of seed is unavoidably lost. When it is dibbled instead of being sown in the common way, two pecks of seed wheat will yield as large a crop as two bushels, and thus quadruple the proportion of the return to the quantity of seed put into the ground. In the *Philosophical Transactions* for 1768, an account is given of an experiment, in which, by separating the roots obtained from a single grain of wheat, and transplanting them in a favourable soil, a return was obtained of above 500,000 grains. But, without referring to peculiar instances, or peculiar modes of cultivation, it is known that calculations have often been made, founded on positive experience of the produce of wheat in different soils and countries, cultivated in an ordinary way, and making allowance for all ordinary destruction of seed.

Mr Humboldt [49] has collected some estimates of this kind, from which it appears that France, the north of Germany, Poland, and Sweden, taken generally, produce from five to six grains for one; some fertile lands in France produce fifteen for one; and the good lands in Picardy and the Isle of France, from eight to ten grains for one. Hungary, Croatia, and Sclavonia yield from eight to ten grains for one. In the Regno de la Plata, twelve grains for one are produced; near the city of Buenos

Ayres, sixteen for one; in the northern part of Mexico, seventeen; and in the equinoctial regions of Mexico, twenty-four for one (*Essai Politique sur le Royaume de la Nouvelle Espagne*, Bk IV, ch. 9, p. 98).

Now supposing that in any one country during a certain period, and under the ordinary cultivation, the return of wheat was six grains for one, it would be strictly correct to say, that wheat had the capacity of increasing in a geometrical ratio, of such a nature as to sextuple itself every year. And it might safely be calculated hypothetically, that if, setting out from the produce of one acre, land of the same quality could be prepared with sufficient rapidity, and no wheat were consumed, the rate of increase would be such as completely to cover the whole earthy surface of our globe in fourteen years.

In the same manner, if it be found by experience, that on land of a certain quality, and making allowance for the ordinary mortality and accidents, sheep will increase, on an average, so as to double their numbers every two years, it would be strictly correct to say, that sheep have a natural capacity of increasing, in a geometrical progression, of which the common multiple is two, and the term, two years; and it might safely be said, that if land of the same quality could be provided with sufficient rapidity, and no sheep were consumed, the rate of increase would be such, that if we were to begin with the full number which could be supported on an acre of land, the whole earthy part of the globe might be completely covered with sheep in less than seventy-six years.

If out of this prodigious increase of food, the full support of mankind were deducted, supposing them to increase as fast as they have ever yet increased in any country, the deduction would be comparatively inconsiderable; and the rate of increase would still be enormous, till it was checked, either by the natural want of will on the part of mankind to make efforts for the increase of food, beyond what they could possibly consume, or, after a certain period, by their absolute want of power to prepare land of the same quality, so as to allow of the same rate of progress.

Owing to these two causes combined, we see that, notwithstanding this prodigious *power* of increase in vegetables and animals, their actual increase is extremely slow; and it is obvious, that, owing to the latter cause alone, and long before a final stop was put to all further progress, their actual rate of increase must of necessity be very greatly retarded, as it would be impossible for the most enlightened human efforts to make all the soil of the earth equal in fertility to the average quality of land now in use; while the practicable approaches towards it would require so much time as to occasion, at a very early period, a constant and great check upon what their increase would be, if they could exert their natural powers.

Elevated as man is above all other animals by his intellectual faculties, it is not to be supposed that the physical laws to which he is subjected should be essentially different from those which are observed to prevail in other parts of animated nature. He may increase slower than most other animals; but food is equally necessary to his support; and if his natural capacity of increase be greater than can be permanently supplied with food from a limited territory, his increase must be constantly retarded by the difficulty of procuring the means of subsistence.

The main peculiarity which distinguishes man from other animals, in the means of his support, is the power which he possesses of very greatly increasing these means. But this power is obviously limited by the scarcity of land – by the great natural barrenness of a very large part of the surface of the earth – and by the decreasing proportion of produce which must necessarily be obtained from the continual additions of capital applied to land already in cultivation.

It is, however, specifically with this diminishing and limited power of increasing the produce of the soil, that we must compare the natural power of mankind to increase, in order to ascertain whether, in the progress to the full cultivation and peopling of the globe, the natural power of mankind to increase must not, of absolute necessity, be constantly retarded by the difficulty of procuring the means of subsistence; and if so, what are likely to be the effects of such a state of things.

In an endeavour to determine the natural power of mankind to increase, as well as their power of increasing the produce of the soil, we can have no other guide than past experience.

The great check to the increase of plants and animals, we know from experience, is the want of room and nourishment; and this experience would direct us to look for the greatest actual increase of them in those situations where room and nourishment were the most abundant.

On the same principle, we should expect to find the greatest actual increase of population in those situations where, from the abundance of good land, and the manner in which its produce is distributed, the largest quantity of the necessaries of life is actually awarded to the mass of the society.

Of the countries with which we are acquainted, the United States of America, formerly the North American Colonies of Great Britain, answer most nearly to this description. In the United States, not only is there an abundance of good land, but from the manner in which it has been distributed, and the market which has been opened for its produce, there has been a greater and more constant demand for labour, and a larger portion of necessaries has been awarded to the labourer, than in any of those other countries which possess an equal or greater abundance of land and fertility of soil.

Here, then, we should expect to find that the natural power of mankind to increase, whatever it may be, would be most distinctly marked; and here, in consequence, it appears that the actual rate of the increase of population has been more rapid than in any known country, although, independently of the abundance of good land, and the great demand for labour, it is distinguished by no other circumstances which appear to be peculiarly favourable to the increase of numbers.

It has been stated, that all animals, according to the known laws by which they are produced, must have a capacity of increasing in a geometrical progression. And the question with regard to man is, what is the rate of this geometrical progression?

Fortunately, in the country to which we should naturally turn our eyes for an exemplification of the most rapid rate of increase, there have been four enumerations of the people, each at the distance of ten years; and though the estimates of the increase of population in the North American Colonies at earlier periods were of sufficient authority, in the absence of more certain documents, to warrant most important inferences, yet as we now possess such documents, and as the period they involve is of sufficient length to establish the point in question, it is no longer necessary to refer to earlier times.

According to a regular census made by order of Congress in 1790, which there is every reason to think is essentially correct, the white population of the United States was found to be 3,164,148. By a similar census in 1800, it was found to have increased to 4,312,841. It had increased then, during the ten years from 1790 to 1800, at a rate equal to 36·3 per cent, a rate which, if continued, would double the population in twenty-two years and about four months and a half.

According to a third census in 1810, the white population was found to be 5,862,092, which, compared with the population of 1800, gives an increase in the second ten years at the rate of nearly 36 per cent, which, if continued, would double the population in about twenty-two years and a half. (These numbers are taken from Dr Seybert's *Statistical Annals*, p. 230.) [50]

According to the fourth census in 1820, the white population was found to be 7,861,710, which, compared with the population of 1810, gives an increase in the third ten years, at a rate per cent of 34·1, which, if continued, would double the population in twenty-three years and seven months. (The number is taken from the American *National Calendar* for 1822, and has since been compared with the original census as published for the use of the members of Congress.)

If we compare the period of doubling according to the rate of increase in the most unfavourable ten years of this series with twenty-five years, we shall find the difference such as fully to cover all the increase of population which would have taken place from immigration, or the influx of strangers.

It appears from a reference to the most authentic documents which can be collected on both sides of the Atlantic, that the emigration to the United States, during the last thirty years, from 1790 to 1820, falls decidedly short of an average of 10,000 a year. Dr Seybert, the best authority on the other side of the water, states that, from 1790 to 1810, it could not have been so much as 6,000 a year. Our official accounts of the number of emigrants to the United States from England, Ireland, and Scotland, during the ten years from 1812 to 1821, inclusive, give an average of less than 7,000, although the period includes the extraordinary years 1817 and 1818, in which the emigrations to the United States were much greater than they were ever known to be before or after, up to 1820. The official American accounts, as far as they go, which is only for two years from 30th September, 1819, tend to confirm this average, and allowing fully for the emigrants from other European countries, the general average will still be under the ten thousand. (American *National Calendar* for 1821, p. 237, and *North American Review* for October 1822, p. 304.)

A new mode has, however, lately been suggested of estimating the amount of increase in any country derived from emigration. It has been justly stated, that when a census is taken every ten years, and the population is distinguished into those above, and those below, ten years of age, all above ten years of age, exclusive of immigrants, must have existed in the census immediately preceding, and, consequently, after having made a proper allowance for the mortality during these ten years, the excess above the remaining number must be attributed to immigration. If we had the means of estimating with accuracy the loss which would be sustained in America in ten years by a population not increased by additional births, this mode of estimating the amount of immigration would be unobjectionable, and often very useful. (This mode was suggested by Mr Booth in Mr Godwin's enquiry of *Population.*)

But, unfortunately, the means are deficient. Even the annual mortality in the United States is not known. It was supposed, by Dr Price, (Vol. II, p. 50, 7th ed.) to be 1 in 50; by Mr Barton, in the *Transactions of the Society* at Philadelphia, (Vol. III, No. 7), 1 in 45;[51] and it is stated by Mr Bristed, in his work on *America and her Resources* (p. 20),[52] that the annual deaths average through the United States is 1 in 40, in the healthiest districts 1 in 56, and in the most unhealthy 1 in 35.

If, however, we could ascertain accurately the average annual mortality, we should still be unable to ascertain the amount of the loss in question, as, under any given law of mortality, it would depend so very much upon the rate at which the population was increasing. The truth of this observation will be placed in a striking light by the following short table, with which we have been favoured by a very able calculator, Mr Milne, author of a well-known *Treatise on Annuities and Assurances*.[53] It is constructed on the supposition that the population, in each case, is always subject to the same law of mortality as that which prevailed in all Sweden and Finland during the five years ended with 1805, and that the number of births in the present year, in each case, is 10,000.

	The Population constantly the same	The Population increasing, and having increased in geometrical progression for more than 100 years, so as to double itself every	
		50 years	25 years
Total population 10 years since	393,848	230,005	144,358
Total above 10 years of age now	320,495	195,566	125,176
Died during the term of 10 years, out of those living at its commencement	73,353	34,439	18,182
Being one of	5·3692	6·6786	7·9396

We see from this table, that, under the same law of mortality, the difference of loss sustained in ten years, by a people not increased by fresh births, would, in the three cases supposed of a stationary population, a population doubling in fifty years, and a population doubling in twenty-five years, be as 1 in 5·3692, 1 in 6·6786, and 1 in 7·9396; and that when the population is doubling itself in twenty-five years, the loss would be very little more than one-eighth.

But the censuses must be allowed to form a prima facie evidence, that the population of the United States has, for some time, been going on doubling itself in twenty-five years; and assuming this evidence to be true, which we are warranted in doing till better evidence is produced on the other side, it will appear that the amount of immigration, deduced from the rule here referred to, is less than 10,000 a year.

Thus the white population of the United States in 1800 was 4,312,841 (Seybert's *Statistical Annals*, p. 23). This population without further accession of births, would, in 1810, be diminished one-eighth, or reduced to 3,773,736. In 1810, the population above ten years of age was 3,845,389; and subtracting the former number from the latter, the difference, or amount of immigration, will be 71,653, or 7,165 a year.

Again, the white population of 1810 was 5,862,092, which, diminished by one-eighth in ten years, would be 5,129,331. The population above ten years of age in 1820, was 5,235,940 (American *National Calendar* for 1822, p. 246). Subtracting the former from the latter, the difference, or amount of immigration, is 106,608, or 10,660, a year; showing, as we should expect, a greater amount of immigration from 1810 to 1820 than from 1800 to 1810, but even in the latter ten years, and including emigrations from Canada, as well as all other countries, little exceeding 10,000.

Altogether, then, we can hardly err in defect, if we allow 10,000 a year for the average increase from immigration during the twenty-five years from 1795 to 1820, and applying this number to the slowest period of increase, when the rate was such as to double the population in twenty-three years and seven months, it may be easily calculated, that in the additional year and five months, a population of 5,862,000 would have increased to an amount much more than sufficient to cover an annual influx of 10,000 persons, with the increase from them at the same rate.

Such an increase from them, however, would not take place. It appears from an account in the *National Calendar* of the United States for the year 1821, that, of the 7,001 persons who had arrived in America from the 30th of September 1819 to the 30th of September 1820, 1,959 only were females, and the rest, 5,042, were males – a proportion which, if it approaches towards representing the average, must very greatly reduce the number from which any increase ought to be calculated. The details for the next year were not then printed, but it is known that the whole number of passengers arriving in the United States was 10,722, of which 2,415 were from the United States, leaving 8,307 foreigners (*American Review* for October 1822, p. 304).

If, however, we omit these considerations; if we suppose a yearly emigration from Europe to America of 10,000 persons for the twenty-five years, from 1795 to 1820, the greatest part of which time Europe was involved in a most extensive scene of warfare requiring all its population; and further, if we allow for an increase of all the emigrants during the *whole period*, at the fullest rate, the remaining numbers will still be sufficient to show a doubling of the population in less than twenty-five years.

The white population of 1790 was 3,164,148. This population, according to the rate at which it was increasing, would have amounted to about 3,694,100 in 1795; and supposing it to have just doubled itself in the twenty-five years, from 1795 to 1820, the population in 1820 would have been 7,388,200. But the actual white population of 1820 appears, by the late census, to be 7,861,710, showing an excess of 473,510, whereas an emigration of 10,000 persons annually, with the increase from them at 3 per cent, a rate which would double a population in less than twenty-four years, would only amount to 364,592.

But the most striking confirmation of the censuses of the United States, and the most remarkable proof of the rate of increase being occasioned almost exclusively by procreation, have been furnished to us by Mr Milne. In his work on *Annuities and Assurances*, which contains much valuable and interesting information on the subject of population, he had noticed the effects of the frequent pressure of want on the labouring classes of Sweden; which, by increasing the proportion of deaths, rendered the law of mortality, so accurately observed in that country by Professors Wargentin and Nicander, inapplicable to other countries more favourably circumstanced.[54] But the law of mortality was observed to be gradually improving from the time that Dr Price constructed his Swedish table; and the period from 1800 to the end of 1805 was so free from scarcities and epidemics, and the healthiness of the country had been further so much improved by the introduction of vaccination, that he justly thought the law of mortality, as observed during these five years, might suit countries where the condition of the people was known to be much better than it had generally been in Sweden. On these grounds he applied the Swedish law of mortality, during the term mentioned, to the hypothesis of a population which had been increasing by procreation, in geometrical progression, for more than a hundred years, so as to double every twenty-five years. Assuming this population to be one million, he distributed it, according to such a supposed law of mortality, into the different ages referred to in the American censuses, and then compared them with the same number of persons distributed according to the actual returns of the ages in the American censuses for the three periods of 1800, 1810, and 1820.

The results are as follows:

DISTRIBUTION OF A POPULATION OF 1,000,000 PERSONS IN THE UNDER-MENTIONED INTERVALS OF AGE

	According to			
		United States		
Between the Ages of	The Hypothesis	Census of 1800	Census of 1810	Census of 1820
0 & 10	337,592	334,556	344.024	333,995
10 & 16	145,583	154,898	156,345	154,913
16 & 26	186,222	185,046	189,227	198,114
26 & 45	213,013	205,289	190,461	191,139
45 & 100	117,590	120,211	119,943	121,839
0 & 100	1,000,000	1,000,000	1,000,000	1,000,000
Under 16	483,175	489,454	500,369	488,908
Above 16	516,825	510,546	499,631	511,092

The general resemblance in the distribution of the ages in the three different censuses to each other, and to the hypothesis, clearly proves –

First, that the distribution of the ages, in the different

enumerations, must be made with some care, and may, therefore, be relied on as in the main correct.

Second, that the law of mortality assumed in the hypothesis cannot deviate essentially from the law of mortality which prevails in the United States; and,

Third, that the actual structure of the American population differs very little from what it would be if it were increasing regularly from procreation only, in geometrical progression, so as to double itself every twenty-five years; and that we may, therefore, safely infer that it has been very little disturbed by immigration.

If to these proofs of the rapid increase of population which has actually taken place we add the consideration that this rate of increase is an average applying to a most extensive territory, some parts of which are known to be unhealthy; that some of the towns of the United States are now large; that many of the inhabitants must be engaged in unwholesome occupations, and exposed to many of those checks to increase which prevail in other countries; and further, that in the western territories, where these checks do not occur, the rate of increase is more rapid than the general average, after making the fullest allowance for immigration, it must appear certain, that the rate at which the population of the whole of the United States has actually increased for the last thirty years must fall very decidedly short of the actual capacity of mankind to increase under the most favourable circumstances.

The best proof that can be obtained of the capacity of mankind to increase at a certain rate is their having really increased at that rate. At the same time, if any peculiarly rapid increase which had appeared to take place in a particular country were quite unsupported by other evidence, we might be disposed to attribute it to error or accident, and might scarcely be justified in founding important conclusions upon it. But this is far from being the case in the present instance. The rate of increase which has at times taken place in other countries, under the operation of great and obvious checks to the progress of population, sufficiently shows what might be expected if these checks were removed.

The countries most resembling the United States of America are those territories of the New World which lately belonged to Spain. In abundance and fertility of soil they are indeed superior; but almost all the vices in the government of the mother country were introduced into her colonial possessions, and particularly that very unequal distribution of landed property which takes place under the feudal system. These evils, and the circumstance of a very large part of the population being Indians in a depressed state, and inferior in industry and energy to Europeans, necessarily prevent that rapid increase of numbers which the abundance and fertility of the land would admit of. But it appears from the instructive and interesting account of New Spain, which Mr Humboldt has not long since given to the public, that for the last half of the eighteenth century, the excess of the births above the deaths, and the progress of the population, have been very great. The following are the proportions of burials to baptisms in the registers of eleven villages, the details of which were communicated to Mr Humboldt by the curates:

	Burials	Baptisms
At Dolores	100	253
Singuilucan	100	234
Calymaya	100	202
Guanaxuato	100	201
St Anne	100	195
Marsil	100	194
Queretaro	100	188
Axapuzco	100	157
Yguala	100	140
Malacatepec	100	130
Panuco	100	123

The mean proportion is 100 to 183.

But the proportion which Mr Humboldt considers as best suited to the whole of the population is 100 to 170.

In some of the villages above mentioned, the proportion of the births to the population is extraordinarily great, and the proportion of deaths very considerable, showing, in a striking point of view, the early marriages and early deaths of a tropical climate, and the more rapid passing away of each generation.

The details which Mr Humboldt has given of the population of New Spain are highly interesting, as they are the first of any consequence which the public has yet received of a tropical climate. The peculiarities which mark them are exactly of the kind which might have been expected, though the proportion of births is still greater than we could have ventured to suppose.

At Queretaro, it appears that the baptisms were to the population as 1 to 14, and the burials as 1 to 26. At Guanaxuato, including the neighbouring mines of St Anne and of Marsil, the baptisms were to the population as 1 to 15, and the burials as 1 to 29.

The general result from all the information which could be collected was, that the proportion of births to the population, for the whole of the kingdom of New Spain, was as 1 to 17, and of the deaths as 1 to 30. These proportions of births to deaths, if they were continued, would double the population in twenty-seven and a half years.

Mr Humboldt further observes, that the information which he had collected respecting the proportions of the births to the deaths, and of these to the whole population, proves, that if the order of nature were not interrupted by some extraordinary and disturbing causes, the population of New Spain ought to double itself every nineteen years. (*Essai Politique sur le Royaume de la Nouvelle Espagne*, Bk II, ch. 4, pp. 330 passim).

It is known, however, that these causes do occur in the actual state of things: consequently we cannot consider the actual rate of the increase of population in New Spain as greater than according to the former calculation. But a rate of increase such as to double the population in twenty-seven and a half years, in spite of all the obstacles enumerated by Mr Humboldt, is very extraordinary. It is next to the increase of the United States, and greatly superior to any that can be found in Europe.

Yet in Europe the tendency to increase is always very strongly marked, and the actual increase for periods of some length is sometimes much greater than could be expected beforehand, considering the obstacles to be overcome.

It appears from Suessmilch, that the population of Prussia and Lithuania, after the great plague in 1709 and 1710, doubled itself in about forty-four years, from the excess of the births above the deaths enumerated in the registers (*Göttliche Ordnung*, Vol. I, Table XXI).

In Russia, the whole population in 1763 was estimated, by enumeration and calculation, at twenty millions, and in 1796 at thirty-six millions. This is a rate of increase which would occasion a doubling in less than forty-two years (Tooke's *View of the Russian Empire*, Vol. II, p. 126).[55]

In 1695, the population of Ireland was estimated at 1,034,000. According to the late returns in 1821, it had increased to the prodigious amount of 6,801,827. This is an example of an actual increase for 125 years together, at a rate which would double the population in about forty-five years; and this has taken place under the frequent pressure of great distress among the labouring classes of society, and the practice of frequent and considerable emigration.

But for the proof of the power of population to increase under great obstacles of the preventive, as well as of the positive, kind, we need not go out of Great Britain. The rate of increase since our enumerations have commenced has been very remarkable for a country which was considered as well peopled before, and some of the details accompanying the returns tend strikingly to illustrate the principle of population.

The population of Great Britain, according to the late enumerations, was, in 1801, 10,942,646, and, in 1811, 12,596,803 (*Population Abstract, 1821*, 'Preliminary Observations', p. 8). This is a rate of increase, during the ten years, of rather above 15 per cent, a rate which, if continued, would double the population in between forty-nine and fifty years.

By the last enumeration of 1821, it appears that the population was 14,391,631 (*Population Abstract, 1821*, loc. cit.), which, compared with the population of 1811, gives a rate of increase during the ten years of 14·25 per cent, a rate which would double the population in about fifty-two years.

According to these numbers, the rate of increase during the last ten years was slower than that of the first; but it appears from the excess of the number of males above females in the enumeration of 1811, so opposite to the state of the population in 1801 and 1821, when the females exceeded the males, particularly at the latter period, that of the large number added to the population for the army, navy, and registered merchant ships in 1811, a considerable proportion must have been foreigners. On this account, and on account of the further difficulty of knowing what part of this number might properly belong to Ireland, it has been proposed to estimate the rate per cent at which the population has increased in each of the ten years by the females only; and according to this mode of computation the population increased during the first period at the rate of 14·02 per cent, and during the second at the rate of 15·82 (*Population Abstract, 1821*, loc. cit.). This last rate of increase would double the population in less than forty-eight years.

The only objection to this mode of computation is, that it does not take into consideration the greater destruction of the males during the war. In 1801, the females exceeded the half of the population by 21,031, and in 1821 by 63,890, while, at the intermediate period, owing to the causes above mentioned, the females fell short of the half of the males by 35,685.

When, however, a proper distribution has been made of the army and navy among the resident population, and taking England and Wales alone, it appears that from 1801 to 1811 the population increased at the rate of 14·5 per cent, and from 1811 to 1821, at the rate of 16·5 per cent (*Population Abstract, 1821*, p. 32). At the former of these rates, the period of doubling would be rather above fifty years; at the latter, under forty-six years; and taking the whole period, the time of doubling would be about forty-eight years. Yet in Great Britain there is a much larger proportion of the population living in towns, and engaged in occupations considered as unhealthy, than in any other known country of the same extent. There are also the best reasons for believing that in no other country of the same extent is there to be found so great a proportion of late marriages, or so great a proportion of persons remaining unmarried, as in Great Britain. And if, under these circumstances, a demand for labour and an increase of the funds for its maintenance could for twenty years together occasion such a rate of increase as, if continued, would double the population in forty-eight years, and quadruple it in ninety-six years, it is in the highest degree probable, that if the encouragements to marriage and the means of supporting a family were as great as in America, the period of doubling in Great Britain would not be more than twenty-five years, even in spite of her great towns and manufactories; and would be decidedly less if these obstacles were removed.

Taking, therefore, into consideration the actual rate of increase which appears from the best documents to have taken place over a very large extent of country in the United States of America, very variously circumstanced as to healthiness and rapidity of progress; considering, further, the rate of increase which has taken place in New Spain, and also in many countries of Europe, where the means of supporting a family, and other circumstances favourable to increase, bear no comparison with those of the United States; and adverting particularly to the great increase of population which has taken place in this country during the last twenty years, under the formidable obstacles to its progress which must press themselves upon the attention of the most careless observer, it must appear, that the assumption of a rate of increase such as would double the population in twenty-five years, as representing the natural progress of population when not checked by the difficulty of procuring the means of subsistence, or other peculiar causes of premature mortality, must be very decidedly within the truth.

It may be safely asserted, therefore, that population, when unchecked, increases in a geometrical progression of such a nature as to double itself every twenty-five years. This statement, of course, refers to the general result, and not to each intermediate step of the progress. Practically, it would sometimes be slower, and sometimes faster.

It would be unquestionably desirable to have the means of comparing the natural rate of the increase of population when unchecked with the possible rate of the increase of food in a limited territory, such as that in which man is actually placed; but the latter estimate is much more difficult and uncertain than the former. If the rate of the increase of population at a particular period of some little extent can be ascertained with tolerable exactness, we have only to suppose the continuance of the same encouragements to marriage, the same facility of supporting a family, the same moral habits, with the same rate of mortality, and the increase of the population at the same rate, after it had reached a thousand millions, would be just as probable as at any intermediate and earlier period; but it is quite obvious that the increase of food in a limited space must proceed upon a principle totally different. It has been already stated that, while land of good quality is in great abundance, the rate at which food might be made to increase would far exceed what is necessary to keep pace with the most rapid increase of population which the laws of nature in relation to human kind permit. But if society were so constituted as to give the fullest scope possible to the progress of cultivation and population, all such lands, and all lands of moderate quality, would soon be occupied; and when the future increase of the supply of food came to depend upon the taking of very poor land into cultivation, and the gradual and laborious improvement of the land already cultivated, the rate of the increase of food would certainly have a greater resemblance to a decreasing geometrical ratio than an increasing one. The yearly increment of food would, at any rate, have a constant tendency to diminish, and the amount of the increase of each successive ten years would probably be less than that of the preceding.

Practically, however, great uncertainty must take place. An unfavourable distribution of produce, by prematurely diminishing the demand for labour, might retard the increase of food at an early period, in the same manner as if cultivation and population had been further advanced; while improvements in agriculture, accompanied by a greater demand for labour and produce, might for some time occasion a rapid increase of food and population at a later period, in the same manner as if cultivation and population had been in an earlier stage of their progress. These variations, however, obviously arise from causes which do not impeach the general *tendency* of a continued increase of produce in a limited territory to diminish the *power* of its increase in future.

Under this certainty with regard to the general *tendency*, and uncertainty in reference to particular periods, it must be allowable, if it throws light on the subject, to make a supposition respecting the increase of food in a limited territory, which, without pretending to accuracy, is clearly more favourable to the power of the soil to produce the means of subsistence for an increasing population than any experience which we have of its qualities will warrant.

If, setting out from a tolerably well-peopled country such as England, France, Italy, or Germany, we were to suppose that, by great attention to agriculture, its produce could be permanently increased every twenty-five years by a quantity equal to that which it at present produces, it would be allowing a rate of increase decidedly beyond any probability of realization. The most sanguine cultivators could hardly expect that, in the course of the next 200 years, each farm in this country on an average would produce eight times as much food as it produces at present, and still less that this rate of increase could continue, so that each farm would produce twenty times as much as at present in 500 years, and forty times as much in 1,000 years. Yet this would be an arithmetical progression, and would fall short, beyond all comparison, of the natural increase of population in a geometrical progression, according to which the inhabitants of any country in 500 years, instead of increasing to twenty times, would increase to above a million times their present numbers.

It will be said, perhaps, that many parts of the earth are as yet very thinly peopled, and, under proper management, would allow of a much more rapid increase of food than would be possible in the more fully inhabited states of Europe. This is unquestionably true. Some parts of the earth would no doubt be capable of producing food at such a rate as to keep pace for a few periods with an unrestricted increase of population. But to put this capacity fully into action is of all things the most difficult. If it is to be accomplished by the improvement of the actual inhabitants of the different parts of the earth in knowledge, in government, in industry, in arts, and in morals, it is scarcely possible to say how it ought to be commenced with the best prospect of success, or to form a conjecture as to the time in which it could be effected.

If it is to be accomplished by emigration from the more improved parts of the world, it is obvious that it must involve much war and extermination, besides all the difficulties usually attendant upon new settlements in uncivilized countries; and these alone are so formidable, and for a long time so destructive, that, combined with the unwillingness which people must always naturally feel to quit their own country, much distress would be suffered at home before relief would be sought for in emigration.

But, supposing for a moment that the object could be fully accomplished, that is, supposing that the capacity of the earth to produce the necessaries of life could be put fully into action, and that they were distributed in the proportions most favourable for the growth of capital, and the effective demand for labour, the increase of population, whether arising from the increase of the inhabitants of each country, or from emigrants issuing from all those countries which were more advanced in cultivation, would be so rapid, that, in a period comparatively quite short, all the good lands would be occupied, and the rate of the possible increase of food would be reduced much below the arithmetical ratio above supposed.

If, merely during the short period which has elapsed since our Revolution of 1688, the population of the earth had increased at its natural rate when unchecked, supposing the number of people at that time to have been only 800 millions, all the land of the globe, without making allowance for deserts, forests, rocks, and lakes, would on an average be equally populous with England and Wales at present. This would be accomplished in five doublings, or 125 years; and one or two doublings more, or a period less than that which has elapsed since the beginning of the reign of James the First,[56] would produce the same effect from the overflowings of the inhabitants of those countries, where, owing to the further progress of cultivation, the soil had not the capacity of producing food so as to keep pace with the increase of an unrestricted population.

Whatever temporary and partial relief, therefore, may be derived from emigration by particular countries in the actual state of things, it is quite obvious, that, considering the subject generally and largely, emigration may be fairly said not in any degree to touch the difficulty. And, whether we exclude or include emigration, – whether we refer to particular countries, or to the whole earth – the supposition of a future capacity in the soil to increase the necessaries of life every twenty-five years by a quantity equal to that which is at present produced, must be decidedly beyond the truth.

But, if the natural increase of population, when unchecked by the difficulty of procuring the means of subsistence, or other peculiar causes, be such as to continue doubling its numbers in twenty-five years; and the greatest increase of food, which, for a continuance, could possibly take place on a limited territory like our earth in its present state, be at the most only such as would add every twenty-five years an amount equal to its present produce; it is quite clear that a powerful check on the increase of population must be almost constantly in action.

By the laws of nature man cannot live without food. Whatever may be the rate at which population would increase if unchecked, it never can actually increase in any country beyond the food necessary to support it. But, by the laws of nature in respect to the powers of a limited territory, the additions which can be made in equal periods to the food which it produces must, after a short time, either be constantly decreasing, which is what would really take place, or, at the very most, must remain stationary, so as to increase the means of subsistence only in an arithmetical progression. Consequently, it follows necessarily that the average rate of the *actual* increase of population over the greatest part of the globe, obeying the same laws as the increase of food, must be totally of a different character from the rate at which it would increase *if unchecked*.

The great question, then, which remains to be considered, is the manner in which this constant and necessary check upon population practically operates.

If the soil of any extensive well-peopled country were equally divided amongst its inhabitants, the check would assume its most obvious and simple form. Perhaps each farm in the well-peopled countries of Europe might allow of one or even two doublings, without much distress, but the absolute impossibility of going on at the same rate is too glaring to escape the most careless thinker. When, by extraordinary efforts, provision had been made for four times the number of persons which the land can support at present, what possible hope could there be of doubling the provision in the next twenty-five years?

Yet there is no reason whatever to suppose that anything besides the difficulty of procuring in adequate plenty the necessaries of life should either indispose this greater number of persons to marry early, or disable them from rearing in health the largest families. But this difficulty would of necessity occur, and its effect would be either to discourage early marriages, which would check the rate of increase by preventing the same proportion of births, or to render the children unhealthy from bad and insufficient nourishment, which would check the rate of increase by occasioning a greater proportion of deaths; or, what is most likely to happen, the rate of increase would be checked, partly by the diminution of births, and partly by the increase of mortality.

The first of these checks may, with propriety, be called the *preventive check* to population; the second, the *positive check*; and the absolute necessity of their operation in the case supposed is as certain and obvious as that man cannot live without food.

Taking a single farm only into consideration, no man would have the hardihood to assert that its produce could be made permanently to keep pace with a population increasing at such a rate as it is observed to do for twenty or thirty years together at particular times and in particular countries. He would, indeed, be compelled to acknowledge, that if, with a view to allow for the most sanguine speculations, it has been supposed that the additions made to the necessaries produced by the soil in given times might remain constant, yet that this rate of the increase of produce could not possibly be realized; and that, if the capacity of the soil were at all times put properly into action, the additions to the produce would, after a short time, and independently of new inventions, be constantly decreasing, till, in no very long period, the exertions of an additional labourer would not produce his own subsistence.

But what is true, in this respect, in reference to a single farm, must necessarily be true of the whole earth, from which the necessaries of life for the actual population are derived. And what would be true in respect to the checks to population, if the soil of the earth were equally divided among the different families which inhabit it, must be true, under the present unequal division of property, and variety of occupations. Nothing but the confusion and indistinctness arising from the largeness of the subject could make persons deny, in the case of an extensive territory, or the whole earth, what they could not fail to acknowledge in the case of a single farm, which may be said fairly to represent it.

It may be expected, indeed, that in civilized and improved countries, the accumulation of capital, the division of labour, and the invention of machinery, will extend the bounds of production; but we know from experience, that the effect of these causes, which are quite astonishing in reference to some of the *conveniencies* and *luxuries* of life, are very much less efficient in producing an increase of *food*; and although the saving of labour and an improved system of husbandry may be the means of pushing cultivation upon much poorer lands than could otherwise be worked, yet the increased quantity of the necessaries of life so obtained can never be such as to supersede, for any length of time, the operation of the preventive and positive checks to population. And not only are these checks as absolutely necessary in civilized and improved countries as they would be if each family had a certain portion of land allotted to it, but they operate almost exactly in the same way. The distress which would obviously arise in the most simple state of society from the natural tendency of population to increase faster than the means of subsistence in a limited territory, is brought home to the higher classes of an improved and populous country in the difficulty which they find in supporting their families in the same rank of life with themselves; and to the labouring classes, which form the great mass of society, in the insufficiency of the real wages of common labour to bring up a large family.

If in any country the yearly earnings of the commonest labourers, determined, as they always will be, by the state of the demand and the supply of necessaries compared with labour, be not sufficient to bring up in health the largest families, one of the three things before stated must happen; either the prospect of this difficulty will prevent some, and delay other, marriages; or the diseases arising from bad nourishment will be introduced, and the mortality be increased; or the progress of population will be retarded, partly by one cause, and partly by the other.

According to all past experience, and the best observations which can be made on the motives which operate upon the human mind, there can be no well-founded hope of obtaining a large produce from the soil but under a system of private property. It seems perfectly visionary to suppose that any stimulus short of that which is excited in man by the desire of providing for himself and family, and of bettering his condition in life, should operate on the mass of society with sufficient force and constancy to overcome the natural indolence of mankind. All the attempts which have been made since the commencement of authentic history, to proceed upon a principle of common property, have either been so insignificant that no inference can be drawn from them, or have been marked by the most signal failures; and the changes which have been effected in modern times by education do not seem to advance a single step towards making such a state of things more probable in future. We may, therefore, safely conclude, that while man retains the same physical and moral constitution which he is observed to possess at present, no other than a system of private property stands the least chance of providing for such a large and increasing population as that which is to be found in many countries at present.[57]

But though there is scarcely any conclusion which seems more completely established by experience than this, yet it is unquestionably true, that the laws of private property, which are the grand stimulants to production, do themselves so limit it as always to make the actual produce of the earth fall very considerably short of the *power* of production. On a system of private property no adequate motive to the extension of cultivation can exist, unless the returns are sufficient not only to pay the wages necessary to keep up the population, which, at the least, must include the support of a wife and two or three children, but also afford a profit on the capital which has been employed. This necessarily excludes from cultivation a considerable portion of land, which might be made to bear corn. If it were possible to suppose that man might be adequately stimulated to labour under a system of common property, such land might be cultivated, and the production of food and the increase of population might go on till the soil absolutely refused to grow a single additional quarter, and the whole of the society was exclusively engaged in procuring the necessaries of life. But it is quite obvious that such a state of things would inevitably lead to the greatest degree of distress and degradation. And, if a system of private property secures mankind from such evils, which it certainly does, in a great degree, by securing to a portion of the society the leisure necessary for the progress of the arts and sciences, it must be allowed that such a check to the increase of cultivation confers on society a most signal benefit.

But it must perhaps also be allowed, that, under a system of private property, cultivation is sometimes checked in a degree, and at a period, not required by the interest of society. And this is particularly liable to happen when the original divisions of land have been extremely unequal, and the laws have not given sufficient facility to a better distribution of them. Under a system of private property, the only effectual demand for produce must come from the owners of property; and though it be true that the effectual demand of the society, whatever it may be, is best supplied under the most perfect system of liberty, yet it is not true that the tastes and wants of the effective demanders are always, and necessarily, the most favourable to the progress of national wealth. A taste for hunting and the preservation of game among the owners of the soil will, without fail, be supplied, if things be allowed to take their natural course; but such a supply, from the manner in which it must be effected, would inevitably be most unfavourable to the increase of produce and population. In the same manner, the want of an adequate taste for the consumption of manufactured commodities among the possessors of surplus produce, if not fully compensated by a great desire for personal attendance, which it never is, would infallibly occasion a premature slackness in the demand for labour and produce, a premature fall of profits, and a premature check to cultivation.

It makes little difference in the actual rate of the increase of population, or the necessary existence of checks to it, whether that state of demand and supply which occasions an insufficiency of wages to the whole of the labouring classes be produced prematurely by a bad structure of society, and an unfavourable distribution of wealth, or necessarily by the comparative exhaustion of the soil. The labourer feels the difficulty nearly in the same degree, and it must have nearly the same results, from whatever cause it arises. Consequently, in every country with which we are acquainted where the yearly earnings of the labouring classes are not sufficient to bring up in health the largest families, it may be safely said, that population is actually checked by the difficulty of procuring the means of subsistence. And, as we well know that ample wages, combined with full employment for all who choose to work, are extremely rare, and scarcely ever occur except for a certain time when the knowledge and industry of an old country is applied under favourable circumstances to a new one, it follows, that the pressure arising from the difficulty of procuring subsistence is not to be considered as a remote one, which will be felt only when the earth refuses to produce any more, but as one which not only actually exists at present over the greatest part of the globe, but, with few exceptions, has been almost constantly acting upon all the countries of which we have any account.

It is unquestionably true, that in no country of the globe have the government, the distribution of property, and the habits of the people, been such as to call forth, in the most effective manner, the resources of the soil. Consequently, if the most advantageous possible change in all these respects could be supposed at once to take place, it is certain that the demand for labour, and the encouragement to production, might be such as for a short time, in some countries, and for rather a longer time in others, to lessen the operation of the checks to population which have been described. It is specifically this truth constantly obtruding itself upon our attention which is the great source of delusion on this subject, and creates the belief that man could always produce from the soil much more than sufficient to support himself and family. In the actual state of things, this power has perhaps always been possessed. But for it we are indebted wholly to the ignorance and bad government of our ancestors. If they had properly called forth the resources of the soil, it is quite certain that we should now have but scanty means left of further increasing our food. If merely since the time of William the Conqueror [58] all the nations of the earth had been well governed, and if the distribution of property and the habits both of the rich and the poor had been the most favourable to the demand for produce and labour, though the amount of food and population would have been prodigiously greater than at present, the means of diminishing the checks to population would unquestionably be less. That difficulty in procuring the necessaries of life which is now felt in the comparatively low wages of labour almost all over the world, and is occasioned partly by the necessary state of the soil, and partly by a premature check to the demand for produce and labour, would then be felt in a greater degree, and would less admit of any relaxation in the checks to population, because it would be occasioned wholly and necessarily by the state of the soil.

It appears, then, that what may be called the proportionate amount of the necessary checks to population depends very little upon the efforts of man in the cultivation of the soil. If these efforts had been directed from the first in the most enlightened and efficient manner, the checks necessary to keep the population on a level with the means of subsistence, so far from being lightened, would, in all probability, be operating with greater force; and the condition of the labouring classes, so far as it depends on the facility of procuring the means of subsistence, instead of being improved, would, in all probability, be deteriorated.

It is to the laws of nature, therefore, and not to the conduct and institutions of man, that we are to attribute the necessity of a strong check on the natural increase of population.

But, though the laws of nature which determine the rate at which population would increase if unchecked, and the very different rate at which the food required to support population could continue to increase in a limited territory, are undoubtedly the causes which render necessary the existence of some great and constant check to population, yet a vast mass of responsibility remains behind on man and the institutions of society.

In the first place, they are certainly responsible for the present scanty population of the earth. There are few large countries, however advanced in improvement, the population of which might not have been doubled or tripled, and there are many which might be ten, or even a hundred, times as populous, and yet all the inhabitants be as well provided for as they are now, if the institutions of society, and the moral habits of the people, had been for some hundred years the most favourable to the increase of capital, and the demand for produce and labour.

Secondly, though man has but a trifling and temporary influence in altering the proportionate amount of the checks to population, or the degree in which they press upon the actual numbers, yet he has a great and most extensive influence on their character and mode of operation.

It is not in superseding the necessity of checks to population in the progress of mankind to the full peopling of the earth (which may with truth be said to be a physical impossibility), but in directing these checks in such a way as to be the least prejudicial to the virtue and happiness of society, that government and human institutions produce their great effect. Here we know, from constant experience, that they have great power. Yet, even here, it must be allowed, that the power of government is rather indirect than direct, as the object to be attained depends mainly upon such a conduct on the part of individuals as can seldom be directly enforced by laws, though it may be powerfully influenced by them.

This will appear, if we consider more particularly the nature of those checks which have been classed under the general heads of preventive and positive.

It will be found that they are all resolvable into *moral restraint, vice*, and *misery*. And if, from the laws of nature, some check to the increase of population be absolutely inevitable, and human institutions have any influence upon the extent to which each of these checks operates, a heavy responsibility will be incurred, if all that influence, whether direct or indirect, be not exerted to diminish the amount of vice and misery.

Moral restraint, in application to the present subject, may be defined to be, abstinence from marriage, either for a time or permanently, from prudential considerations, with a strictly moral conduct towards the sex in the interval. And this is the only mode of keeping population on a level with the means of subsistence which is perfectly consistent with virtue and happiness. All other checks, whether of the preventive or the positive kind, though they may greatly vary in degree, resolve themselves into some form of vice or misery.

The remaining checks of the preventive kind are: the sort of intercourse which renders some of the women of large towns unprolific; a general corruption of morals with regard to the sex, which has a similar effect; unnatural passions and improper arts to prevent the consequences of irregular connections. These evidently come under the head of vice.

The positive checks to population include all the causes, which tend in any way prematurely to shorten the duration of human life, such as unwholesome occupations; severe labour and exposure to the seasons; bad and insufficient food and clothing arising from poverty; bad nursing of children; excesses of all kinds; great towns and manufactories; the whole train of common diseases and epidemics; wars, infanticide, plague, and famine. Of these positive checks, those which appear to arise from the laws of nature may be called exclusively misery; and those which we bring upon ourselves, such as wars, excesses of all kinds, and many others, which it would be in our power to to avoid, are of a mixed nature. They are brought upon us by vice, and their consequences are misery.

Some of these checks, in various combinations, and operating with various force, are constantly in action in all the countries with which we are acquainted, and form the immediate causes which keep the population on a level with the means of subsistence.

A view of these checks, in most of the countries of which we have the best accounts, was taken in the *Essay on Population*. The object was to trace, in each country, those checks which appeared to be most effective in repressing population; and to endeavour to answer the question, generally, which had been applied, particularly, to New Holland by Captain Cook, namely, 'By what means is the population of this country kept down to the number which it can subsist?'[59]

It was hardly to be expected, however, that the general accounts of countries which are to be met with should contain a sufficient number of details of the kind required to enable us to ascertain what portion of the natural increase of population each individual check which could be traced had the power to overcome. In particular, it was not to be expected, that any accounts could inform us of the degree in which moral restraint prevails, when taken in its strictest sense. It is necessary, therefore, to attend chiefly to the greater or smaller number of persons who remain unmarried, or marry late; and the delay of marriage, owing to the difficulty of providing for a family, when the degree of irregularity to which it may lead cannot be ascertained, may be usefully called the prudential restraint on marriage and population. And this will be found to be the chief mode in which the preventive check practically operates.

But if the preventive check to population – that check which can alone supersede great misery and mortality – operates chiefly by a prudential restraint on marriage; it will be obvious, as was before stated, that direct legislation cannot do much. Prudence cannot be enforced by laws, without a great violation of natural liberty, and a great risk of producing more evil than good. But still, the very great influence of a just and enlightened government, and the perfect security of property in creating habits of prudence, cannot for a moment be questioned. The principal causes and effects of these habits are thus stated in the *Principles of Political Economy Considered, with a View to their Practical Application*, ch. 4, p. 250:[60]

From real high wages, or the power of commanding a large portion of the necessities of life, two very different results may follow; one, that of a rapid increase of population, in which case the high wages are chiefly spent in the maintenance of large and frequent families; and the other, that of a decided improvement in the modes of subsistence, and the conveniences and comforts enjoyed, without a proportionate acceleration in the rate of increase.

In looking to these different results, the causes of them will evidently appear to be the different habits existing among the people of different countries, and at different times. In an inquiry into the causes of these different habits we shall generally be able to trace those which produce the first result to all the circumstances which contribute to depress the lower classes of the people, which make them unable or unwilling to reason from the past to the future, and ready to acquiesce for the sake of present gratification, in a very low standard of comfort and respectability; and those which produce the second result, to all the circumstances which tend to elevate the character of the lower classes of society, which make them approach the nearest to beings who 'look before and after', and who consequently cannot acquiesce patiently in the thought of depriving themselves and their children of the means of being respectable, virtuous, and happy.

Among the circumstances which contribute to the character first described, most efficient will be found to be despotism, oppression, and ignorance; among those which contribute to the latter character, civil and political liberty, and education.

Of all the causes which tend to encourage prudential habits among the lower classes of society the most essential is unquestionably civil liberty. No people can be much accustomed to form plans for the future, who do not feel assured that their industrious exertions, while fair and honourable, will be allowed to have free scope; and that the property which they either possess or may acquire will be secured to them by a known code of just laws impartially administered. But it has been found by experience that civil liberty cannot be permanently secured without political liberty. Consequently, political liberty becomes almost equally essential; and in addition to its being necessary in this point of view, its obvious tendency to teach the lower classes of society to respect themselves, by obliging the higher classes to respect them, must contribute greatly to the good effects of civil liberty.

With regard to education, it certainly might be made general under a bad form of government, and might be very deficient under one in other respects good; but it must be allowed that the chances, both with regard to its quality and its prevalence, are greatly in favour of the latter. Education alone could do little against insecurity of property; but it would powerfully assist all the favourable consequences to be expected from civil and political liberty, which could not indeed be considered as complete without it.

The varying prevalence of these habits, owing to the causes above referred to, combined with the smaller or greater mortality occasioned by other customs, and the varying effect of soil and climate, must necessarily produce great differences in different countries, and at different periods, in the character of the predominant checks to population and the force of each. And this inference, which inevitably follows from theory, is fully confirmed by experience.

It appears, for instance, from the accounts we have received of ancient nations, and of the less civilized parts of the world, that war and violent diseases were the predominant checks to their population. The frequency of wars, and the dreadful devastations of mankind occasioned by them, united with the plagues, famines, and mortal epidemics of which there are records, must have caused such a consumption of the human species that the exertion of the utmost power of increase must, in many cases, have been insufficient to supply it; and we see at once the source of those encouragements to marriage, and efforts to increase population, which, with inconsiderable exceptions, distinguished the legislation and general policy of ancient times. Yet there were some few men of more extended views, who, when they were looking to the settlement of a society in a more improved state, were fully aware, that, under the most beautiful form of government which their imagination could conceive, the greatest poverty and distress might be felt from a too rapid increase of population. And the remedies which they proposed were strong and violent in proportion to the greatness of the evil which they apprehended. Even the practical legislators who encouraged marriage seemed to think that the supplies of children might sometimes follow too rapidly for the means of supporting them; and it appears to have been with a view to provide against this difficulty, and of preventing it from discouraging marriage, that they frequently sanctioned the inhuman practice of infanticide.

Under these circumstances, it is not to be supposed that the prudential restraint on marriage should have operated to any considerable extent. Except in a few cases where a general corruption of morals prevailed, which might act as a preventive check of the most vicious kind, a large portion of the procreative power was called into action, the occasional redundancy from which was checked by violent causes. These causes will be found resolvable almost wholly into vice and misery; the first of which, and a large portion of the second, it is always in the power of man to avoid.

In a review of the checks to population in the different states of modern Europe, it appears that the positive checks to population have prevailed less, and the preventive checks more, than in ancient times, and in the more uncultivated parts of the world. The destruction occasioned by war has unquestionably abated, both on account of its occurring, on the whole, less frequently, and its ravages not being so fatal, either to man or the means of his support, as they were formerly. And although, in the earlier periods of the history of modern Europe, plagues, famines, and mortal epidemics were not infrequent, yet, as civilization and improvement have advanced, both their frequency and their mortality have been greatly reduced, and in some countries they are now almost unknown. This diminution of the positive checks to population, as it has been certainly much greater in proportion than the actual increase of food and population, must necessarily have been accompanied by an increasing operation of the preventive checks; and probably it may be said with truth, that, in almost all the more improved countries of modern Europe, the principal check which at present keeps the population down to the level of the actual means of subsistence is the prudential restraint on marriage.

Yet in comparing together the accounts and registers of the different countries of modern times, we shall still find a vast difference in the character and force of the checks which are mainly in action; and it is precisely in this point of view that these accounts afford the most important instruction. Some parts of Europe are yet in an unimproved state, and are still subject to frequent plagues and mortal epidemics. In these countries, as might be expected, few traces are to be found of the prudential restraint on marriage. But even in improved countries, the circumstances may be such as to occasion a great mortality. Large towns are known to be unfavourable to health, particularly to the health of young children; and the unwholesomeness of marshy situations may be such as in some cases to balance the principle of increase, even when nearly the whole of the procreative power is called into action, which is very seldom the case, in large towns.

Thus in the registers of twenty-two Dutch villages given by Suessmilch, the mortality (occasioned, as may be supposed, chiefly by the natural unhealthiness of the country) was as high as 1 in 22 or 23, instead of the more common proportion of 1 in 35 or 40; and the marriages, instead of being in the more usual proportion to the population of 1 in about 108 or 112, were in the extraordinary high proportion of 1 in 64, shewing a most unusual frequency of marriage, while, on account of the great mortality, the number of inhabitants was nearly stationary, and the births and deaths about equal (*Göttliche Ordnung*, Vol. I, ch. 4, section 57, p. 128. This very large proportion of marriages could not all have been supplied from the births in the country, but must have been occasioned in part by the influx of strangers).

On the other hand, in Norway, where the climate and modes of living seem to be extremely favourably to health, and the mortality was only 1 in 48, the prudential restraint on marriage was called more than usually into action, and the marriages were only 1 in 130 of the population (*Essay on Population*, Vol. I, p. 260, 6th ed.).

These may be considered as extreme cases, but the same results in different degrees are observable in the registers of all countries; and it is particularly to be remarked, that in those countries where registers of births, deaths, and marriages have been kept for a considerable time, the progressive diminution of mortality occasioned by the introduction of habits more favourable to health, and the consequent diminution of plagues and

mortal epidemics, hav been accompanied by a smaller proportion of marriages and births. Suessmilch has given some striking
instances of the gradual diminution in the proportion of the
number of marriages during a part of the last century (*Göttliche
Ordnung*, Vol. I, p. 134, passim).

In the town of Leipsic, in the year 1620, the annual marriages
were to the population as 1 to 82; from the year 1741 to 1756,
they were as 1 to 123.

In Augsburgh, in 1510, the proportion of marriages to the
population was 1 in 86; in 1750 as 1 to 120.

In Dantzic, in the year 1705, the proportion was as 1 to 89;
in 1745 as 1 to 118.

In the Dukedom of Magdeburgh, in 1700, the proportion
was as 1 to 87; from 1752 to 1755, as 1 to 125.

In the principality of Halberstadt, in 1690, the proportion
was as 1 to 88; in 1756 as 1 to 122.

In the Dukedom of Cleves, in 1705, the proportion was 1 to
83; in 1755, 1 to 100.

In the Churmark of Brandenburgh, in 1700, the proportion
was 1 to 76; in 1755, 1 to 108.

(Some of these high proportions of marriages could not have
taken place except under a shorter duration of human life, and
a great proportion of second and third marriages, which have
always a most powerful effect. In all considerable towns, also,
the inhabitants of the neighbouring country increase the lists
of marriages.)

Instances of this kind are numerous, and they tend to shew
the dependence of the marriages on the deaths in all old
countries. A greater mortality almost invariably produces a
greater number of early marriages; and it must be equally certain, that, except where the means of subsistence can be adequately increased, a greater proportion of early marriages must
occasion a greater mortality.

The proportion of yearly births to the whole population
must evidently depend principally on the proportion of marriages and the age at which they are contracted; and it appears,
consequently, from registers, that in countries which will not
admit of any considerable increase of population, the births and

marriages are mainly influenced by the deaths. When an actual decrease of population is not taking place, the births will always supply the vacancies made by death, and exactly so much more as the increasing wealth of the country and the demand for labour will admit. Everywhere in the intervals of plagues, epidemics, and destructive wars, the births considerably exceed the deaths; but while from these and other causes the mortality in different countries is extremely various, it appears from registers that, with the allowance above stated, the births vary in the same proportion. (Suessmilch, *Göttliche Ordnung*, Vol. I, p. 225; *Essay on Population*, Vol. I, p. 331, 6th ed.)

Thus, in thirty-nine villages of Holland, where the deaths, at the time to which the registers refer, were about 1 in 23, the births were also 1 in 23. In fifteen villages round Paris, the births bore the same or even a greater proportion to the whole population, on account of a still greater mortality, the births being 1 in 22·7, and the deaths the same. In the small towns of Brandenburgh, which were in an increasing state, the mortality was 1 in 29, and the births 1 in 24·7. In Sweden, where the mortality was about 1 in 34·5, the births were 1 in 28. In 1,056 villages of Brandenburgh, in which the mortality was about 1 in 39 or 40, the births were about 1 in 30. In Norway, where the mortality was 1 in 48, the births were 1 in 34.

Of all the countries reviewed in the *Essay on Population*, there is none which so strikingly illustrates the most important fact of the dependence of the proportions of marriages and births on the deaths, and the general principles of population, as Switzerland. It appears that between 1760 and 1770 an alarm prevailed respecting the continued depopulation of the country; and to ascertain the point, M. Muret, minister of Vevay, made a very laborious and careful search into the registers of different parishes, from the time of their first establishment. He compared the number of births which had taken place during three different periods of seventy years each, the first ending in 1620, the second in 1690, and the third in 1760. And finding by this comparison that the number of births was less in the second period than in the first, and less in the third period than in the second, he considered the evidence of a continued depopulation of the country from the year 1550 as incontrovertible. (*Mémoires, etc.*, Société Économique de Berne, 1776, p. 15 passim; *Essay on Population*, Vol. I, p. 338 passim, 6th ed.) But the accounts which he himself produces clearly shew that, in the earlier periods to which he refers, the mortality was very much greater than in the latter; and, that the greater *number* of births found in the registers formerly was not owing to a greater population, but to the greater *proportion* of births which almost always accompanies a greater mortality.

It appears from accounts, which are entirely to be depended on, that during the last period, the mortality was extraordinarily small, and the proportion of children reared from infancy to puberty extraordinarily great. At the time when M. Muret wrote his paper, in 1766, the proportion of deaths to the population in the Pays de Vaud was 1 in 45, of births 1 in 36, and of marriages 1 in 140. These are all very small proportions of births, deaths, and marriages, compared with other countries; but the state of things must have been totally different in the sixteenth and seventeenth centuries. M. Muret gives a list of all the plagues which had prevailed in Switzerland from 1520, from which it appears that this dreadful scourge desolated the country at short intervals during the whole of the first period, and extended its occasional ravages to within twenty-two years of the termination of the second. We may safely conclude, that in these times, the average mortality was very much greater than at present. But what puts the question beyond a doubt is the great mortality which prevailed in the neighbouring town of Geneva in the sixteenth century, and its gradual diminution in the seventeenth and eighteenth. It appears from calculations, (published in the *Bibliothèque Britannique*, Vol. IV, p. 328), that in the sixteenth century, the probability of life, or the age to which half of the born lived, was only 4·883, or under four years and eleven months; and the mean life, or the average number of years due to each person 18·511, or about eighteen years and a half. In the seventeenth century, the probability of life in Geneva was 11·607, about eleven years and seven months; the mean life 23·358, or twenty-three years and four months. In the eighteenth century, the probability of life had increased to 27·183, twenty-seven years and two months; and the mean life to thirty-two years and two months.

There can be no doubt, from the prevalence of the plague, and its gradual extinction as noticed by M. Muret, that a diminution of mortality of the same kind, though not perhaps to the same extent, must have taken place in Switzerland; but if with a mortality which could not have been less than 1 in 30 or 32 the proportion of births had been what it was when M. Muret wrote, it is quite evident that the country would have been rapidly depopulated. But as it is known, from the actual amount of births found in the registers, that this was not the case, it follows as a necessary consequence, that the greater mortality of former times was accompanied by a greater proportion of births. And this at once shews the error of attempting to determine the actual population, either of different countries, or of different periods in the same country, by the amount of the births; and the strong tendency of population to fill up all vacancies, and very rarely to be limited by any other cause than the difficulty of supporting a family.

Switzerland and the Pays de Vaud afford other most striking instances of the dependence of the births on the deaths; and the accounts of them are perhaps more to be depended upon, as they appear to contradict the preconceived opinions of the person who collected them.

Speaking of the want of fruitfulness in the Swiss women, M. Muret says, that Prussia, Brandenburgh, Sweden, France, and indeed every country the registers of which he had seen, give a greater proportion of baptisms to the number of inhabitants than the Pays de Vaud, where this proportion is only as 1 to 36. He adds, that from calculations lately made in the Lyonois, it appeared that in Lyons itself the proportion of baptisms was 1 in 28, in the small towns 1 in 25, and in the villages 1 in 23 or 24. What a prodigious difference, he exclaims, between the Lyonois and the Pays de Vaud, where the most favourable proportion, and that only in two small parishes of extraordinary fecundity, is not above 1 in 26, and in many parishes it is considerably less than 1 in 40. The same difference, he remarks, takes place in the mean life. In the Lyonois it is little above twenty-five years; while in the Pays de Vaud, the lowest mean life, and that only in a single marshy and unhealthy parish, is 29.5 years, and in many places it is above forty-five years. He says (*Mémoires, etc.*, Société Économique de Berne, 1766, p. 48 passim):

But whence comes it, that the country where children escape the best from the dangers of infancy, and where the mean life, in whatever way the calculation is made, is higher than in any other, should be precisely that in which the fecundity is the smallest? How comes it again, that of all our parishes, the one which gives the mean life highest should also be the one where the tendency to increase is the smallest?

To resolve this question, M. Muret says:

I will hazard a conjecture, which, however, I give only as such. Is it not that, in order to maintain in all places a proper equilibrium of population, God has wisely ordered things in such a manner as that the force of life in each country should be in the inverse ratio of its fecundity? In fact, experience verifies my conjecture. Leyzin (a village in the Alps), with a population of 400 persons, produces but a little above eight children a year. The Pays de Vaud, in general, in proportion to the same number of inhabitants, produces 11, and the Lyonois 16. But if it happen that at the age of twenty years, the 8, the 11, and the 16 are reduced to the same number, it will appear that the force of life gives in one place what fecundity does in another. And thus the most healthy countries, having less fecundity, will not over-people themselves, and the unhealthy countries, by their extraordinary fecundity, will be able to sustain their population.

These facts and observations are full of the most important instruction, and strikingly illustrate the principle of population. The three gradations in the proportion of births which are here so distinctly presented to our view may be considered as representing that variety in the proportion of births which is known to take place in different countries, and at different periods; and the practical question is, whether, when this variety prevails without a proportionate difference in the rate of increase, which is almost universally the case, we are to suppose, with M.

Muret, that a special providence is called into action to render women less prolific in healthy countries, and where improved habits of cleanliness have banished plagues and mortal epidemics; or to suppose, as experience warrants, that the smaller mortality of healthy and improved countries is balanced by the greater prevalence of the prudential restraint on marriage and population.

The subject is seen with particular clearness in Switzerland, on account of the population of some of the districts being stationary. The number of inhabitants on the Alps was supposed to have diminished. This was probably an error; but it is not improbable that they should have remained stationary, or nearly so. There is no land so little capable of providing for an increasing population as mountainous pastures. When they have been once fully stocked with cattle, little more can be done; and if there be neither emigration to take off the superabundant numbers, nor manufacturers wherewith to purchase an additional quantity of food, the deaths must equal the births.

This was the case with the Alpine parish of Leyzin before referred to, where, for a period of thirty years, the mortality and the proportion of births almost accurately kept pace with each other; and where, in consequence, if the positive checks to population had been unusually small, the preventive checks must have been unusually great. In the parish of Leyzin, according to M. Muret, the probability of life was as high as sixty-one years (*Mémoires, etc.*, Société Économique de Berne, 1766, Table V, p. 65 of the Tables); but it is obvious that this extraordinary degree of healthiness could not *possibly* have taken place under the actual circumstances of the parish with respect to the means of subsistence, if it had not been accompanied by a proportionate action of the prudential restraint on marriage; and, accordingly, the births were only 1 in 49, and the number of persons below sixteen was only one in four of the population.

There can be little doubt that in this case the extreme healthiness of the people, arising from their situation and employments, had more effect on producing the prudential check to population than the prudential check in producing the extreme healthiness; yet it is quite certain that they must constantly act and react upon each other, and that if, when the circumstances are such as to furnish no adequate means for the support of an increased population, and no relief in emigration, the prudential check does not prevail, no degree of natural healthiness could prevent an excessive mortality. Yet to occasion such a mortality, a much greater degree of poverty and misery must have taken place than in districts less favourably circumstanced with regard to health; and we see at once the reason why, in countries of mountainous pasture, if there be no vent in emigration, the necessity of the prudential check should be more strongly forced on the attention of the inhabitants, and should, in consequence, prevail to a greater degree.

Taking countries in general, there will necessarily be differences as to natural healthiness in all the gradations, from the most marshy habitable situations to the most pure and salubrious air. These differences will be further increased by the nature of the employments of the people, their habits of cleanliness, and their care in preventing the spread of epidemics. If in no country was there any difficulty in obtaining the means of subsistence, these different degrees of healthiness would make a great difference in the progress of population; and as there are many countries naturally more healthy than the United States of America, we should have instances of a more rapid increase than that which has there taken place. But as the actual progress of population is, with very few exceptions, determined by the relative difficulty of procuring the means of subsistence, and not by the relative natural powers of increase, it is found by experience that, except in extreme cases, the actual progress of population is little affected by unhealthiness or healthiness, but that these circumstances shew themselves most powerfully in the character of the checks which keep the population down to the level of the means of subsistence, and occasion that sort of variety in the registers of different countries which was noticed in the instances mentioned by M. Muret.

The immediate cause of the increase of population is the excess of the births above the deaths; and the rate of increase, or the period of doubling, depends upon the proportion which the excess of the births above the deaths bears to the population.

The excess of births is occasioned by, and proportioned to, three causes; first, the prolificness of the marriages; second, the proportion of the born which lives to marry; and, third, the earliness of these marriages compared with the expectation of life, or the shortness of a generation by marriage and birth, compared with the passing away of a generation by death.

In order that the full power of increase should be called into action, all these circumstances must be favourable. The marriages must be prolific, owing to their being contracted early; the proportion of the born living to marry must be great, owing both to the tendency to marriage, and the great proportion of births rising to the age of puberty; and the interval between the average age of marriage and the average age of death must be considerable, owing to the great healthiness of the country, and the expectation of life being high. (By 'early' is not meant a premature age; but if women marry at nineteen or twenty, there cannot be a doubt that, on an average, they will have a greater number of births than if they had married at twenty-eight or thirty.) Probably these three causes, each operating with the greatest known force, have never yet been found combined. Even in the United States, though the two first causes operate very powerfully, the expectation of life, and, consequently, the distance between the age of marriage and the average age of death, is not so favourable as it might be. In general, however, the excess of births which each country can admit being very far short of the full power of increase, the causes above mentioned contribute to the required supply in very various proportions, according to the different circumstances and habits of each state.

One of the most interesting and useful points of view in which registers can be considered is in the proofs which they afford of the varying prevalence of the prudential check to marriage and population in different countries and places. It has been not an uncommon opinion, and has even been strongly expressed of late years, although the subject has been much better understood than formerly, that the labouring classes of people, under the circumstances in which they are placed, cannot reasonably be expected to attend to prudential considerations in entering upon the marriage state. But that this opinion does them great injustice is not only obvious to common observation, by which we can scarcely fail to see that numbers delay marriage beyond the period when the passions most strongly prompt to it, but it is proved by the registers of different countries, which clearly shew, either that a considerable number of persons of a marriageable age never marry, or that they marry comparatively late, and that their marriages are consequently less prolific than if they had married earlier. As the prudential restraint on marriage may take place in either of these ways, it may prevail nearly in the same degree with a different proportion of marriages to the whole population; and further, with the same proportion of marriages there may be a very different proportion of births and rate of increase. But on the supposition of the same natural prolificness in the women of most countries, the smallness of the proportion of births will generally indicate with tolerable correctness the degree in which the prudential check to population prevails, whether arising principally from late and consequently unprolific marriages, or from a large proportion of the population dying unmarried.) It is impossible to form any judgement of the natural prolificness of women in different countries from the proportion of births to marriages in their registers, because those proportions are always prodigiously affected by the rate of increase, the number of second and third marriages, and the proportion of *late* marriages. The registers of a country might mark four births to a marriage, and yet the women, who in country situations marry at twenty, might have on an average seven or eight births.)

We must refer, then, to the different proportions of births in different countries as the best criterion of the different degrees in which the prudential restraint on marriage operates. These proportions vary from about 1 in 36 to about 1 in 19, or even 17, in different countries, and in a much greater degree in different parishes or districts.

A particular parish in the Alps has already been mentioned, where the births were only a forty-ninth part of the population; and it appears by the late returns of the parish registers of England and Wales, that the births in the county of Monmouth are only 1 in 47, and in Brecon, 1 in 53; which, after making ample allowance for omissions, would shew the prevalence of the prudential restraint on marriage in a high degree.

If in any country all were to marry at twenty or twenty-one, the proportion of the births would probably be more than 1 in 19; and this result would be still more certain if the resources of the country could not support an accelerated rate of increase, than if the means of subsistence were in the greatest abundance, and the demand for labour as effectual as it has ever been in the United States. On the latter supposition, taking the births at one-nineteenth, and the expectation of life the same as it is in England, the effect would be to occasion a most rapid increase of population; and the period of doubling, instead of being about forty-six or forty-eight years, would be less than in America. On the other hand, if the resources of the country could not support a more rapid increase than that which has taken place in England and Wales during the ten years previous to the census of 1821, the effect would be a great diminution in the expectation of life. If the births were 1 in 19, instead of 1 in 30, the same rate of increase would take place as at present, if the annual mortality were increased to about 1 in 26.5; and in that case, the expectation of life would be reduced in the proportion of from 41, or, as is more probable, from above 45 to less than 26. (This may be presumed from the small annual mortality in this country during the ten years from 1810 to 1820). This is the kind of effect which must inevitably follow the absence of the prudential check to marriage and population; and it cannot be doubted that a considerable part of the premature mortality which is found to take place in all parts of the world is occasioned by it. The laws of nature, in application to man as a reasonable being, show no tendency to destroy half of the human race under the age of puberty. This is only done in very particular situations, or when the constant admonitions which these laws give to mankind are obstinately neglected.

It has been said, that a tendency in mankind to increase at such a rate as would double the population in twenty-five years, and, if it had full scope, would fill the habitable globe with people in a comparatively short period, cannot be the law of nature, as the very different rate of increase which is actually found to take place must imply such an excessive degree of mortality and destruction of life as to be quite irreconcileable with actual facts and appearances. But the peculiar advantage of a law of increase in a geometrical progression is, that though its power be absolutely immense, if it be left unchecked, yet, when this becomes impossible, it may be restrained by a comparatively moderate force. It can never, of course, happen, that any considerable part of that prodigious increase which might be produced by an uninterrupted geometrical progression should exist, and then be destroyed. The laws of nature which make food necessary to the life of man, as well as of plants and animals, prevent the continued existence of an excess which cannot be supported, and thus either discourage the production of such an excess, or destroy it in the bud, in such a way as to make it scarcely perceptible to a careless observer. It has been seen, that, in some countries of Europe, where the actual progress of the population is slower than in many others, as in Switzerland and Norway, for instance, the mortality is considerably less. Here, then, the necessity of a greater check to the natural progress of population produces no increase of mortality. And it appears, further, that even the degree of mortality which in each year would be sufficient to destroy that excess of births which would naturally be produced if all married young, and all could be supported, might take place, and often does take place in particular situations, and yet is very little noticed. About the middle of last century, the mortality of Stockholm and London was about 1 in 20. This is a degree of mortality which would probably keep the births on a level with the deaths, even though all married at twenty. And yet numbers resorted both to Stockholm and London from choice; the greater part probably not aware that, by so doing, they would shorten their own lives and those of their children; and the rest thinking that the difference was not worth attending to, or was at least balanced by the advantages of society and employment which the town presented. There is nothing, therefore, in the actual state of the mortality observed to take place in different countries and situations which, in the slightest degree, contradicts the supposition of a natural tendency to increase quite as great as that which has been stated.

It has been further remarked, that as, in point of fact, it very rarely happens that mankind continues to increase in a geometrical progression of any kind, and only in a single instance in such a one as to double the population in twenty-five years, it is useless and absurd to lay any stress upon *tendencies* which never, for any length of time together, produce their natural effects. But it might really as well be said, that we are not to estimate the natural rate of increase in wheat or sheep, as it is quite certain that their natural tendency to increase has never practically continued to develop itself for so long a time together as that of mankind. Both as a physical, and even economical, question, it is curious and desirable to know the natural law of increase which prevails among the most important plants and animals. In the same view, it must be still more interesting to know the natural law of increase with respect to man. It may be said, indeed, with truth, that the actual appearances all around us – the varying rate of increase in different countries, its very slow progress, or stationary state in some, and its very rapid progress in others – must be a mass of anomalies, and quite contrary to the analogies of all the rest of animated nature, if the natural tendency of mankind to increase be not, at the least, as great as that which is developed under the most favourable circumstances, while in all others it is kept down by the varying difficulties which the state of the soil and other obstacles oppose to it. But the question, as it applies to man, assumes at once a tenfold importance, in reference to the moral and political effects which must result from those checks to increase, the existence and operation of which, in some form or other, no human exertions can by possibility prevent. A field is here opened for the most interesting inquiries which can engage the friends of human happiness.

But, as a preliminary to these inquiries, it is obvious that we must know the degree of force to be overcome, and the varying character of the checks which, in the different countries of the world, are practically found to overcome it; and, for this purpose, the first step must be an endeavour to ascertain the natural law of population, or the rate at which mankind would increase under the fewest known obstacles. Nor can this tendency to increase ever safely be lost sight of in the subsequent inquiries, which have for their object the improvement of the moral condition of man in society.

The existence of a tendency in mankind to increase, if unchecked, beyond the possibility of an adequate supply of food in a limited territory, must at once determine the question as to the natural right of the poor to full support in a state of society where the law of property is recognized. The question, therefore, resolves itself chiefly into a question relating to the necessity of those laws which establish and protect private property. It has been usual to consider the right of the strongest as the law of nature among mankind as well as among brutes; yet, in so doing, we at once give up the peculiar and distinctive superiority of man as reasonable being, and class him with the beasts of the field. In the same language, it may be said, that the cultivation of the earth is not natural to man. It certainly is not to man, considered merely as an animal without reason. But, to a reasonable being, able to look forward to consequences, the laws of nature dictate the cultivation of the earth, both as the means of affording better support to the individual, and of increasing the supplies required for increasing numbers: the dictates of those laws of nature being thus evidently calculated to promote the general good, and increase the mass of human happiness. It is precisely in the same way, and in order to attain the same object, that the laws of nature dictate to man the establishment of property, and the absolute necessity of some power in the society capable of protecting it. So strongly have the laws of nature spoken this language to mankind, and so fully has the force of it been felt, that nothing seems to be thought so absolutely intolerable to reasonable beings as the prevalence in the same society of the right of the strongest; and the history of all ages shows, that if men see no other way of putting an end to it than by establishing arbitrary power in an individual, there is scarcely any degree of tyranny, oppression, and cruelty, which they will not submit to from some single person and his satellites, rather than be at the mercy of the first stronger man who may wish to possess himself of the fruit of their labour. The consequence of this universal and deeply-seated feeling, inevitably produced by the laws of nature, as applied to reasonable beings, is, that the almost certain consequence of anarchy is despotism.

Allowing, then, distinctly, that the right of property is the creature of positive law, yet this law is so early and so imperiously forced on the attention of mankind, that, if it cannot be called a natural law, it must be considered as the most natural as well as the most necessary of all positive laws; and the foundation of this pre-eminence is its obvious tendency to promote the general good, and the obvious tendency of the absence of it to degrade mankind to the rank of brutes.

As property is the result of positive law, and the ground on which the law which establishes it rests is the promotion of the public good, and the increase of human happiness, it follows, that it may be modified by the same authority by which it was enacted, with a view to the more complete attainment of the objects which it has in view. It may be said, indeed, that every tax for the use of the government, and every county or parish rate, is a modification of this kind. But there is no modification of the law of property, having still for its object the increase of human happiness, which must not be defeated by the concession of a right of full support to all that might be born. It may be safely said, therefore, that the concession of such a right, and a right of property, are absolutely incompatible, and cannot exist together.

To what extent assistance may be given, even by law, to the poorer classes of society when in distress, without defeating the great object of the law of property, is essentially a different question. It depends mainly upon the feelings and habits of the labouring classes of society, and can only be determined by experience. If it be generally considered as so discreditable to receive parochial relief, that great exertions are made to avoid it, and few or none marry with a certain prospect of being obliged to have recourse to it, there is no doubt that those who were really in distress might be adequately assisted, with little danger of a constantly increasing proportion of paupers; and, in that case, a great good would be attained, without any proportionate evil to counterbalance it. But if, from the numbers of the dependent poor, the discredit of receiving relief is so diminished as to be practically disregarded, so that many marry with the almost certain prospect of becoming paupers, and the proportion of their numbers to the whole population is, in consequence, continually increasing, it is certain, that the partial good attained must be much more than counterbalanced by the general deterioration in the condition of the great mass of the society, and the prospect of its daily growing worse: so that, though from the inadequate relief which is in many cases granted, the manner in which it is conceded, and other counteracting causes, the operation of poor laws, such as they exist in England, might be very different from the effects of a full concession of the right, and a complete fulfilment of the duties resulting from it; yet such a state of things ought to give the most serious alarm to every friend to the happiness of society, and every effort consistent with justice and humanity ought to be made to remedy it. But whatever steps may be taken on this subject, it will be allowed that, with any prospect of legislating for the poor with success, it is necessary to be fully aware of the natural tendency of the labouring classes of society to increase beyond the demand for their labour, or the means of their adequate support, and the effect of this tendency to throw the greatest difficulties in the way of permanently improving their condition. (The grand objection to the language used respecting the 'right of the poor to support' is, that, as a matter of fact, we do not perform what we promise, and the poor may justly accuse us of deceiving them.)

It would lead far beyond the limits which must be prescribed to this summary, to notice the various objections which have been made by different writers to the principles which have been here explained. Those which contain in them the slightest degree of plausibility have been answered in the late editions of the *Essay on Population*, particularly in the Appendix to the fifth and sixth, to which we refer the reader. In the answer to Mr Arthur Young,[61] the question of giving land to cottagers is discussed; and it is a curious fact that, after proposing a plan of this kind, Mr Young is obliged to own, 'that it might be

prudent to consider the misery to which the progressive population might be subject, as an evil which it is absolutely and
physically impossible to prevent.' The whole of the difficulty, in
fact, lies here. The grand distinction between colonies in England and Ireland, and colonies in Canada, is, that in the one
case there will be no demand for the progressive population
from the colonists, and the redundancy of labour after a short
time will be aggravated; in the other, the demand will be great
and certain for a long time, and the redundancy in the emigrat-
ing countries essentially relieved. The answer to Mr Weyland,[62]
in the Appendix, contains much that is applicable to present
objections. We will only, therefore, further notice the objection
which has been made by some persons on religious grounds;
for, as it is certainly of great importance that the answer which
has been given to it should be kept in mind, we cannot refuse
a place to a condensed statement of it at the end of this summary.

It has been thought, that a tendency in mankind to increase
beyond the greatest possible increase of food which could be
produced in a limited space, impeaches the goodness of the
Deity, and is inconsistent with the letter and spirit of the scriptures. If this objection were well founded, it would certainly be
the most serious one which has been brought forward; but the
answer to it appears to be quite satisfactory, and it may be com-
pressed into a very small compass.

First, it appears that the evils arising from the principle of
population are exactly of the same kind as the evils arising from
the excessive or irregular gratification of the human passions in
general, and may equally be avoided by moral restraint. Consequently, there can be no more reason to conclude, from the
existence of these evils, that the principle of increase is too strong,
than to conclude, from the existence of the vices arising from the
human passions, that these passions are all too strong, and require diminution or extinction, instead of regulation and
direction.

Second, it is almost universally acknowledged that both the
letter and spirit of revelation represent this world as a state of
moral discipline and probation. But a state of moral discipline

and probation cannot be a state of unmixed happiness, as it necessarily implies difficulties to be overcome, and temptations to be resisted. Now, in the whole range of the laws of nature, not one can be pointed out which so especially accords with this scriptural view of the state of man on earth, as it gives rise to a greater variety of situations and exertions than any other, and marks, in a more general and stronger manner, and nationally as well as individually, the different effects of virtue and vice, – of the proper government of the passions, and the culpable indulgence of them. It follows, then, that the principle of population, instead of being inconsistent with revelation, must be considered as affording strong additional proofs of its truth.

Last, it will be acknowledged that in a state of probation, those laws seem best to accord with the views of a benevolent Creator which, while they furnish the difficulties and temptations which form the essence of such a state, are of such a nature as to reward those who overcome them, with happiness in this life as well as in the next. But the law of population answers particularly to this description. Each individual has, to a great degree, the power of avoiding the evil consequences to himself and society resulting from it, by the practice of a virtue dictated to him by the light of nature, and sanctioned by revealed religion. And, as there can be no question that this virtue tends greatly to improve the condition, and increase the comforts, both of the individuals who practise it, and, through them, of the whole society, the ways of God to man with regard to this great law are completely vindicated.

EDITOR'S NOTES ON THE *FIRST ESSAY*
AND THE *SUMMARY*

(1) DAVID HUME (1711–76) was the great Scottish philosopher and historian. But Malthus is here thinking of him as the author not of *A Treatise of Human Nature* (1739–40) or of *A History of England* (1754–61) but rather of the *Political Discourses* (1752). These included several important contributions to political economy which have recently been collected, along with relevant extracts from Hume's correspondence with Montesquieu, Turgot, and Adam Smith, by E. Rotwein as *David Hume: Writings on Economics*, Nelson, 1955. Hume's essay 'Of the Populousness of Ancient Nations', first published in 1752 as one of these *Political Discourses*, was a landmark in demographic studies, since in it Hume was the first writer to question effectively the traditional assumption of the greater populousness of the ancient as compared with the modern world.

ADAM SMITH (1723–90) is famous chiefly as the author of *An Inquiry into the Nature and Causes of the Wealth of Nations*, published in the year of Hume's death. But Adam Smith was for many years Professor of Moral Philosophy in the University of Glasgow, and in 1759 had published two volumes on *The Theory of Moral Sentiments*. He was also a personal friend of Hume. He deliberately courted the disfavour of the orthodox in 1777 by putting out an account of Hume's last illness and death in which he paid tribute to Hume's character. The scandal in this case was that Hume – faithful to the family motto 'True to the end' – continued unshaken in his fearless assurance of mortality. This constancy disappointed among others James Boswell, who visited the sickbed in hopes of being able to report to Dr Johnson something more agreeable to their shared assumptions.

ROBERT WALLACE (1697–1771) was yet another Scot, but this time a Minister of the Kirk. His main publications were *A Dissertation on the Numbers of Mankind in Ancient and Modern Times* (1753), *Characteristics of the Present State of Great Britain* (1758), and *Various Prospects of Mankind, Nature and Providence* (1761). Wallace showed Hume a draft of the first of these in the summer of 1751, and Hume reciprocated this respectful courtesy by showing Wallace the manuscript of his own essay 'Of the Populousness of Ancient Nations'.

(2) The reference is to Adam and Eve in Milton's epic poem:

> The world was all before them, where to choose
> Their place of rest, and Providence their guide:
> They hand in hand with wandering steps and slow
> Through Eden took their solitary way.

Paradise Lost, Bk XII, lines 646–9.

(3) ALARIC, King of the Visigoths, died in A.D. 410. In 401 he had led his armies into northern Italy, driving the Roman Emperor Honorius from Milan to Ravenna. In 409 he besieged Rome; in 410 he besieged it again, after which his men enjoyed three days of rape and pillage. Augustine's *City of God* was written in part as an attempt to answer the charge that these Roman disasters were consequences of the conversion of the Empire to Christianity.

ATTILA (*c.* 406–53), King of the Huns, led several invasions of the Eastern Roman Empire between 440 and 450, and succeeded in extracting tribute from the Emperor Theodosius. In 451 he turned his attentions to the West, but suffered a setback at Orleans. These achievements earned him the title *flagellum Dei*, 'The Scourge of God'.

ZINGIS KHAN is Genghis Khan (1162–1227), King of the Mongols. He conquered central Asia, and armies commanded by his lieutenants reached as far as the shores of the Adriatic.

(4) JULIUS CAESAR (100–44 B.C.) led the armies which conquered Gaul – the modern France – for Rome. By the time of his assassination he had become in effect the first Roman Emperor, though the Imperial period is usually counted as beginning with the reign of his natural great-nephew and adopted son Augustus.

(5) WILLIAM PITT (1759–1806) was Prime Minister at the time of the publication of the *First Essay*. This is the younger Pitt, son of the great Earl of Chatham. Pitt became Chancellor of the Exchequer at the age of twenty-three and Prime Minister before he had turned twenty-five. It was this administration which recognized the United States of America and ended the War of Independence. Later and until his death he was the leader of British resistance to the expansion of Revolutionary and Napoleonic France. He was, as this and other references in Malthus suggest, by no means the all-black domestic reactionary which spokesmen for the export of the French Revolution presented him as being. It was, for instance, during one of his adminis-

trations that public executions were abolished and Roman Catholics were admitted to commissions in the Army and to the Bar; he attempted to pass a Bill for the reform of Parliamentary suffrage; and in 1801 he resigned on the issue of his failure to secure a further measure of Roman Catholic emancipation.

(6) This is ADMIRAL ANTONIO DE ULLOA, the author of a work translated into English by J. Adams, and first published in London in 1758, as *A Voyage to South America*.

(7) MONTEZUMA (1466–1520) was the King of the Aztecs at the time of the Spanish Conquest. He was killed in an affray which occurred while he was a captive of Cortes and his conquistadors.

(8) RICHARD PRICE (1723–91) was a Welsh dissenting minister. He is a considerable figure in the history of moral philosophy by virtue of his *Review of the Principal Questions and Difficulties in Morals* (1758). In this book he took issue with Hume. Price's commendable controversial manners were well expressed in his later statement to Hume: 'I am not, I hope, inclined to dislike any person merely for a difference in opinion, however great; or to connect worth of character and God's favour with any particular set of sentiments.' See E. C. Mossner, *The Life of David Hume*, Nelson, 1954, p. 394.

The reference here is to Price's *Observations on Reversionary Payments*. This was first published in 1771 and not, as incorrectly stated in the *Dictionary of National Biography*, in 1769. But the same source has the authority of later editions by Price himself for calling it a *Treatise* and not *Observations*. Price was, like Hume, sympathetic to the American Revolution. In 1776 he published some *Observations on the Nature of Civil Liberty, the Principles of Government and the Justice and Policy of the War with America*. In 1780 he produced an *Essay on the Population of England from the Revolution to the Present Time*, and in 1787 a presentation of *Evidence for a Future Period in the State of Mankind, with the Means and Duty of Promoting it*.

Price has a further claim to fame in that two of his public addresses helped to provoke the classic *Reflections* of Edmund Burke. Their full title is *Reflections on the Revolution in France and on the Proceedings in Certain Societies in London Relative to that Event, in a Letter Intended to have been sent to a Gentleman in Paris*. The central part of these proceedings was the address given on 4 November 1789 by 'Doctor Price, non-conforming minister of eminence ... at the dissenting meeting house of the Old Jewry', after which the speaker himself moved a resolution for transmission to the French National Assembly.

The pamphlet which Malthus here confesses to not having was a *Discourse on the Christian Union*, published in 1761 by Dr Ezra Styles. In a letter of 4 February 1799 Malthus includes this in a list of works which he would like to acquire, adding that it is 'hard to get'. It is indeed, for the British Museum has no copy.

(9) LOUIS XIV (1638–1715) was King of France from the age of five until his death. Whether or not he did actually say 'L'État, c'est moi' (I am the State), the famous phrase does epitomize his policies and attitudes. It was he who in 1685 revoked the Edict of Nantes, by which a measure of toleration had been accorded the French Protestants. The ravages mentioned here occurred in the course of a series of wars against coalitions organized first by Holland and later by Britain.

(10) 'Indostan', like 'Hindustan', is an obsolete word for the Indian sub-continent.

(11) The Lisbon earthquake occurred on All Saints' Day, 1755. The dimensions of this catastrophe shocked all Europe, and made it one of the major ideological talking-points of the period. Thus the Portuguese Jesuits immediately interpreted the earthquake as salutary Divine retribution for the people's sins, while sceptics pointed to it as an impossible difficulty for theodicy. (It features in *Candide* as part of Voltaire's satirical challenge to the central paradox of the *Theodicy* of Leibniz, that if God is omnipotent and good then all must be for the best in this best of all possible worlds.) The Lima earthquake of 28 October 1746 achieved no comparable literary fame.

(12) The reference is to *Die Göttliche Ordnung in den Veränderungen des Menschlichen Geschlechts, aus der Geburt, dem Tode und der Fortplantzung Desselben Erwiesen* by J. P. Suessmilch. The third edition was published in Berlin in 1765. I take all this information from the Catalogue of the British Museum Library, and I have systematized the rather erratic spellings of Malthus accordingly. This was another of the books which he listed in the letter mentioned in Note 8, above. He wanted a translation: 'If it should be in German, it will be of no use to me.'

(13) THOMAS SHORT (*c.* 1690–1772) was a Scottish doctor of medicine. He published *A Rational Discourse on the Inward Uses of Water* in 1725 and *A Dissertation on Tea* in 1730, but his contributions to population studies are *New Observations on the Bills of Mortality* in 1750 and *A Comparative History of the Increase and Decrease of Mankind* in 1767.

(14) ELIZABETH I (1533–1603) succeeded to the throne on the death of her half-sister Mary Tudor. The latter by conscientiously murderous persecutions earned from those who did not share her religious convictions the apt traditional epithet 'Bloody'. The accession of the Protestant Elizabeth was hailed immediately as the beginning of a new era, and it continued to be celebrated as such long after her death.

(15) GREGORY KING (1648–1712) was a genealogist, engraver, and statistician. He was also responsible for laying out part of what is now Soho. Soho Square was formerly King's Square; while the name 'Greek Street', it has been suggested, derives from an original 'Greg Street'. The reference here is presumably to King's *A Scheme of the Rates and Duties Granted to his Majesty upon Marriages, Births, and Burials, and upon Bachelors and Widowers for the Term of Five Years from May 1st 1695*. This was published in 1695 as a folio volume, and the five years were counted backwards. Since I have not succeeded in getting a sight of this work I cannot say for certain whether the date 1693 given in the text is incorrect. King also wrote *Natural and Political Observations and Conclusions upon the State and Condition of England 1696*. But these seem not to have been published until just after the *First Essay*.

(16) 'Gentoo' is a now obsolete Anglo-Indian word for 'a pagan inhabitant of Hindustan'. It covered all Hindus but excluded Muslims.

(17) Precisely this happened not in England but in Ireland, with ultimately catastrophic results. See C. Woodham-Smith, *The Great Hunger*, H. Hamilton, 1962. Roman Catholic Ireland reacted to the trauma of its terrible potato famine in the middle forties of the last century in two ways, both of which the Malthus of the *Second Essay* must have approved: first, by exploiting the unusual opportunities of emigration to all the other English-speaking countries; and, second, by practising on an heroic scale moral restraint in the strict technical

sense. One result has been that for generations that part of Ireland has combined an outstandingly high average age of marriage and an outstandingly low marriage rate with apparently almost unrestricted fertility within these relatively late and few marriages. It is wryly appropriate that the Catholic General Editor of the Everyman Library chose a philoprogenitive fellow Catholic, himself of Irish origin, to edit their new edition of the *Second Essay*, edited by M. P. Fogarty, Dent and Dutton, 1958.

(18) The allusion is to one of Shakespeare's less familiar history plays:

> This is the state of man: today he puts forth
> The tender leaves of hope; tomorrow blossoms,
> And bears his blushing honours thick upon him;
> The third day comes a frost, a killing frost . . .

Henry VIII, III, ii, 15–18.

(19) The well-schooled Malthus was certainly aware that Sir Isaac Newton (1642–1727) intended the *Principia* to constitute, among other things, a decisive counterblast against the programme for science proposed by the French philosopher and scientist René Descartes (1596–1650). Descartes was seen as a spokesman for rationalism, in a technical philosophical sense of the word. A rationalist in this sense is defined as one who holds that there are self-evident and non-tautological truths from which we can deduce substantial conclusions about the way things have been, are, and will be. The opposite here is a philosophical empiricist. He denies this rationalist claim, and urges that it is only through experience that we can acquire knowledge of the universe around us.

So we find Descartes in his *Discourse on the Method* (1637) describing an earlier work – suppressed on the news of the persecution of Galileo – in which he says: 'I pointed out what the laws of nature are, and, without basing my arguments on any other principle other than the infinite perfection of God, I tried to demonstrate all those about which there could be any doubt, and to show that these laws are such that even if God had created several universes he would not have known how to have one in which they are not observed' (Part V). By contrast Newton offers as the epitome of his own empiricism four 'Rules of Reasoning in Philosophy'. It was these rules, which come in Book III, which Hume and all the other would-be Newtons of the moral sciences took as their guide. The full title of the *Principia* – the work which once for all defined classical physics – is *Philosophiae*

Naturalis Principia Mathematica (1687); and it embodies an allusion to Descartes' *Principles of Philosophy* (1644).

(20) See I Corinthians, xv, 51–2: 'Behold, I show you a mystery; we shall not sleep, but we shall all be changed, in a moment, in the twinkling of an eye, at the last trump: for the trumpet shall sound, and the dead shall be raised incorruptible, and we shall be changed.'

(21) Malthus was surely aware that the idea of small heads and legs had already been abandoned in favour of that of more meat in the best joints by the pace-setters in selective sheep-breeding. His next few pages do a lot to justify Karl Pearson's tribute to Malthus as 'the strewer of seed which reached its harvest in the ideas of Charles Darwin and Francis Galton' (*Annals of Eugenics*, Vol. I, October 1925, frontispiece). Francis Galton was a cousin of Darwin, like him a Fellow of the Royal Society, and was a student of *Hereditary Genius* (Macmillan, 1896), and an advocate of the selective breeding of human beings. It was he who, for this policy and for the studies associated with it, introduced the term 'eugenics'.

(22)   Say first, of God above, or man below,
         What can we reason, but from what we know?

                              Alexander Pope, *Essay on Man*, 1, 17–18.

(23) The following extract is from 'The Lucubrations of Isaac Bicker-staff, Esq.' in the *Tatler*, No. 75 (29 September–1 October 1709). It is believed to have been written by Addison and Steele:

I would not be tedious in this discourse, but cannot but observe that our race suffered very much about three hundred years ago by the marriage of one of our heiresses with an eminent courtier who gave us spindle-shanks and cramps in our bones; in so much that we did not recover our health and legs until Sir Walter Bickerstaff married Maud the Milkmaid, of whom the then Garter King of Arms (a facetious person) said (pleasantly enough) 'that she had spoiled our blood but mended our constitutions'.

(24) The words come from a speech by Shakespeare's Prospero:

         . . . the baseless fabric of this vision,
         The cloud-capped towers, the gorgeous palaces,
         The solemn temples, the great globe itself,
         Yea, all which it inherit shall dissolve,
         And, like this insubstantial pageant faded,
         Leave not a wrack behind. We are such stuff
         As dreams are made on . . .

                              The Tempest, IV, i, 451.

(25) The second sentence of this passage should read : 'They are alike hostile to intellectual *and moral* improvement', which – except for my italics – is what is found in the first and third editions (Vol. II, p. 810 and Vol. II, p. 464, respectively). This is, I think, the only case in the *First Essay* of an error in reporting resulting in unfairness to the author reported.

(26) Malthus was, as I have said already in my Introduction, later proud to number Archdeacon William Paley (1748–1805) as one of his most distinguished converts. Paley's three famous books were *The Principles of Moral and Political Philosophy* (1785), *A View of the Evidences of Christianity* (1794), and *Natural Theology, or Evidences of the Existence and Attributes of the Deity* (1802). The first contains a satire on property, which earned its author the nickname 'Pigeon Paley', and which he was assured must cost him his chances of a bishopric: 'the weakest, perhaps, and worst pigeon of the flock' controls and wastes all the grain. It is the third, and not the second, which, in developing the traditional Argument to Design for the existence of God, makes famous and effective use of the wonders of the human eye.

As an illustration of Paley's impact and influence consider another passage from Charles Darwin's autobiography, which refers to his time as an undergraduate at Cambridge: 'in order to pass the B.A. examination, it was, also, necessary to get up Paley's *Evidences of Christianity*, and his *Moral Philosophy* ... I am convinced that I could have written out the whole of the *Evidences* ... The logic of this book and as I may add of his *Natural Theology* gave me as much delight as did Euclid' (C. Darwin, *Autobiography*, ed. N. Barlow, Collins, 1958, p. 59).

(27) FOSTER POWELL (1732–93) was the champion walker of his century. He is reputed to have walked from Shoreditch to York Minster and back as late as 1792 in 135 hours 15 minutes, breaking his own earlier record. For this he got ten pre-inflationary pounds, the largest sum he ever received.

(28) RICHARD BROTHERS (1757–1824), had served in the Royal Navy under Rodney, and retired on half-pay in 1783. In 1792 he wrote to the King and the Cabinet claiming to be the Prince of the Hebrews, descended from King David, and destined to rebuild Jerusalem. Instead he was arrested on a charge of treason in 1795,

and confined as a criminal lunatic till 1806. In the very year of the *First Essay* one of his followers had executed on his instructions, at a cost of £1,200, a plan of the New Jerusalem. The name of the Prophet Brothers remained a household word for some time. The historian T. B. Macaulay refers to him twice, once in the essay on Mackintosh (1835) and once in that on Ranke (1840).

(29) THESEUS was a legendary King of Athens, who volunteered to go as one of an annual tribute of fourteen human sacrificial victims to Crete. There with the help of Ariadne, the daughter of the King Minos, he killed the Minotaur – the Monster of the Labyrinth. Achilles was the hero of Homer's *Iliad*, a Greek warrior in the ten-year Trojan War. Archaeologists have now discovered some basis for these legends of a Royal Cretan Labyrinth and of a Graeco-Trojan War.

(30) The allusion is to Godwin's *Political Justice* (Bk. VIII, ch. 7; in the first edition, Vol. II, p. 868).

(31) The word 'puddling' means literally, as you might expect, splashing with or in (presumably muddy) water. It occurs in *Othello*, III, iv, : 'has puddled his clear spirit'.

(32) The reference is to *Political Justice*, 3rd ed., Bk. VIII, ch. 9.

(33) Ibid., Vol. I, p. 86.

(34) The reference here is, of course, not to the French Revolution of 1789 but to our own Glorious Revolution of 1688. It is called glorious partly because it was largely bloodless, but mainly because it established a Protestant and constitutionally limited monarchy in place of a developing Roman Catholic despotism.

(35) JOHN HOWLETT (1731–1804) was, like Malthus himself, a clergyman of the established church. He published several works on population: *An Examination of Dr Price's Essay on the Population of England and Wales* (1781); *An Enquiry into the Influence which Enclosures have had on the Population of England* (1786); *An Essay on the Population of Ireland* (1786); a pamphlet on Pitt's speech in the House of Commons on 12 February 1796, on the condition of the poor; and *The Insufficiency of the Causes to which the Increase of our Poor and the Poor's Rates have been Generally Ascribed* (1788).

(36) These French economists, of whom much more will be heard in Chapter XVII, are the Physiocrats. The most relevant part of *The Wealth of Nations* is chapter 9 of Book IV: 'Of the agricultural systems, or of those systems of political economy which represent the produce of land as either the sole or the principal source of the revenue and wealth of every country'. The word 'physiocracy' was coined by his disciple Dupont de Nemours as a name for the doctrines of François Quesnay (1697–1774), a contributor to the French *Encyclopaedia* and the man who introduced the slogan 'laissez faire, laissez passer' into economics. Mirabeau and, up to a point, Turgot can also be rated as Physiocrats.

(37) EUCLID of Alexandria flourished there during the reign of the first Ptolemy (323–283 B.C.). It was he who systematized the sort of plane geometry which we now call Euclidean. His *Elements* was still the standard text-book in English schools in the first decade of the present century, and my mother tells me that the subject itself was then known there not as geometry but as Euclid. By offering for the first time the realized ideal of a deductive system the *Elements* became one of the great landmarks of intellectual history.

(38) HENRY VIII was King of England (1509–47). Although it was he who early won from the Pope the title of 'Defender of the Faith', which his Protestant successors still so incongruously retain, later his demand to be granted a divorce from one of his six wives led to a breach with Rome. He then established under his headship a church which was completely Anglican and independent but otherwise orthodox. (The whole story can be compared most illuminatingly with that of Marshal Tito's first breach with Stalin's secular and Russian Vatican.)

(39) SISYPHUS was the legendary founder and first King of Corinth. Homer in the Odyssey tells how as a great sinner he was punished in Hades by being required to push uphill a huge marble block, which just as he was reaching the top always rolled down again.

(40) 'Vindicate the ways of God to man' is not a misquotation of Milton's 'And justify the ways of God to men' (*Paradise Lost*, 1, 26). It comes from the line of Pope's *Essay on Man* immediately preceding those quoted in Note 22, above.

(41) See Isaiah LV, 8–9: 'For my thoughts are not your thoughts, neither are your ways my ways, saith the Lord. For as the heavens are higher than the earth, so are my ways higher than your ways, and my thoughts than your thoughts'. In the next paragraph the quotation is from Job XI, 7: 'Canst thou by searching find out God? Canst thou find out the Almighty unto perfection?'

(42) POPE PIUS XII in his Encyclical letter *Humani Generis* usefully reminded us of what is involved in the traditional Catholic doctrine of Original Sin: 'Christians cannot lend their support to a theory which involves the existence, after Adam's time, of some earthly race of men, truly so called, who were not descended ultimately from him, or else supposes that "Adam" was the name given to some group of our primordial ancestors. It does not appear how such views can be reconciled with the doctrine of Original Sin, as this is guaranteed to us by the Church. Original Sin is the result of a sin committed in actual historical fact, by an individual man named Adam; and it is a quality native to all of us, only because it has been handed down by descent from him.' (Compare Romans V, 12–19, and Council of Trent, Session V, Canons 1–4: I use the translation of Monsignor Ronald Knox, Catholic Truth Society, London, 1950.)

(43) *Essay concerning Human Understanding*, II, xx, 6. This work (1690) is a philosophical classic. John Locke (1632–1704) was also, as author of *Two Treatises of Civil Government* (1690), the ideological spokesman of the Glorious Revolution, and directly and indirectly a main influence on those who shaped the American Constitution.

(44) ALEXANDER THE GREAT (356–23 B.C.) came to the throne of Macedonia in 336 B.C. and proceeded to conquer all Greece, most of West Asia, and Egypt. Tamberlane (1336–1405) was a conquering King of Samarkand, whose exploits are the subject of a play by Christopher Marlowe.

(45) What Shakespeare actually says, through the mouth of Enobarbus, is:

> Age cannot wither her, nor custom stale
> Her infinite variety: other women cloy
> The appetites they feed; but she makes hungry
> Where most she satisfies . . .

Antony and Cleopatra II, ii, 243–6.

(46) *Ecclesiastes* I, 9. Malthus is accepting the view, dominant until the last century, that this was in fact written by Solomon.

(47) This is a remarkably advanced passage, the significance of which seems not to have been noticed. Malthus as an ordained clergyman of the Church of England is here quite explicitly, calmly, and unequivocally rejecting the doctrine of Hell as a punishment of everlasting torment. It was this 'damnable doctrine' which reconciled Darwin to his loss of religious faith: 'I can indeed hardly see how anyone ought to wish Christianity to be true . . .' (*Autobiography*, ed. N. Barlow, Collins, 1958, p. 87).

My colleague Mr John Briggs in the Department of History at Keele has drawn my attention to the fact that as late as 1853 the Council of King's College, London required F. D. Maurice to resign his Chair because his *Theological Essays*, published earlier that year, had attacked this doctrine of the endlessness of future punishment as superstitious and not sanctioned by the strictest interpretation of the Thirty-nine Articles of Religion.

(48) The *Essay on Man*, I, 95–6.

(49) This is F. H. ALEXANDER VON HUMBOLDT (1769–1859) the geographer. He is not to be confused with his elder brother K. W. von Humboldt (1767–1835), a distinguished philologist and Prussian statesman. The book mentioned was first published in two volumes in French and also in English in 1811. It later counted as Part III of the collected edition of this Humboldt's main geographical and scientific work (with A. Bonpland) which appeared in thirty volumes as *Voyage aux Regions Equinoxiales du Nouveau Continent Fait en 1799–1804*. The expression 'Nouvelle Espagne' refers of course to Spanish America, which had not at that time won its independence.

(50) ADAM SEYBERT (1773–1825) published in Philadelphia in 1818, while serving as a Democrat member of the Congress, *Statistical Annals: embracing views of the population, commerce, navigation . . . revenues . . . public debt and sinking fund of the United States of America; founded on official documents*. And even that is an abbreviated version of his full title! The period covered is 4 March 1779–20 April 1818.

(51) PROFESSOR B. S. BARTON (1776–1815), sometime President

of the Philadelphia Medical Society and author of works on the rattlesnake, goitre, and the breeding habits of the opossum.

(52) JOHN BRISTED, of the Inner Temple, published this *America and her Resources* in London in 1818.

(53) JOSHUA MILNE (1776–1851) published his *A Treatise on the Valuation of Annuities and Assurances on Lives and Survivorships* in two octavo volumes in London in 1815, and it brought about a revolution in actuarial science.

(54) PROFESSOR WARGENTIN furnished information on Swedish demography to Price, and Professor Nicander – his successor in the same chair at Stockholm – later did the same for Malthus. See the *Second Essay*, Chapter 2 of Book II.

(55) WILLIAM TOOKE, the elder (1744–1820) published a *View of the Russian Empire during the Reign of Catherine II, and to the Close of the Present Century* in London in 1799.

(56) JAMES I of England and VI of Scotland ruled from the death of Queen Elizabeth I in 1603 until his own death in 1625.

(57) I suppose it is passages of this sort which provoke such tendentious pseudo-history as the following, which I happened to meet while I was working on these notes: 'He read Malthus, his *Essay on Population*. In it Malthus tried to justify the existence of poverty in an era of capitalist competition.' This comes in an article on 'Popper's Falsifiability and Darwin's Natural Selection' by K. K. Lee in *Philosophy* 1969, p. 294. No doubt to those in a Marxist tradition it appears that there is no call to be fair to anyone who can be dismissed as a 'reactionary element' and an 'enemy of socialism'.

(58) WILLIAM, Duke of Normandy led the last successful invasion of England, defeating the Saxon army under King Harold at the Battle of Hastings in A.D. 1066, and establishing himself as King William I.

(59) JAMES COOK (1728–79) was the naval explorer of the coasts of Australia, New Zealand and the Pacific generally. Malthus in the *Second Essay* gives the question which Cook in his *First Voyage* asked of New Holland as: 'By what means are the inhabitants of this

country reduced to such a number as it can subsist' (*Second Essay*, Vol. I, p. 67).

(60) This book is by Malthus himself, published in 1820. See my Introduction, p. 14.

(61) ARTHUR YOUNG (1741–1820) was primarily an improving agricultural writer. He published many books of which *Travels in France* (1792) remains the best known, being a major source for the condition of France just before the French Revolution of 1789. By the time he crossed swords with the author of the *Second Essay* Young was past his prime.

(62) JOHN WEYLAND (1774–1854) published a criticism of Malthus under the title *The Principles of Population and Production as they are Affected by the Progress of Society with a View to Moral and Political Consequences* (1820). His main point was substantially the same inept misunderstanding as was considered on pp. 31–3 of the Introduction, above.

SUGGESTIONS
FOR FURTHER READING

No previous editor of the *First Essay* seems to have set himself to the not very onerous task of locating the few unidentified quotations and annotating all the references to people. The nearest approach to this modest ideal was made by James Bonar in the facsimile edition prepared for the Royal Economic Society (Macmillan, 1926). The *Second Essay* is best read in the original sixth edition; but, failing that, there is an edition by M. P. Fogarty in the Everyman Library (Dent and Dutton, 1958). The short but useful 'A Letter to Samuel Whitbread, Esq., M.P., on His Proposed Bill for the Amendment of the Poor Laws' is included along with some excellent modern material in *Introduction to Malthus*, edited by D. V. Glass (C. A. Watts, 1953).

The same James Bonar who edited the facsimile edition of the *First Essay* also wrote the valuable study *Malthus and His Work* (G. Allen and Unwin, 1885, second edition, 1924) as well as *Theories of Population from Raleigh to Arthur Young* (G. Allen and Unwin, 1931). A more recent work on Malthus and his impact is G. F. MacCleary *The Malthusian Population Theory* (G. Allen and Unwin, 1953).

Two recent collections of work on our contemporary population problems are *Population Evolution and Birth Control*, edited by Garrett Hardin (W. H. Freeman, San Francisco, 1964, second edition, 1969) and *Population in Perspective*, edited by Louise B. Young (Oxford University Press, 1968).

INDEX OF PERSONAL NAMES

Note. This index covers the Introduction, the texts, and the notes, but not the tables of contents. It also omits the names of Gods and of fictitious, mythological or legendary human persons.

READ MORE IN PENGUIN

In every corner of the world, on every subject under the sun, Penguin represents quality and variety – the very best in publishing today.

For complete information about books available from Penguin – including Puffins, Penguin Classics and Arkana – and how to order them, write to us at the appropriate address below. Please note that for copyright reasons the selection of books varies from country to country.

In the United Kingdom: Please write to *Dept. JC, Penguin Books Ltd, FREEPOST, West Drayton, Middlesex UB7 OBR.*

If you have any difficulty in obtaining a title, please send your order with the correct money, plus ten per cent for postage and packaging, to *PO Box No. 11, West Drayton, Middlesex UB7 OBR*

In the United States: Please write to *Consumer Sales, Penguin USA, P.O. Box 999, Dept. 17109, Bergenfield, New Jersey 07621-0120.* VISA and MasterCard holders call 1-800-253-6476 to order all Penguin titles

In Canada: Please write to *Penguin Books Canada Ltd, 10 Alcorn Avenue, Suite 300, Toronto, Ontario M4V 3B2*

In Australia: Please write to *Penguin Books Australia Ltd, P.O. Box 257, Ringwood, Victoria 3134*

In New Zealand: Please write to *Penguin Books (NZ) Ltd, Private Bag 102902, North Shore Mail Centre, Auckland 10*

In India: Please write to *Penguin Books India Pvt Ltd, 706 Eros Apartments, 56 Nehru Place, New Delhi 110 019*

In the Netherlands: Please write to *Penguin Books Netherlands bv, Postbus 3507, NL-1001 AH Amsterdam*

In Germany: Please write to *Penguin Books Deutschland GmbH, Metzlerstrasse 26, 60594 Frankfurt am Main*

In Spain: Please write to *Penguin Books S. A., Bravo Murillo 19, 1° B, 28015 Madrid*

In Italy: Please write to *Penguin Italia s.r.l., Via Felice Casati 20, I–20124 Milano*

In France: Please write to *Penguin France S. A., 17 rue Lejeune, F–31000 Toulouse*

In Japan: Please write to *Penguin Books Japan, Ishikiribashi Building, 2–5–4, Suido, Bunkyo-ku, Tokyo 112*

In Greece: Please write to *Penguin Hellas Ltd, Dimocritou 3, GR–106 71 Athens*

In South Africa: Please write to *Longman Penguin Southern Africa (Pty) Ltd, Private Bag X08, Bertsham 2013*

READ MORE IN PENGUIN

A CHOICE OF CLASSICS

The Brothers Karamazov Fyodor Dostoyevsky

A drama of parricide and intense family rivalry, *The Brothers Karamazov* is Dostoyevsky's acknowledged masterpiece. It tells the story of the murder of a depraved landowner and the ensuing investigation and trial.

Selections from the Carmina Burana
A verse translation by David Parlett

The famous songs from the *Carmina Burana* (made into an oratorio by Carl Orff) tell of lecherous monks and corrupt clerics, drinkers and gamblers, and the fleeting pleasures of youth.

Fear and Trembling Søren Kierkegaard

A profound meditation on the nature of faith and submission to God's will, which examines with startling originality the story of Abraham and Isaac.

Selected Prose Charles Lamb

Lamb's famous essays (under the strange pseudonym of Elia) on anything and everything have long been celebrated for their apparently innocent charm. This major new edition allows readers to discover the darker and more interesting aspects of Lamb.

The Picture of Dorian Gray Oscar Wilde

Wilde's superb and macabre novel, one of his supreme works, is reprinted here with a masterly Introduction and valuable Notes by Peter Ackroyd.

Frankenstein Mary Shelley

In recounting this chilling tragedy Mary Shelley demonstrates both the corruption of an innocent creature by an immoral society and the dangers of playing God with science.

READ MORE IN PENGUIN

A CHOICE OF CLASSICS

Evelina Frances Burney

Subtitled *The History of a Young Lady's Entrance into the World*, the novel records in letters its young heroine's encounters with society, both high and low, in London and at fashionable watering places. It is acutely observant of the social laws regarding power, authority and authorship, which the author herself partly had to subvert.

The Republic Plato

The best-known of Plato's dialogues, *The Republic* is also one of the supreme masterpieces of Western philosophy, whose influence cannot be overestimated.

Brigitta and Other Tales Adalbert Stifter

Each of these four stories is set in a recognizable world depicted with measured realism. But once the reader has learned to look beneath the calm, apparently seamless surface of the narrative, and, in Stifter's words, 'to see with the heart', strange tensions are revealed.

The Poems of Exile Ovid

Exiled from Rome for his scandalous erotic verse and a mysterious (probably political) misdemeanour, Ovid spent his declining years in the remote Black Sea port of Tunis, trying to use poetry to win a reprieve.

The Birth of Tragedy Friedrich Nietzsche

Dedicated to Richard Wagner, *The Birth of Tragedy* created a furore on its first publication in 1871; it has since become one of the seminal books of European culture.

Madame Bovary Gustave Flaubert

With *Madame Bovary* Flaubert established the realistic novel in France while his central character of Emma Bovary, the bored wife of a provincial doctor, remains one of the great creations of modern literature.

READ MORE IN PENGUIN

A CHOICE OF CLASSICS

READ MORE IN PENGUIN

A CHOICE OF CLASSICS

Molière	**The Misanthrope/The Sicilian/Tartuffe/A Doctor in Spite of Himself/The Imaginary Invalid**
	The Miser/The Would-be Gentleman/That Scoundrel Scapin/Love's the Best Doctor/Don Juan
Michel de Montaigne	**Essays**
Marguerite de Navarre	**The Heptameron**
Blaise Pascal	**Pensées**
	The Provincial Letters
Abbé Prevost	**Manon Lescaut**
Rabelais	**The Histories of Gargantua and Pantagruel**
Racine	**Andromache/Britannicus/Berenice**
	Iphigenia/Phaedra/Athaliah
Arthur Rimbaud	**Collected Poems**
Jean-Jacques Rousseau	**The Confessions**
	A Discourse on Inequality
	Emile
Jacques Saint-Pierre	**Paul and Virginia**
Madame de Sevigné	**Selected Letters**
Stendhal	**Lucien Leuwen**
	Scarlet and Black
	The Charterhouse of Parma
Voltaire	**Candide**
	Letters on England
	Philosophical Dictionary
Emile Zola	**L'Assomoir**
	La Bête Humaine
	The Debacle
	The Earth
	Germinal
	Nana
	Thérèse Raquin

READ MORE IN PENGUIN

A CHOICE OF CLASSICS

Francis Bacon	**The Essays**
George Berkeley	**Principles of Human Knowledge/Three Dialogues between Hylas and Philonous**
James Boswell	**The Life of Samuel Johnson**
Sir Thomas Browne	**The Major Works**
John Bunyan	**The Pilgrim's Progress**
Edmund Burke	**Reflections on the Revolution in France**
Frances Burney	**Evelina**
Margaret Cavendish	**The Blazing World and Other Writings**
William Cobbett	**Rural Rides**
William Congreve	**Comedies**
Thomas de Quincey	**Confessions of an English Opium Eater**
	Recollections of the Lakes and the Lake Poets
Daniel Defoe	**A Journal of the Plague Year**
	Moll Flanders
	Robinson Crusoe
	Roxana
	A Tour through the Whole Island of Great Britain
Henry Fielding	**Amelia**
	Jonathan Wild
	Joseph Andrews
	Tom Jones
John Gay	**The Beggar's Opera**
Oliver Goldsmith	**The Vicar of Wakefield**

READ MORE IN PENGUIN

A CHOICE OF CLASSICS

William Hazlitt	**Selected Writings**
George Herbert	**The Complete English Poems**
Thomas Hobbes	**Leviathan**
Samuel Johnson/	
James Boswell	**A Journey to the Western Islands of Scotland and The Journal of a Tour of the Hebrides**
Charles Lamb	**Selected Prose**
George Meredith	**The Egoist**
Thomas Middleton	**Five Plays**
John Milton	**Paradise Lost**
Samuel Richardson	**Clarissa**
	Pamela
Earl of Rochester	**Complete Works**
Richard Brinsley Sheridan	**The School for Scandal and Other Plays**
Sir Philip Sidney	**Selected Poems**
Christopher Smart	**Selected Poems**
Adam Smith	**The Wealth of Nations**
Tobias Smollett	**The Adventures of Ferdinand Count Fathom**
	Humphrey Clinker
Laurence Sterne	**The Life and Opinions of Tristram Shandy**
	A Sentimental Journey Through France and Italy
Jonathan Swift	**Gulliver's Travels**
	Selected Poems
Thomas Traherne	**Selected Poems and Prose**
Sir John Vanbrugh	**Four Comedies**

READ MORE IN PENGUIN

A CHOICE OF CLASSICS

Matthew Arnold	**Selected Prose**
Jane Austen	**Emma**
	Lady Susan/The Watsons/Sanditon
	Mansfield Park
	Northanger Abbey
	Persuasion
	Pride and Prejudice
	Sense and Sensibility
William Barnes	**Selected Poems**
Anne Brontë	**Agnes Grey**
	The Tenant of Wildfell Hall
Charlotte Brontë	**Jane Eyre**
	Shirley
	Villette
Emily Brontë	**Wuthering Heights**
Samuel Butler	**Erewhon**
	The Way of All Flesh
Thomas Carlyle	**Selected Writings**
Arthur Hugh Clough	**Selected Poems**
Wilkie Collins	**The Moonstone**
	The Woman in White
Charles Darwin	**The Origin of Species**
	The Voyage of the *Beagle*
Benjamin Disraeli	**Sybil**
George Eliot	**Adam Bede**
	Daniel Deronda
	Felix Holt
	Middlemarch
	The Mill on the Floss
	Romola
	Scenes of Clerical Life
	Silas Marner
Elizabeth Gaskell	**Cranford/Cousin Phillis**
	The Life of Charlotte Brontë
	Mary Barton
	North and South
	Wives and Daughters

READ MORE IN PENGUIN

A CHOICE OF CLASSICS

Charles Dickens	**American Notes for General Circulation**
	Barnaby Rudge
	Bleak House
	The Christmas Books (in two volumes)
	David Copperfield
	Dombey and Son
	Great Expectations
	Hard Times
	Little Dorrit
	Martin Chuzzlewit
	The Mystery of Edwin Drood
	Nicholas Nickleby
	The Old Curiosity Shop
	Oliver Twist
	Our Mutual Friend
	The Pickwick Papers
	Selected Short Fiction
	A Tale of Two Cities
Edward Gibbon	**The Decline and Fall of the Roman Empire**
George Gissing	**New Grub Street**
	The Odd Women
William Godwin	**Caleb Williams**
Thomas Hardy	**The Distracted Preacher and Other Tales**
	Far from the Madding Crowd
	Jude the Obscure
	The Mayor of Casterbridge
	A Pair of Blue Eyes
	The Return of the Native
	Tess of the d'Urbervilles
	The Trumpet-Major
	Under the Greenwood Tree
	The Woodlanders

READ MORE IN PENGUIN

A CHOICE OF CLASSICS

Lord Macaulay	**The History of England**
Henry Mayhew	**London Labour and the London Poor**
John Stuart Mill	**The Autobiography**
	On Liberty
William Morris	**News from Nowhere** and **Selected Writings and Designs**
John Henry Newman	**Apologia Pro Vita Sua**
Robert Owen	**A New View of Society and Other Writings**
Walter Pater	**Marius the Epicurean**
John Ruskin	**'Unto This Last' and Other Writings**
Walter Scott	**Ivanhoe**
	Heart of Midlothian
Robert Louis Stevenson	**Kidnapped**
	Dr Jekyll and Mr Hyde and Other Stories
William Makepeace Thackeray	**The History of Henry Esmond**
	The History of Pendennis
	Vanity Fair
Anthony Trollope	**Barchester Towers**
	Can You Forgive Her?
	The Eustace Diamonds
	Framley Parsonage
	He Knew He Was Right
	The Last Chronicle of Barset
	Phineas Finn
	The Prime Minister
	The Small House at Allington
	The Warden
	The Way We Live Now
Oscar Wilde	**Complete Short Fiction**
Mary Wollstonecraft	**A Vindication of the Rights of Woman**
	Mary and Maria
	Matilda
Dorothy and William Wordsworth	**Home at Grasmere**